1980

University of St. Francis
G   301.435 B161
Baird. Janet H.,
T

T4-ALA-716

L I B R A R Y
College of St. Francis
JOLIET, ILL.

Presented by

DR. SCHOLL FOUNDATION

THESE HARVEST YEARS

These
Harvest Years

EDITED BY

Janet H. Baird

LIBRARY
College of St. Francis
JOLIET, ILL.

Essay Index Reprint Series

BOOKS FOR LIBRARIES PRESS
FREEPORT, NEW YORK

Copyright 1951 by
Doubleday and Company, Inc.

Reprinted 1972 by arrangement

Library of Congress Cataloging in Publication Data

Baird, Janet H   ed.
    These harvest years.

    (Essay index reprint series)
    CONTENTS: The new philosophy of maturity, by
M. Gumpert.--How to keep your mind limber, by
O. S. English.--How to reach the harvest years, by
E. P. Boas. ₒetc.₃
    1. Old age--Addresses, essays, lectures. I. Title
₋HQ1061.B3 1972₋   301.43'5   74-167308
ISBN 0-8369-2581-5

PRINTED IN THE UNITED STATES OF AMERICA
BY
NEW WORLD BOOK MANUFACTURING CO., INC.
HALLANDALE, FLORIDA 33009

G
301.435
B161

PREFACE

THIS BOOK is designed as a realistic guide toward a longer and more active life. It represents the thinking of pioneers in the fields of geriatrics and gerontology (words which still strike our ears with an unfamiliar sound, but which are fast becoming parts of our common language).

These pioneers have set up the first signposts along the road that leads to the exciting and productive adventure of not only a longer life, but a more rewarding one.

At the present time, older people are the fastest-growing group in our population. We have more persons over the age of forty than ever before in human history, and it is estimated that within the next thirty years there will be 20,000,000 of us over the age of sixty-five! Whether we are to be 20,000,000 depleted, discouraged old people or 20,000,000 wise and active men and women enjoying the most enriched period of our lives depends on what we do now to prepare for our harvest years.

Until now we have arbitrarily said that up to the age of sixty-five we are employable, worth-while, and productive people. And we have as arbitrarily said that at the age of sixty-six we suddenly cease to be any of these desirable things, and should be relegated to retirement. These attitudes had their foundation back in the days when we expected to lose our

90078

v

looks, our hair, and our teeth by the time we were forty and to
creep as best we could through our next twenty years.

Modern medicine and new discoveries in other sciences have
changed all this. The eleven authors present in this book are
among those who have contributed mightily to raising the
plane of human development. Through their studies we can
learn how to make the maximum use of the knowledge, experience, and wisdom which we as individuals have accumulated
during our earlier years.

This new knowledge is based on years of individual study
and research and, even more important, upon the experience of
these experts in living their own lives. The authorities who have
contributed to this volume as authors are the most convincing
proof to us as readers of what we can expect of our harvest
years. Without exception, they have lived through their own first
forty years and are living their second forty with even greater
enthusiasm and accomplishment. Every hour of their days is
filled with new projects, new undertakings, new studies,
and new activities. Their own busy lives demonstrate the truth
of their philosophies, each of which reflects the important part
that our mental attitudes play in determining our physical well-
being and our capacity for making the most of our later years.

These specialists in the many phases of living have not set
forth mere theories nor discussed the problems which face us
with empty, high-sounding phrases. They have set forth a
practical blueprint of the things each of us must know if we
are to prepare for the years ahead.

Of all the sections in this book, my own on "How to Look
as Good as You Feel" is the only one not based on original research. It is a compilation of the material which has come to
me as executive director of the Foundation for Forty Plus Living, Inc., a clearinghouse for information on all aspects of
longer living.

It has been a great privilege to work with these forward-looking leaders, many of whom predicted the present revolutionary change in our way of life as much as twenty years ago and began then the investigations which are giving us so many of today's answers. These studies are now showing that if, like Mr. Walter Pitkin, we are to find life does indeed begin at forty, we must prepare for it long before we reach this particular birthday.

What do each of us want in the years which come after forty? It is within our power to plan what kind of older people we will be. We can lay the foundation now for the maintenance of our health, our spiritual values, and our economic security throughout the later, the harvest, years. This book, we hope, will help.

Janet H. Baird

New York
1951

CONTENTS

THESE HARVEST YEARS

THE NEW PHILOSOPHY OF MATURITY

by

MARTIN GUMPERT, M.D.

THE discovery of the harvest years has come to this country as a tremendous surprise. Suddenly we have waked up to awareness that the United States, which for so long has been the symbol of youth, is populated by an increasing number of older people—there will soon be twenty million of them beyond the customary age of retirement. The miraculous increase of the average human life span since the turn of this century has been a world-wide trend. But nowhere are its social and cultural implications of such tremendous impact as here. We have to realize that a revolution has come to us overnight—from a rather unexpected quarter—and that we must radically change long-standing patterns of our society: we shall be forced to do so by conflict and crisis if we do not undertake to make these changes voluntarily and intelligently.

How are things now, in the present stage of transition? We find we are still bound by superstitious discrimination against the aged. We dread thinking of ourselves as growing older, as being the aged of tomorrow. We are afraid of death, but we do little to prevent premature death. We cling to the concept of retirement as determined by a fixed number of years regardless of our biological condition. We expect the elderly person to lead a passive, sedate, empty life, dependent on the good will and charity of others. We deprive him of his civic rights and duties; we deny him work, income, and influence, and relegate him to a state of incapacity and disability. As a result, the mature person in our country today may face tragedy and despair from the emotional, economic, and social defeats he has to suffer. Our society devotes itself to educating the young and to promoting the middle-aged adult, but for the older person we have nothing but a charitable institution. We advise or enforce retirement; we paternalistically recommend the practice of often rather childish hobbies. Our mental asylums and old-age homes are overflowing with a steadily mounting stream of the old-age segment of our population, and in these "homes"—which are often nothing but sorry dumping grounds, anterooms of death—very little is done in the way of treatment or even of social and psychological adjustment to later years.

But this situation *is* changing. More and more of us realize that our present behavior toward the elderly is a completely unrealistic one. All of us know older persons who are mentally and physically vigorous; active citizens, who refuse to be buried alive, are aware of their rights and responsibilities and refuse to give them up. Even under present unjust conditions, the older age group is growing in social influence and in political power. Government, industry, mental-health organizations, have become aware of the fact that something must be done to salvage the productive qualities of the older person and to integrate this neglected period of living into our public life. The problem is certainly not an altruistic one. Are we going to have a gigantic old-age asylum in which a great (and growing) segment of our population is supported by a shrinking wage-earning group, or will we make room for our older citizens, keeping them in active business and professional life, leading independent, useful lives? We must make our decision here and now . . . today.

In recent decades medicine has developed a special field of interest—geriatrics. Contrasted to the specialist in pediatrics, or children's diseases, the specialist in geriatrics deals with the ailments of the later years. This new branch of medical science has been able to show that the physical deteriorations of these years are not, as we still tend to believe, the unavoidable consequences of the process of growing older.

Each age period of our life span is subject to the attack of specific ailments. Children may develop rickets, and are vulnerable to a number of infections—chicken pox, measles, whooping cough—which as a rule do not affect the older person. Elderly people are subject to arteriosclerotic changes which are almost never seen in childhood. The ailments of later years are often of the chronic degenerative type affecting the heart, the circulatory system, the joints, the kidneys. But diseases they are, and as such they can be prevented, arrested, or cured. It is true that the fantastic advances which medicine has made in recent years have mostly benefited the fight against acute infectious diseases: pneumonia, tuberculosis, syphilis, diphtheria, et cetera. But of late the attention of medical research has been vigorously turning toward a better knowledge of chronic diseases and their treatment. Arteriosclerosis is now recognized as a pathological process—that is, an illness—which, though intimately connected with aging, is not an unavoidable change of the aging tissue. The recent discoveries of powerful hormones of the pituitary gland and the adrenal cortex have already brought decisive relief for sufferers from arthritis and allied diseases which only a short time ago were considered hopeless.

There is small doubt that in the near future we will invade and solve the mystery of cancer, that efficient drugs and better diagnostic methods will reduce deaths from coronary disease, and that many other illnesses which now threaten the enjoyment of life in later years will be eliminated or amenable to treatment. The active part of geriatrics, called gerontotherapy (Dr. Harry Benjamin), or de-aging (Dr. C. Ward Crampton), will bring health and happiness to the aged.

Wherever medicine has abandoned its passive and pessimistic attitude toward the older patient it has been rewarded with success. When I was a young student, an older person in need of a major operation was often abandoned and left to die. In my experience the average patient of a highly advanced age is, today, often a better surgical risk than the middle-aged person. Mental afflictions of the cerebral arteriosclerotic type, which were once considered completely hopeless and unfit for treatment, may now, in many instances, be considerably improved. They merely needed the active attention of the medical therapist.

However, medicine alone cannot accomplish this vital job of making the later years the most rewarding ones. A rejuvenation of the public mind as to the process of aging is urgently needed as well. Aging starts long before we appear to grow old. Chronic degenerative diseases of which old people die usually have their slow onset between the ages of thirty and forty. This is the most favorable time for prevention and cure. The average person must be educated to the potential benefits of preventive medicine and work closely with the physician of his confidence, following medical advice and managing his life before an emergency arises. A patient who is driven to his doctor by unbearable pain or complete disability often comes too late.

We might be even more radical. Growing older does not start merely in middle age; it starts with the first day of existence. Since our life expectancy has been so enormously prolonged we are in the position of a man who suddenly finds that his day lasts forty-eight hours instead of twenty-four. Such an individual would have to change the scheme and the routine of his whole day, from early morning until late at night. He would have more time for work, more time for leisure, and would have to move at a different pace. Scientists seem to agree that the normal human life span lies between 100 and 125 years. Very few specimens of our human race have ever attained this normal limit of healthy life, because they have succumbed prematurely to disease. But in the near future the centenarian will no longer be a freak of whom we ask the foolish question—"How on earth did you do it?"—for there will be thousands of centenarians, and for the first time in history we will have, as a cultural group, the great opportunity of witnessing wisdom and maturity as a mass phenomenon, no longer as a queer exception.

But wisdom does not come from heaven; it is the rarest and most precious fruit of human harvest. A young fool will never be a wise old man. The great gift of a longer life is, today, still largely wasted. There are millions of elderly souls who bitterly regret looking backward—they have gravely mismanaged their lives and would give everything for the chance of starting all over again. But at the time when they believe they have discovered how they should have lived, they are too weak, too sick, or too insecure to utilize their experience and their wisdom. The real tragedy of maturity is the tragedy of a squandered and misdirected youth and middle age. The dangerous and pitiful deterioration of later life is not the product of the aging process, but of a stagnant and inert period of maturity.

Throughout history there have been heroic examples of famous elderly men who have maintained their creativeness and productivity up to the most advanced age and have produced works of art and science of the highest order, who have exercised power and authority at a time when the majority of their contemporaries were incapacitated by senility. How did they accomplish this miracle? By handling their lives as a continuous unit of mental and emotional development, by never retiring, by never ceasing to learn.

One does not need to be a specimen of robust health and heavy muscles. The overcoming of physical deficiencies often increases resistance to death and decay. Our physical faculties start to decline at the age of twenty, and a boxer of thirty is professionally an old man. But our mental capacity grows to its full development only around the age of thirty-five, and it maintains its high level practically unlimited to the most advanced age—provided it is not artificially stopped. However, most people today stop learning and renounce mental training and emotional development with their graduation from high school, at an age before they start thinking. They are indeed poor prospects for old age.

What then can be done? Let us spread the good word that old age is no longer necessarily decrepit, ugly, feeble-minded, and miserable. I have yet to find the young man or woman who answers "yes" to the question of whether he wants to grow very old. In our civilization old age is looked at with horror and pity. There is no temptation to look forward to a long life. The fault lies with us.

Almost every American family has some sort of old-age trouble. There is old Grandpa, or poor Granny, or there are parents or in-laws who are difficult, depressed, indigent, or ailing, and nobody knows what to do with them. These old people are unemployed, despondent, bored, grudging, and in some cases, as the stubborn holders and consumers of financial resources, feared and hated. Nobody, at any rate, seems to like them, and anyone who is not liked inevitably becomes disagreeable. We know a great deal today about child psychology, and great advances are being made in the mental hygiene of the younger adult. About older people we seem to know next to nothing, and even psychotherapists have neglected them shamefully. No wonder many elderly people develop a deep-rooted neurosis which is closely connected with their increasing years. Unless we recognize old age as the potential high point of life, in truth, the harvest years, which can attain dignity, authority, independence, and which deserves the most intelligent social and medical consideration, we shall not be able to change this unfortunate attitude.

The best work on this subject was written by Cicero in "Cato or an Essay on Old Age"—proving that geriatrics is nothing new; it was an urgent problem as long as two thousand years ago. Cicero reports that Solon, being questioned by the tyrant Pisistratus as to what inspired him with boldness to oppose his ruler's unjust laws, bravely replied, "My old age." "Old age," Cicero continues, "may be animated with more courage and fortitude than is usually found even in the prime of life." This kind of courage is needed by the mature men and women of our time. They must beat down discrimination based solely, and unreasonably, on number of years; and we must all help in this battle.

I am always much ashamed when I am told as a professional secret that a patient has been forced to understate his age ten years or so in order even to be admitted for an interview by some prospective employer. The time will come when healthy maturity will be an asset, something to be proud of, when those who possess it will speak up honestly and boldly.

We do not know yet what the older person of tomorrow will look like, because there are so very few really healthy old people around, and even they suffer from the bias which changes this age group into a depressed "minority" with all the imposed anxieties and inferiority complexes that go with such status. But an older person will, of course, have to manage his life differently from that of an adolescent or middle-aged person. We must remember, however, that there are deficiencies and assets attached to each period of our life span—inexperience in youth, special responsibilities and adjustments in middle life.

Let me close with some simple rules for the elderly who want to lead an active and productive existence in their so-called declining years.

1. Keep up physical and mental activity without intermission. Nothing is more dangerous than the lowered vitality that results from stagnation and resignation. Therefore, try to acquire new skills, new interests, new knowledge. I have elsewhere defined aging as a state in which one does more and more things for the last time, fewer and fewer for the first time. Try to reverse this process: continue to do as many things as possible for the first time and try to give up as little as possible. It is complete nonsense to believe that an older person is unable to learn. If learning has been his lifelong habit, he need never give up this habit. His memory may become slightly impaired, especially if it is not well trained. But there are other compensations, of better comprehension and greater experience, which are lacking in younger people.

2. Plan to try to save energy in everything, because the resources of hidden energy are diminished with time. Make a point of reaching the same end with a smaller expenditure of effort and physical strength. Standardize your movements and your tempo. Be aware of all the danger signals of undue fatigue: trembling, drowsiness, breathlessness, sweating, headache, consciousness of the heart. In principle an older person can do what he could do as a younger person, though he may need more time in which to accomplish it.

3. Do not long for retirement and do not retire. The concept of retirement from life seems to me damaging if it is not required by urgent physical necessity. It may be wonderful to

abandon a boring or overstrenuous routine job, but do so only if it is in order to pursue a better and more adequate and more stimulating activity. But beware of hobbies except as a pastime; beware of reduced and childish modes of living.

4. Plan to lengthen your intervals of rest and to shorten those of exercise, because easily exhausted available energies must be more thoroughly and more frequently restored. Divide your day into equal periods of energy output and rest. Don't overdo rest, either. Consider the prolonged effect of exercise and rest on your body reserves, with advancing age, and plan accordingly. Avoid monotonous and tasteless diets, sudden heat and cold (overhot tubs, a cold shower or dip in the ocean), be cautious with sleeping drugs, sedatives, and laxatives—use drugs only if medically indicated. Elderly people are as sensitive to drugs as are small children.

5. Try not to neglect the common rules of physical training: as, for instance, the fact that a warming-up period at the beginning of a race and the so-called "end-spurt" can be applied to increase the efficiency and output of all work and activity. Try to use your personal-efficiency experience wisely within the limits of your diminished physical strength.

6. Try to avoid boredom and monotony. Maintain the standards of your physical appearance and improve your manners with age. Be generous and tolerant. Watch out for spots on your vest! Sloppiness is often the first sign of a deteriorating personality.

These recommendations may be far from philosophy, but they do contain, I believe, some grains of proven medical wisdom prescribed to the modern older man and woman. If we attack the new problems of increasing age with wisdom, boldness, and optimism, the elderly may look forward to a fine future. And it will be our own future, for we are, all of us, the elderlies of tomorrow.

HOW TO KEEP YOUR MIND LIMBER

by

O. SPURGEON ENGLISH, M.D.

THIS moment may mark the first time that you have given serious thought to the idea that you are growing older. When you were twelve such an idea was filled with delightful and long-anticipated possibilities. Your next birthday meant that you would be in your teens and could no longer be considered a mere child. Once in your teens, you longed to be twenty-one, for this meant freedom from parental control and the undeniable right to "live your own life." It meant that you had legal standing in the community, the opportunity to travel, to earn your living, to marry and establish a home of your own. But somewhere between the ages of twenty-one and twenty-five your attitude about growing older began to change.

If you are a man, you may have begun to wonder if you were going to achieve that rather questionable American ideal of making enough money to retire and take it easy by the time you were forty-five. At the age of thirty you may have become conscious of your receding hairline and the fact that your tennis game was losing a little of its snap. By thirty-five you may have begun to refer wryly to yourself as "getting to be an old man." And then suddenly you were forty!

A man usually reacts to his fortieth birthday in one of two ways: it may hit him as crushing and undeniable proof that he is growing old and will soon be on the shelf, or he may find, with considerable surprise, that being forty is not so very different except that he seems to have a little more sense and judgment and a clearer idea of the goals toward which he is working. In either event, being forty is a state of mind rather than a chronological number of years.

The same is true, of course, of women. At twenty-five an unmarried girl may begin to speculate uneasily about "being too old to get a husband." By thirty she feels that she must have a well-established career to avoid being classed as an old maid. And by forty she has firmly decided to list her age as thirty-eight for the rest of her natural life!

Up to now it has done little good to point to the Shaws and Goethes, the Einsteins and the Baruchs, the Bernhardts and the Barrymores and say, "Look how much living, how much work, how much enthusiasm can be experienced long after forty or fifty or sixty!" It was too easy to brush them aside as the "exceptions," as the rare individuals who just refused to grow old.

We have resisted the idea that none of us need grow old and useless unless we will it, and that we bring many of the infirmities of age upon ourselves. We have stubbornly refused to recognize this truth although the evidence has been everywhere about us. Think for a moment of the people you know who were old men and women at thirty-five and you will see that years have little relation to youthfulness.

We say of such young people grown old that they are "set in their ways," that they are "resistant to change," that they "refuse to see anyone else's point of view," and that they think there "is no way but their way." All of which are just other ways of stating that they have lost their flexibility and that their minds are no longer limber. It is at the *moment that an individual loses his flexibility* that old age begins! It can be at twenty-five, thirty-five or sixty-five, but it doesn't *have* to happen even at ninety-five!

Let's forget about chronological age for a moment and see where we stand on the scale of flexibility, since that is the true measure of youthfulness and meaningful maturity. Take stock of your mental elasticity by answering these few questions:

1. Have you changed your point of view recently on any major question, or are you clinging to the basic set of ideas you grew up with, determined to keep them intact no matter how much the evidence that they need revision?
2. Do you like younger people, or are you afraid that they will offer too much competition in either business or social relationships? Do you feel that their youthful enthusiasm may outweigh your more mature wisdom, know-how, or charm?
3. How do you feel about the "younger generation"? Do you get along well with children, or do you deplore their ways and feel that child-rearing methods in your day were better?
4. Have you taken a trip lately, and if you did take one, did you thoroughly enjoy it? Can you recall the eagerness with which you used to anticipate any change of surroundings and the wealth of new ideas and impressions that you brought back from even a casual bus trip or ferryboat ride? Take a careful look at your present traveling attitudes, for they are one of the true barometers of age. Travelers, unless handicapped by physical limitations, who "can't wait to get home and settle back to normal living" are really getting old, even though they may have experienced only thirty-two birthdays. They are already beginning to narrow down their interests and screen out many pleasant, stimulating incidents from their lives.
5. Do you have any special interests, hobbies, or recreations? There is much to be said for that old saw about "read any good books lately?" Have you explored any new ways of thought or dipped into religious attitudes that may be differ-

ent from your own? Have you seen a play or movie that gave
you something different to think about, other than the usual
"boy-meets-girl" theme? Under this heading, housewives
should take stock of their cooking habits. What about new
recipes—do you try them out, or are your meals based on a
fairly standard pattern? Do you ever experiment with unfamiliar vegetables or unusual cuts of meat?

6. What happens if you have to change your plans suddenly or
alter your usual routine? If such situations upset you unduly,
you may be sure that your rigidity, and hence your age, is
showing rather dangerously.

7. Do you often feel left out of things, and that other people
don't pay enough attention to you? This is one of the most
frequent complaints of age and one of the most needless ones.
Inflexible men and women, whatever their age, overlook the
fact that human beings are most apt to do the things they
want to do and ignore the others. Therefore, if older people
crave affection (and every one of us does), it behooves them
to behave in such a way that other people will *want* to give it
to them.

8. When you have the attention of another person are you inclined to talk too much and fail to listen with genuine interest
to what he has to say? This is another of the unfailing signs
of age, and I have seen it in secretaries of twenty-seven as well
as in grandfathers of seventy-two.

9. Do you frequently do a kindness for a neighbor, a relative, or
for anyone with whom you are in contact? This does not
mean a "business favor," which implies a similar favor in
return, but a simple act of making life a little better for someone else when it is within your power to do so. One of the
youngest women of advanced years that I ever knew operated
her whole life on the principle of "Why are we living except
to make life easier for each other?" She was a far cry from a
do-gooder, but her philosophy kept her so young in heart and
so active in body that when the minister announced her age

at her funeral, he was questioned about his accuracy! Without actually thinking about her age, her associates had assumed that she was in her late fifties, when in reality she was closer to eighty! The too frequently encountered attitude of "trying to make things as tough for people as possible" will age an individual faster than rheumatism or a poor digestion!

10. Are you contributing something to the world you live in, or are you content to sit on the side lines, convinced that it is going to pot and there is very little that you or anyone else can do about it?

Put a little check mark beside the questions which you feel apply most particularly to your present mental attitudes. It will give you sort of a rough inventory of what stock you have on hand, what needs refurbishing, and where you need to lay in a completely new line. Don't wait until later to do something about it. You are no longer at the place in your life where a tolerant parent can overlook your weaknesses in the belief that you will outgrow them.

You can't depend upon yourself to outgrow anything from now on, and unpleasant character traits tend to become more marked with the passing years. There are a number of reasons for this, but let us consider the two most obvious ones.

The first reason that we are so apt to become less attractive to others as we grow older is because here in America we do not have a philosophy of continuous self-improvement throughout life. We regard the years between kindergarten and legal voting age as the period during which we should acquire knowledge, and from that point on we make little effort to accumulate any more. It is often said that the thoughts we have gathered by the time we are twenty-five we make last for the rest of our lives.

The great universities have long known that it is the exceptional graduate indeed who continues his studies once he has

his diploma in his hand. It has been only very recently, however, that any serious steps have been taken to change this
unfortunate situation. Up until a few years ago the annual
meetings of the "old grads" were energetic but pathetic attempts on the part of middle-aged men to get together and
drink as much liquor and tell as many stories as they had in
their undergraduate days. They grew nostalgic over the glories
of departed football teams and overanxious about the prospects
of the present ones and woke up the next morning painfully
aware that it is not possible to turn back the clock.

The whole process was a negative thing, because the old
graduates were trying to go backward instead of moving forward, which is the only direction in which a mentally healthy
person can move. Today, in many of the large colleges, the
annual meetings of the graduate students are opportunities
and spurs to increased learning. There are seminars and
discussion groups at which men and women of all ages find
themselves absorbing new ideas and rediscovering old ones.
They limber up parts of their minds grown stiff with disuse
and come away refreshed and revitalized. They return to their
regular pursuits with a feeling of "being in touch with the
times," rather than as "old duffers who can't keep up with the
young fellers any more."

The idea that all of life is a continuous and unbroken process
of learning is still too new to the American scene for more than
a fortunate few to benefit from it. The term *adult education*
is still somewhat uninviting to those who look back on their
school days with no great enthusiasm. But adult education
need not be carried on in formal classes; it can be an individual
undertaking as well as a group project and can embrace learning new homemaking arts, needlework, and dog raising just as
well as following new scientific trends and taking Great Books
courses. Those who remain young at any age are the men and

women who have realized that when one stops *learning* one in truth stops *living*.

The second major reason why our undesirable character traits become more evident as time goes by is because too many men and women feel that the mere possession of years and a few gray hairs gives them the right to assert their opinions and even to inflict them on others.

Mothers-in-law have attained their unenviable reputation by trying to run their married children's lives. Older office-workers have alienated their fellow workers by insisting that "things be done around here the way they always have been." I remember one woman who tried to clinch every argument by saying that she had a great many more gray hairs than the person to whom she was talking and there could be no doubt, therefore, that she was in a better position to know what was right!

Such thoughtless presumption on the part of older people does little to endear them to younger ones. Almost all human beings have smarted to some degree as children under the too rigid authority of their parents, and it is not surprising that when they come to occupy positions of authority they may enjoy turning the tables on older associates to make them suffer in turn. Older men and women who feel that younger people are antagonistic to them should analyze their own attitudes carefully to see if they are behaving in such a way as to make young people want to get back at them.

How to Get Along with the Coming Generation

The whole question of getting along with the younger generation is such an important part of growing older that it deserves a separate discussion.

In our present society three living generations in a family is not unusual, and living great-grandparents are going to be present in increasing numbers in the future. If the differences of opinion and behavior habits among these several generations are to operate side by side as a harmonious unit, we must all begin now to acquaint ourselves with what the generation on the step below us is doing and thinking.

Here again the quality of *flexibility* will stand us in good stead, for the flexible person will be able to remember how he or she felt at that same earlier period of life. It will be possible to recall the things that seemed important then, and thus it will be easier to appreciate the motives and actions of those who are following in our footsteps.

It is true that young people appear to change and certainly to become better informed with each generation as our knowledge of educational techniques and systems for transmitting news and information become greater. But the underlying drives and uncertainties, the dreams and aspirations, the hurts and disappointments, remain very much the same from one generation to another. Human beings are, after all, human beings, unchanged from generation to generation or from place to place.

If you have already discovered that you "just can't understand the coming generation," you had better set out right now with an open mind to learn something about it. Don't let yourself become so preoccupied with earning money or acquiring a more exalted position that you do not have time to cultivate children and young people. You will retain your own youthfulness far more fully and genuinely if you associate with the very young in years, who have a surprising fund to give to their elders.

You must do so, however, with an open mind, so that what they have to give can really penetrate into your thinking and consciousness. Let the more inspired type of schoolteacher be your guide in this. The really great teachers are those who can establish a two-way flow of ideas between their young students and themselves. The schoolteachers who become crabbed and tense and unloved are those who direct their stream of facts at the class and do not permit anything of the youth and beauty and clear-mindedness of their young charges to bounce back to them. To such teachers, the imparting of knowledge is a dreary, unrewarding business by which they earn enough money to sustain their dreary, unrewarding lives. To them children are the invention of Satan, created for the express purpose of making life miserable for their betters. And the children, sensing this attitude when it exists in teachers, parents, or relatives, seldom fail to fulfill their elders' worst expectations!

If you feel you have become a little rusty in the art of establishing contact with children, or with some individual child, you might start by *respectfully* asking their opinion on some matter. That is a sure-fire way of bridging the gap between strange adults, and children are very like us, only smaller. So get their opinion on something and see how it squares up with yours. Only don't try to tear it down by insisting that yours is better. Remember how touchy you are about your own opinions.

Glance through the books and comics they are reading, so that you can discover why they find them so interesting. Again, don't criticize their choice of reading matter unless you are prepared to put something better and equally enthralling in its place.

Inquire about their activities, their companions, and their interests. They may not be able to discuss these subjects in the most entertaining way, but don't give them a hint that you are bored or impatient to get back to your own thoughts or conversation. (This is not to be construed as a blanket invitation to let the small fry interrupt and take over legitimate adult conversations—this applies to the time that you are devoting to keeping in touch with younger people and younger thought.)

If you are trying to win the interest and respect of children, don't expect them to treat you with any more deference than you are willing to show them. The genuine attention and affection of children must be *earned*, it can't be *demanded*. This is the shoal upon which so many parents and grandparents go aground. Children are much too clear-sighted to be fooled by mere years masquerading as kindly wisdom and affection. You have to show real interest in them and their activities before you can expect them to take a deep and lasting interest in you. Neither blood ties nor a position of authority will carry any real weight if they know that you are chiefly concerned with criticizing them, pointing out their failures and short-comings, ignoring their little triumphs and accomplishments, and trying to impress them with the fact that your ideas are better than theirs. This type of grandparent gets nothing but "duty calls" from the younger generation and lives a lonely, fretful old age because he or she feels left out of the family's activities.

How to Be a Successful Parent and Grandparent

The true measure of your success as a parent comes not when your children are small, but when they are grown. It is then, during your own harvest years, that you reap the rich rewards or taste the bitter fruit of your parenthood.

Again, it has been only during recent years that we have recognized that we are preparing both ourselves and our children for the later years during the brief span that they are little. It is at this point that we establish the attitudes toward ourselves which our children will carry all through life and which will be reflected back to us when they are grown and we are older men and women. It is here, too, that we develop in them the character traits and mental attitudes which can help them make their whole life a process of learning and growth and prepare them in turn for the real enjoyment of their own harvest years.

The preparation for maturity and for some of the problems which arise in the middle years begins early and continues throughout life. The resourceful parent or teacher can show a child many ways to keep time from hanging heavily on his hands. Such a child learns very early that life is an exciting adventure and that many roads are open to him to fulfill his natural creative urges and to make use of his boundless energy. The habit of inquiring, of learning, of seeking and expecting to find answers to his questions becomes fixed and continues always as a habit of thought and action. Such a child is not afraid to tackle new problems or to find himself in unfamiliar surroundings. His natural flexibility has been encouraged and strengthened and he will retain it and use it all his life.

How different the years of maturity will be for such a youngster than for the one who has become resigned at an early age to a tasteless, limited, and unproductive existence. We see so many such children sitting alone and listless on a porch step or gazing with empty, dispirited eyes from a window, their natural curiosity blunted, their wills frustrated, and their energies put to drab, unstimulating tasks. Such children have already learned to ask little and expect less from the business of living. They are the ones who will grow up into limited men and women to whom old age will be only a greater and less rewarding burden than childhood.

It is the parents of just such children who are apt to complain in later years about the neglect and ingratitude of their offspring. These are the parents who did little to make childhood the warm, reassuring, and delightful adventure that it should have been, who bemoan the fact that their children do little or nothing to make their old age a time of comfort, joy, and entertainment!

Many parents also make the mistake of taking their children's affection for granted simply because of the blood relationship. As your children grow older you should not impose on them to run errands and do your shopping for you, or to entertain you or call you regularly. At this period in your life you should be prepared to take up new interests (of which we shall have more to say later) and branch out and live for yourself. Don't cling to your children and insist that they let you live solely through them.

You will be included in their plans and activities far more frequently if you are independent and freewheeling than if you complain about the loneliness and drabness of your lot and make them feel they are duty-bound to fill your life with interest, whether they want to or not.

Parents get along much better with their grown-up children when they show appreciation for whatever little attentions are paid to them, rather than taking the attitude that their children are doing little enough for them in return for all the parents have previously done for the children.

Be glad and complimented when they come to you for advice, but don't force it upon them after they are twenty-one. Show that you trust them to know what is best for themselves and to have sense enough to ask for guidance if they feel they need it. If you have been a wise parent, by the time your children have enjoyed twenty-one years of your leadership and example they will have a fairly good idea of what they should do and how they should behave.

If you haven't been a wise and affectionate parent, you can't hope to undo the damage after they are twenty-one and bring about any very radical changes. So in either event it is best to interfere with your grown children as little as possible. They will make mistakes, of course, just as all of us have, and they will learn from these mistakes and go on to make other ones, for such is the process of learning and growth.

As a grandparent you will be faced with the delightful and challenging opportunity of winning the affection and respect of your grandchildren, not on the basis of relationship, but upon your own merits as a human being whose society and companionship is valuable and desirable. Don't try to seduce your grandchildren by overindulgence and too much attention. Don't be the sort of grandparent who is loved only because the children know they can "get away with anything." And above all, don't try to usurp the place of the parents in the child's affection just because you don't agree with the new-fangled way of rearing children.

Be willing to stand or fall as a parent or grandparent on your own merits as a human being with whom other human beings can genuinely enjoy spending time. If you can't do so on these grounds, it's high time you revamped your personality and mental attitudes and tried to increase your own attractiveness rather than complain because others aren't willing to put up with you as you are.

How to Remain an Always Welcome Guest

As we grow older we often find ourselves more and more in the role of the guest and less and less in the role of the host.

Just as the preparation of the big family Thanksgiving dinner will sooner or later devolve upon a younger member of the family, with the former hostess included as a guest, so it is with other social relationships ranging from inclusion in a day's outing to living permanently with other members of the family.

No discussion of how we are best to employ our harvest years would be complete without taking a careful look at the living-with-relatives situation, which can be one of life's real blessings or one of its all-but-unbearable burdens. Such living arrangements produce friction in so many cases that it is only realistic to state at the outset that separate living quarters seem more desirable in most cases. Obviously, the shortage of housing, particularly housing that is suitable for older persons, together with the very real economic problems involved, makes possible for only a limited few the ideal arrangement of older people having their own house or a separate apartment in their children's house.

The present trend toward the development of housing designed for older people, where they are assured of a community of interests and convenient physical surroundings, shows that our thinking has at last caught up with two very basic realities in this situation.

The first is that the interests of the four divisions of people —i.e., children, adolescents, adults, and older people—are sufficiently diverse to necessitate the benefit of each other's company part of the time. But certain interests cannot constantly be shared by these different age groups.

Second, few human beings have yet learned to respect the rights of another to have some privacy and the privilege of doing things his own way. Here it is very often the older generations who are most at fault, since they feel that their added years entitle them to give unasked-for advice, to try to run things, and to be the center of attention. However, the younger generations cannot be absolved from blame on this score either, when they try to force their "modern methods" on older individuals who are quite content to continue doing things in their accustomed way.

To suggest that it would be better for us to live apart from those who are considerably younger than we are and to seek more constant companionship at our own age level may seem at first to be in contradiction to what has been said earlier about the importance of cultivating younger friends and acquaintances. It is true that younger and older generations should work and understand and help each other, but this is often better accomplished if they are not constantly thrown together by the necessity of living under the same roof. Many people function best when they meet and work together for a while and then part for an hour, a day, or a week. If thrown together constantly, regardless of age and differences of interest, friction and tension are almost sure to develop and mutual appreciation, respect, and creativity disappear.

In the distant future, when we know more of human nature and have gained in understanding and patience, we may all dwell in peace. But for the remainder of the present century, at least, it seems that we had better stop insisting that all ages live together willy-nilly and like it. Human personality must reach a higher plane of love and understanding before individuals born twenty or more years apart can live together in harmony. Moreover, we shouldn't be too disturbed by our present inability to accomplish this difficult feat in human relationships. We are improving and striving for better understanding and more communion between different age groups, and one of the most effective ways to achieve it is to accept our role of guest gracefully during our later years.

The best way to remain an always welcome guest is *never to forget that you are one.* Don't take your children's home for granted any more than you take their affection for granted. You wouldn't think of criticizing and dictating while visiting in the home of a casual friend, nor would you ever again invite a guest to your house who walked in and tried to "take over." Don't be guilty of such unforgivably poor manners in the home of your children.

Typical of the tragedy that such lack of manners and consideration can bring on a family is the report of a woman who sought advice from a professional social worker on how to solve the problem of her mother. In explaining that her mother had recently been widowed and wanted to come and live with her, the married daughter said: "I know if Mother moves into our house it will cost me my marriage. She's never been easy to live with, and now that she's older and Father's gone, she's even more difficult. She doesn't get on with the children and she thinks almost everything we do about bringing them up is wrong. She doesn't like our friends and says they have no manners because they don't include her in all their activities. She doesn't like the way I run the house and even interferes with the cleaning woman, who says she'll leave if Mother comes to live with us. If we ask her to help with the dishes she feels we're trying to make a servant of her, but if we don't let her share the household tasks she says she feels useless. When she's around I'm always fighting with my husband and my children because they object to her interference and I feel I have to defend her, because, after all, she is my mother. But I just can't face the prospect of having her spend the rest of her life with us!"

Here, then, is what can happen when an older person fails to live up to the role of a welcome, respected, and beloved guest. The mother in this case would be outraged at her daughter's attitude and label her selfish and lacking in affec-

90078

LIBRARY
College of St. Francis
JOLIET, ILL.

tion. But it is easy to see that it is the mother and not the daughter who is the greater offender on both counts.

When, as the years go by, you find yourself living in someone else's house for a day, a week, or a year—never lose sight of the fact that you are a *guest* in that house and conduct yourself as one. You may be a self-sustaining guest, but whether or not you contribute to the operating expenses of the house, you are a guest and you should never forget it.

The role may be somewhat difficult for you, and you may try to excuse your interference and constant suggestions on the grounds that you had your house for so long that it's very hard to try to live in someone else's. But remember that when you had your own house you ran it in your own way, and your son or daughter or friends want the same privilege in running theirs.

The annual visits of grandparents or in-laws are dreaded only when such older people come to criticize or be a dead weight around the younger people's necks. They are welcomed and anticipated with pleasure when they are genial, pleasant, and helpful; when they come to praise, to appreciate, and to build up. They should be willing to help if help is needed, and, if not, to enjoy themselves and occupy their time with other interests. Grandmothers can make friends with the children and give their daughters a little free time for shopping or visiting friends. They can sew, knit, or contrive something tangible to leave behind them as a lasting reminder of their interest and affection and of the pleasant, productive hours they have spent beneath this particular roof.

Above all, remember your own, and the family's, need for privacy and leave the group to itself for a part of each day. Don't retire to your own room like a martyr with that "I know when I'm not wanted" air that makes everyone feel guilty and uncomfortable, but go in the spirit of a wise human being who recognizes human limitations and wants to see life lived as pleasantly and harmoniously as possible for all concerned.

If you remember your childhood literature, you may recall the delightful grandmother in the story of *Heidi,* whose visits were high lights of each year for the entire household, with the exception of the very rigid and inflexible housekeeper. The grandmother, although well advanced in years, was a wise and cheerful person who kept her own life filled with a variety of interests and who sought to help rather than to impose on those around her. Her daily nap time was a source of keen disappointment to the children, who wanted to be with her constantly, but the grandmother was wise enough to realize that both the children and the adult members of the family would appreciate her presence and her stories more if she disappeared from their midst for a time each day. The nap also gave her an opportunity to restore her energies and freshen her appearance and attire.

The welcome guest is always careful about personal appearance and neatness and also makes an effort to have something of interest to contribute to those who are being visited. One of the most constant complaints about older guests is that they go over the same conversational territory again and again and that they have no new ideas to offer or any interest in hearing about those that others may have.

The complaint is a valid one—none of us like to be bored more than is necessary—but it is also a complaint that older persons can overcome if they are sincerely interested in retaining their position in the affections of their family and friends. The solution lies in that basic principle we mentioned earlier— the need to treat life as a never-ending process of learning, so that we never cease to add to our store of information and knowledge.

How to Acquire New Interests and Fresh Viewpoints

The dull, monotonous older person is, of course, only the narrow, limited younger person grown older. The woman teacher or office worker who begins in her thirties to lose her buoyancy, breadth of vision, sense of humor, optimism, and her friendly feeling for other people will with the years become sensitive, critical, domineering, possessive, and pedantic. When these characteristics progress to such a degree that her business superiors and fellow associates can no longer work in harmony with her, she may lose her job and be bitter about being fired "just because I was getting on in years." Actually her chronological age had little to do with it other than to intensify the negative attitudes present in her long before she was "old."

The same is true of older men of whom we often hear it said, "He can't take directions any more; he acts so upset when new plans are introduced; he's no good at teaching the younger men." Individuals of both sexes may be blamed for stirring up trouble and resentment, for being meddlesome, curious, gossipy, and disagreeable to work with. The individuals themselves may feel greatly put upon and unappreciated. They will say, in the words of the popular song, "Nobody loves you when you're old and gray," but they will fail to see that their own character patterns and lack of flexibility have brought them to this sorry state.

Getting ready to enjoy the harvest years can't begin too early. In the realm of sound family relationships, it is important that physicians who are attending growing families should point out that the child of today will be a grown, independent man or woman in a surprisingly short time and the mother and father had better look ahead right now to what they are going to do with their lives once active parenthood is past!

Young parents may feel that they have many years in which to make up their minds about such matters, but it is the variety of interests and the enthusiasm with which they acquire new ones at this time that determine in large measure whether they will be delightful, lively, and interesting oldsters or dull, querulous old people who can do little more than huddle in the modern equivalent of the chimney corner.

Men, in our present society, really have a more difficult time than women in acquiring new interests throughout life. Women of leisure have long been expected to take up new card games, new pastimes, new handicrafts, and new philanthropic pursuits. Men, on the other hand, who do anything more radical than play golf (which they frequently excuse on the grounds of needing to get a little exercise) may be considered effete, or wasting their time, if they do not devote all their energies to making money.

The end product of this mistaken concept has been the impressive number of financially successful, retired men of fifty, sixty, or seventy who don't know what to do with themselves once they stop working. They realize that they don't need to earn any more money and that they should leave their offices to make room for younger men to move up, but they find the retirement they have longed for a bore. It is dull because they haven't prepared themselves for it by gathering a variety of interests, other than making money, along the way.

An attractive woman in her early thirties came to my office not long ago seeking help for her husband, who she feared was on the verge of a "complete nervous breakdown." The man, who was thirty-six, could no longer eat, sleep, or concentrate on anything. His restlessness and irritability had become an almost unbearable burden both to himself and to his family. He was one of three brothers, all of whom had been persuaded by their father to enter the family's firm upon graduation from college, with the understanding that when they had learned the business it would be turned over to them in three equal shares to operate on their own.

The father, a robust man of seventy-two, had provided handsomely for his own retirement, but now that retirement age was at hand, he steadfastly refused to step aside and let his sons take over. They had worked hard and well, but the father showed no inclination to relinquish any of his authority or to permit the younger men to make any major decisions. His business was his whole life, and active as he was in mind and body, he could not endure the thought of sitting by in idleness, since there was nothing aside from his work in which he took the slightest interest or pleasure. His sons, meanwhile, were forced to continue playing secondary roles long after they had prepared themselves for leadership. As a result, all of them were showing the ill effects of this prolonged frustration, nervous tension, and bitter resentment toward their father, who professed that he was acting for their best interests. Actually he was making nervous wrecks of his sons because of his own failure to provide other interests for himself once the urgent need to make money was past.

The attitude has somehow grown up in this country that while it may be all right for a business executive to sneak away from the office once in a while to see a ball game, it would be unthinkable for him to attend a lecture on organic farming, color photography, or lapidary as a home art! The national ideal of a man keeping his nose strictly to the grindstone, with never a change of pace or a little experimentation with new ideas, leads inevitably to some very dull and blunted older people.

Many a man has cherished a secret desire to learn to play

the violin or to belong to a good choral group or to perfect the magic tricks he started to learn when he was a boy, but he's been afraid of what his associates might think if he did anything about it. Such men glance through the announcements of lectures at the museum, the programs at the concert halls, or the list of activities of special-interest groups, thinking, "That might be a lot of fun; too bad I haven't got time to go in for any of that stuff."

Perhaps they cannot actually spare the time at that moment, but the wise man with an eye to the future will at least clip the announcement or make a note of its contents, so that when the day comes that he does have time, he will have a wealth of suggestions ready at hand of things that once attracted and may still interest him. Such a list will serve as a foundation for his future exploration and save him from the feeling of being lost in an unchartered sea of time that has no real purpose or meaning. It is better not to put these things off too long, though. It is a good idea to try doing now a few of those things you "don't have time for."

The same applies to a woman whose household or business chores prevent her from enjoying many of the cultural and social events in which she feels she would like to indulge. For her, too, a list of things which capture her fancy and interest through the years will provide a starting point for developing a full life for herself when her family or job no longer claims her time.

Such a system acts very much as does a scrapbook for home planners, who may spend years clipping pictures of pleasing architectural details, efficient closets and storage units, and well-planned kitchens, against the day that they finally build their own home. They may not incorporate many of the ideas into the actual building of their house, but the scrapbook has given them a good starting point and made it possible for them to weed out the things they did and did not want. It has also given them untold hours of happy anticipation.

Don't be afraid to experiment a little as you go along and try out some of your ideas in a modest way. If you think life in the country is what you want when you retire, spend as much time in the country as you can during your vacations, to see if you really like it or are just being romanced by the full-color covers on the farm journals and seed catalogues! If you have a long-suppressed desire to express yourself in water colors or oils, join an inexpensive evening art class and find out if your talent is real or imagined. You may find that it isn't really painting but ceramics or modeling in clay that brings you the greatest pleasure, and you will have gained a head start right away on years of fascinating activity.

Just as men will sometimes use the pressure of business affairs as an alibi for not diversifying their interests, women will frequently fall back on housekeeping and motherhood as reasons for not enlarging their field of interests. They may take an exaggerated pride in their tidiness or in the amount of time they devote to their children, thus making a virtue of what is really an admission that they are afraid to go out and mix with other people. They may feel anxiety about going downtown and finding themselves in crowds, or they may feel inadequate in the presence of women who they believe are better informed or smarter looking than themselves. To make up for this feeling, they may indulge in criticizing other women for their many interests and accusing them of neglecting their home duties, even though they wish that they could be like them.

Certainly no one would recommend cultivating a variety of interests at the expense of the family's comfort and security. However, it is possible to find the middle way, which permits a woman to give her home the warmth and security that it must have if it is to be a real home and yet allows some leisure toward developing herself as a woman and a well-rounded human being.

Instead of dreading the later years of life, a man or woman who is even now laying the foundation for the absorbing things he or she is going to do later will anticipate the harvest years as the richly rewarding time that they should be.

Rather than cling to the idea of retirement and idleness as the desirable goal, we should recognize that true retirement is generally a sad illusion. Few of us realize how fortunate we are to be busy, to be occupied, to be contributing, to be in a position of some importance to ourselves and to others. When we are busy we may complain that we are being imposed upon, but when we are no longer busy and have any obligations or responsibilities we complain even more bitterly. Don't look ahead to the time when you will do nothing. Look ahead to the time when you will fill your life with the things you've always wanted most to do!

The Mental Hygiene of Later Life

Dr. Maxwell Gittleson has set up some valuable guideposts to sound mental health in the later years. For the person who would keep his mind as healthy and as active as his body, Dr. Gittleson says it is important:

1. Never to know that one is through.
2. Never to feel superfluous.
3. Never to lack significance.
4. Never to be without use.
5. Never to be without an outlet for the creative urge.
6. Never to be without a word in the affairs of men.

This is an ideal state toward which we are now working, and which, when we have achieved it, will mitigate much of the poor mental health which we now associate with the later years.

Poor mental health, however, is no more inevitable with the passing years than is poor physical health. It can be prevented just as we now know that we do not have to suffer from rheumatism merely because we have celebrated a given number of birthdays. Much of what now passes for mental deterioration and breakdown is in reality only an intensification of undesirable personality characteristics which were already there.

We say of such persons that they have become childish, which really means that they have become almost completely selfish instead of broadening their scope of interests with the years. They become more demanding, more irritable and impatient, more concentrated on their own physical condition, their own creature comforts, until they develop an almost total disregard for everyone else. This is old age at its dreariest, made even more intolerable because in many cases, where there is no real change in personality or in the physical condition of the brain, it is needless and preventable.

In both men and women this marked deterioration in sound mental attitudes sometimes starts with the menopause or change of life. This is even more regrettable since this change is a perfectly normal part of life and should in no way be construed as a weakness or a disease.

The same old wives' tales and lack of understanding which have caused so many women to regard pregnancy as an illness rather than as a normal function of a healthy body have given rise to the many groundless fears about the loss of mental health at the time of the menopause.

Men have not escaped the violence of these rumors either,

and far too many of them live in dread of the approaching climacteric and are ready to go to pieces when they find that that which they have so long feared is upon them.

Whether or not men undergo a change of life in the same sense that a woman does is still being argued in medical circles, and the final answer is awaiting us somewhere in the future. Certainly nothing so sudden and clearly defined as occurs in women happens to men, and the change is so gradual and so long in process that the individual would scarcely be aware of it were it not for the fears which have been built up around it.

Certainly no normal man looks forward to the loss of his sexual capacity, but it is also true that a man who has not attached exaggerated importance to this single function is able to replace his interest in sex with many other things during the latter part of his life.

Here again, in both men and women, we find that the individuals who suffer major disturbances at this time are those who have led narrow, unenriched lives long before the climacteric was upon them. It is the woman whose life has been limited, loveless, and self-sacrificing who becomes irritable, truculent, troublesome, sadistic, and hostile when the menopause makes her forcibly aware that it is no longer possible for her to bear children. On the other hand, those who have had their families and feel that their lives have been well filled welcome the menopause as a time for even freer and more complete sexual expression without concern about pregnancy.

In men this same absence of romantic color and stimulating activities throughout life may manifest itself in an unbecoming interest in extremely young women at the time when they feel that only enough vitality is left for one last fling.

It is understandable that at this time of life those who have enjoyed few of its joys or tasted little of its richness should be in a state of rebellion. Men and women who are satisfied with seeing and doing little are emotionally limited individuals, but when the time for retirement comes they are not always content to live quietly and unobtrusively. Moreover, those who seemed to be satisfied with so little when they were younger may suddenly turn into the most unreasonably demanding older people as they clutch at the prizes that they did not have along the way. All the repressed demands for love, prestige, and gratification now make themselves felt more strongly than ever, and many a family is at a loss to cope with the sudden change that has taken place in one of its heretofore placid older members.

We need a great deal of education in order to learn to live at all age periods and to reap the rewards which each period has to offer those who are prepared to accept them. These are the men and women who are prepared to live fully and generously. At present there is so much wasted energy, so much needless worry, so much striving for unimportant goals, and so many values that have little meaning in terms of human feelings. We need to make a constant effort to define the real essentials in our relations with each other, so that we do not lose sight of the truly important goals amid the many meaningless ones. We need to live all our lives in such a way that we leave room to develop that all-important quality of flexibility which Dr. Gittleson defined when he said:

"The flexible person is one who respects himself without conceit, who has been guided by principles but who has not been a slave to dogma, who has had steadiness of purpose without being hypnotized by an immutable goal, who has bent his energies to making the grade rather than getting to the top first, who has tolerated his weakness while employing his strengths, who has respected his neighbor as well as had pride in himself."

The mental and emotional futures of each of us lie to a large extent in our own hands. It is up to us to develop ourselves so that we may remain useful, either through our physical efforts or our personalities, to people of all ages around us. It is only then that we can claim the right to retain a word in the affairs of men and to know that we shall never be through, never feel superfluous, and never be without an outlet for the urge to do something truly useful and meaningful all our lives—something which will merit appreciation in the eyes of the world and most especially in the eyes of those who love us.

HOW TO REACH THE HARVEST YEARS

by

ERNST P. BOAS, M.D.

THE physical process of aging is a very gradual one. It is a continuing process from the time of our conception, but we are apt to give it little thought until we are inconvenienced by it.

The practice of geriatrics may be said to begin where pediatrics leaves off. For far too many Americans, however, a gap of twenty years or more may exist between the time when their parents took them for regular medical checkups for normal growth and childhood ailments and the moment when they decide that they should have a doctor look them over because they feel their machinery is beginning to falter. In too many cases the damage has already been done and an extensive rehabilitation program may be needed to correct a condition that might have been prevented or rendered unimportant if it had been caught in time.

The Bible tells us that the natural life span of man is threescore years and ten. Today, after some twenty-five hundred years of civilization, this is still very close to the truth, although we see an increasing number of individuals who reach their ninetieth and one hundredth birthdays with a good deal of "go" left in them. This will, no doubt, become more frequent as a better understanding of the care, and particularly the diet, of older people is gained.

The attainment of great age is not nearly so important to us at this point as insuring that all the years we live will be healthy, useful ones. In the words of the Gerontological Society, we want "to add life to years, not years to life."

A considerable amount of confusion exists on this point because so much publicity has been given to the tremendous increase in the average expectation of life at birth during the first half of this century. By this we mean the number of years, on an average, that newborn children may expect to live.

At the time of the American Revolution the average life span in this country was 35.5 years. By 1900 it had risen to fifty years, and today it is sixty-five years for men and seventy-one for women. These figures indicate that there are now much fewer deaths at young ages and that many more young people grow to maturity and middle life, although it is true that there has also been a marked increase in the saving of life at advanced ages.

It seems probable that the application of the present knowledge of medicine and hygiene will make it possible to extend the average life to about seventy-five years, with an increasing number of individuals living into the ninth decade. There is little to be gained, however, in merely prolonging our stay on this planet. The real goal is to maintain our health and vitality for whatever number of years we are here.

There is no particular point in life at which a person "begins to get old." All of life is a never-ending process of growth and repair, and since the body's cells and organs have a remarkable power of renewing themselves, it is each individual's business to see that the body gets all the help and encouragement possible to keep this process in smooth operation. Eventually, like the "wonderful one-hoss shay," the best of bodies will wear out; the trick is to keep it in comfortable working condition right up to the last minute!

A Stitch in Time

There are tremendous differences in the life spans of various animals. Many insects live only a few days in their mature form; rats have an average life span of six years; dogs live about fifteen years and horses about twenty. It is well known that in some human families most of the members, generation after generation, live to a ripe old age, while in other families the individual members are much shorter-lived. It appears, therefore, that longevity is a special attribute and that it is a quality handed down through heredity.

It is safe to say that the life span of any animal or human being is determined in large measure by the pattern of the life curve of the species to which he belongs, modified by the hereditary vigor of the family line of which he happens to be a member. In our present state of incomplete knowledge, we can only generalize on the fact that longevity depends on the vital force liberated in the ovum or egg at the time of fertilization and that aging is due to the gradual running down and weakening of this vital force.

Oliver Wendell Holmes said, "If you are setting out to achieve threescore years and twenty, the first thing to be done is, some years before birth, to advertise for a couple of parents both belonging to long-lived families."

Aside from this advice, the best thing you can do is to become acquainted with the aging and disease tendencies shown in your family history so that you can be on guard against their possible ill effects.

The rate of aging varies in different individuals as well as in different families. Some persons are old from the physical standpoint at fifty while others are physically young at seventy.

We must learn to distinguish between the chronological and physiological age, for it is not so much how many years we have lived, but how well our bodies have withstood the march of time. The soundness of your body depends in considerable measure upon the soundness of your mental outlook, for a disturbed, unhappy mind is a great ally of physical deterioration and decay.

As a rule the human body gives its owner many little warnings before it permits anything of a very serious nature to go wrong. Sudden changes in weight may occur; you may find yourself tiring too readily or becoming irritated over trifles; headaches and other pains may appear too frequently. Breathlessness, insomnia, marked changes in bowel habits and urination, swelling of the joints and legs, lumps and growths on or under the skin may be signals that your body needs help in functioning at its best.

On the other hand, such minor symptoms may be of little significance and an individual may be prey to damaging and needless worry. The wisest plan is to make a yearly visit to your physician and allow him to evaluate your symptoms. Some old soul with a genius for mixing her proverbs once said, "A stitch in time is worth a pound of cure." Certainly no truer word was ever spoken in regard to the practice of geriatrics. It is the stitch in time that leads to longevity, and the stitch should be taken early for both physical and mental well-being. Don't worry about a symptom that might be serious. Find out about it, and then, if it is unimportant, dismiss it completely from your thoughts. Don't join the legions of men and women who literally worry themselves into old age.

The healthy body has a remarkable capacity for self-regulation. At rest, it keeps constant its temperature, its complex chemical processes, its intake of oxygen, the amount of blood circulating in a given unit of time; and it rapidly adjusts all these functions to any sudden change in physical activity. In the more mature body these adjustments cannot be made so quickly and sudden demands upon body reserves cannot be met so readily. Thus older persons do not tolerate excessive heat and cold; their hearts, quite adequate for normal situations, cannot respond when a too demanding load is put upon them. This is true of all bodily functions, as anyone who played tennis in his thirties will attest to in his fifties!

We do not yet know exactly why many of these changes in our physical capacity occur. No doubt many of them are due to the normal wear and tear of ceaseless activity throughout the years. Our bodies may wear out and become shaky like an antique chair or threadbare like an old suit of clothes. There is no direct relationship between the function of the glands of internal secretion and the process of aging, nor is there evidence that a lessening of the male or female sex hormones have anything to do with it.

Some bodily changes which we have heretofore attributed to "old age" may be due to prolonged inadequate or unbalanced diet. It has been shown experimentally in rats that a longer life span can be achieved by an adjustment of food intake. In man, the effects of improper eating habits may accumulate over the years and not become apparent until later in life.

We cannot yet be sure whether the lack of calcium in the bones of older persons is natural in later life or whether it is the result of an insufficient amount of calcium throughout their entire life. We do know that calcium in sufficient quantities is lacking in the average American diet. Lack of calcium is, in fact, one of the most characteristic deficiencies in our present way of eating. But we shall discuss this later when we consider diets.

The optimum vitamin intake is yet to be established, and we cannot say with certainty whether an insufficient vitamin consumption may, with the years, lead to some of the less desirable features of growing older.

We do know that the passing years affect mental and psychological processes in much the same way that they affect our physical beings. Some of the elasticity of response is lost, but it is important to note that the *power to learn does not decline.* An attempt should be made to distinguish between changes which are actually due to slower body responses and those which are due to outside factors, since so many of our mental and emotional reactions are conditioned by the environment in which we live. It is too easy for us to blame everything on "old age," when age itself may have little or nothing to do with it!

It has been generally accepted, for instance, that memory becomes impaired in later life. But memory is a function of attention. An older person, removed from active, competitive life, with no urgent tasks or desires that demand constructive action, pays less attention to what is going on about him. His *ability* to remember is as good as ever; what he lacks is *interest* in using this ability, because he may not have the social stimulus to make him want to remain alert.

What is true of memory is true of other mental and emotional reactions. In heedlessly relegating older persons to positions of unimportance and dependency, society has taken away most of the incentive to "stay alert." This changed status, brought about by forces beyond their control, has created insoluble problems for many older people, problems which need not have existed at all.

We are apt to brand our elders as "conservatives" and charge it up to their inability or unwillingness to learn new tricks or to go along with the times. Actually, the conservative attitude of many older persons is nothing but an expression of their insecurity and need to cling to modes of life and thought that are familiar to them rather than venture into the hazards of the unknown, hazards set up by a hostile society.

Support for the correctness of these views is found in industry's growing tendency to re-evaluate the worth and importance of older workers and to abolish their present wasteful and unjust prejudice against employing men and women who have passed sixty. The Old Age Counseling Center in California, in making a study some years ago of business employees whose work was below standard, reported three striking findings. First, it was found that slowness, lack of co-operation, and resistance to change was found in workers of *all* ages. Second, these characteristics usually had specific causes—such as home worries, hampering habits, unwholesome ideas or emotions, and similar factors not related to old age. Third, the causes behind these maladjustments could be remedied in the older workers, just as they could be in the younger ones, by attacking them at their sources.

Most significant of all, it was discovered that once the cause of the trouble was removed—such as fear of dismissal because of age—the older worker often proved more valuable than ever before and, "far from being ripe for retirement, responded with enthusiasm to increased responsibility."

What, then, can each individual do to minimize the effects of the advancing years? We cannot stay their passage, but we can, to a considerable degree, modify their cumulative effect on the human organism. But to do so we must begin when we are young and not wait until the aging process is nearing its end.

The Healthy Road to Maturity

First of all, take stock of your family background. Obesity, diabetes, arteriosclerosis, high blood pressure, and sometimes cancer, tend to run in families. If there are such tendencies in your family, your physician should know of it, so that he can be on the lookout for their earliest symptoms. By regulating your life, particularly in respect to diet, he will attempt to prevent the development of some of these conditions.

On the other hand, it would be unfortunate to become morbid about contracting a disease that may have afflicted one's parents or grandparents, for these are hereditary *tendencies* and are not *inevitable* so far as they affect any particular individual. It is simply good sense for a person in whose family there is a history of diabetes not to permit himself to become grossly overweight. This, by the way, is sound advice for anyone, since obesity may be an active factor in creating conditions favorable to disease. Don't allow yourself to pile on weight at any period in your life.

The promotion of health in the later years calls for no mysterious measures or occult remedies. It is largely a matter of hygiene, common sense, and a recognition of the fact that from the beginning of childhood the body and its many organs very gradually lose their resiliency and power to cope with excessive strains. Moderation applied to all activities should be our guide, and remember always that it is just as harmful to be oversolicitous about one's health as it is to be careless about it.

Although certain changes in physical and mental responses come with the advancing years, they do not cause illness or death. The body's lessened power of reaction and adaptation to untoward circumstances does, however, favor the development of disease. The loss of elasticity of the lungs and rib cage, for instance, makes it easier for the lungs to accumulate secretions which are favorable to the development of pneumonia. Older persons are more susceptible to heat stroke because of the body's reduced power to regulate its temperature.

The death rate increases eight per cent with each year

throughout life. But illness and death in people of mature years is not due to aging in itself. *Few, if any, people die of old age.* Autopsy studies of people who have died at very advanced ages always show that some disease process or trauma was the cause of death, even if this disease was not suspected during their lifetime.

It becomes a matter of very practical importance, therefore, to distinguish between the gradual, natural process of growing older and the diseases of the later years. Every ailing person, *no matter what his age,* should be given the benefit of all the aid that medical science can offer. Far too often we assume that the illness is but an inevitable sign of aging and that nothing can be done about it. Many such illnesses go unrelieved and many lives are lost because sickness becomes confused with aging. Age, like pregnancy, is not a disease. It is a perfectly healthy, normal, natural part of our complete life pattern. We do not die simply because we have lived a given number of years; we die because our bodies have been attacked by diseases which they do not have the power to overcome.

We live by words and concepts, and when these concepts are not clearly defined and the words are not correctly used, error and disaster may follow. The diseases of later life, such as arteriosclerosis, cancer, chronic rheumatism, and diabetes, are called "degenerative" diseases. The word "degenerative," like the word "aging," has a feeling of hopelessness about it. It brings despair to the patient and often inexcusably checks attempts at cure and rehabilitation. This same sense of inevitability has discouraged scientific research into the nature and causes of these disorders. Yet in the past few years the fields of arteriosclerosis and rheumatism have been thrown wide open by medical investigators who attacked the problem without prejudice, and we appear to be on the threshold of gaining the knowledge needed to control and prevent these major scourges of mankind.

When I am asked by patients to set up some sort of guide-posts to point the way to healthy, active maturity, the following suggestions appear to be the most significant.

The Importance of Work

Work that is gratifying and that enables the individual to maintain himself as a self-sufficient unit of society is the best stabilizer of mental and physical well-being. Nothing is of greater importance than the satisfaction of an interesting and rewarding occupation. As one grows older, however, one should, if possible, ease up on the intensity of one's work, eliminate the unnecessary trimmings, and learn to confine oneself to the essentials. Too much ambition, too intense a drive, overtaxes the body and brings about the increased strains which we mentioned earlier. Such strains may in time speed up the progress of a latent heart condition or a tendency toward high blood pressure.

For the employed older worker who is forced to maintain a pace set by younger workers, it is not always easy to accomplish a change in working tempo. Greater understanding on the part of employers is needed—understanding which will benefit both the worker and the work. For when a worker finishes the day worn out and exhausted it indicates that the task is too heavy for him and requires some readjustment.

The majority of men and women can continue to work indefinitely, as long as their health and strength permit, provided their tasks are well suited to their current physical resources. The present custom of setting sixty or sixty-five years as the age of retirement, and shelving the worker automatically when he reaches this chronological age, is based on an incorrect premise and entails much evil to the individual and to society.

With the steady increase in the percentage of older persons in our population, and with the parallel prolongation of the period of education and apprenticeship of our youth, the economic burden of maintaining the whole population is resting more and more on the age group between twenty-five and sixty-five. It is in the interest of society to provide gainful occupations for its members as long as they have the ability and desire to work.

A readjustment in industry's employment policies will, of necessity, be one of the major developments of the near future. Actual experience and study have shown that for many occupations the older worker is an asset to industry. What he may lose in speed he makes up in increased accuracy, steadiness, lack of absenteeism, and the wisdom of experience. For the worker himself, the opportunity to continue at his job and to maintain his earning power is the very best tonic against the effects of aging.

Frequently, men and women in all walks of life who are abruptly put on the shelf and forced into idleness become ill and die shortly after retirement. This is as true of the bank president and chairman of the board as it is of the office or factory worker. The best preserved, both physically and mentally, of the older age groups are those who continue the pattern of their working lives, as well as their financial independence, into their later years.

The age of sixty-five, instead of being marked as the age of *automatic* retirement, should be established as the year of *voluntary* retirement. The employer should have the option to retire the worker if he no longer measures up to his job or cannot be transferred to a more suitable position; the worker, in turn, should also have the choice of continuing to work or of retiring. A proper employment policy will do as much for many an older person as good medical care or a carefully planned social program. The importance of gainful, satisfying work cannot be overemphasized.

The Importance of Exercise

Properly planned exercise brings the body to a condition resembling that of a trained athlete. Most of us become inexcusably soft with the passing years. In youth strenuous physical exercise is natural, but as one reaches middle life and has passed the age of forty some modification in its form should be made. Tennis, handball, and such vigorous sports are best eliminated, in spite of the fact that there are some who can follow these games when well advanced in years. Golf, swimming, walking, riding, gardening, and work in the wood lot are excellent substitutes. For city dwellers, walking is, of course, the exercise of choice and one that can be used to great advantage to the body.

In order to achieve and maintain harmonious function between the nervous system, the muscular, circulatory, and respiratory apparatus, exercise should be a daily habit and not just something to be indulged in occasionally. Daily exercise improves the efficiency of the body as a machine, increases its reserve strength to meet emergencies, and leads to a general sense of well-being.

With the advancing years there will be a natural tendency to lessen the intensity of physical exertion, and one should yield gracefully to the promptings of the body. No exercise should ever be pushed to the point of exhaustion—its purpose is to strengthen the body, not to wear it out! But unless there is a definite physical reason against it, some form of planned body activity should be a part of every day's schedule. The element of competition should be avoided, for competition may spur one to activities beyond one's strength and put undue strain on the body's equipment.

The Importance of Diet

There are probably more misconceptions and fads about eating than about any other human activity. The intake of food is a source of great pleasure to most people, but it is important chiefly because it provides the fuel, the bodily energy which permits us to operate. It replaces stores of proteins, carbohydrates, and fats that have been used up; it supplies the necessary minerals, such as iron and calcium, water and salts, as well as the vitamins that are so essential for chemical reactions in the body.

The caloric requirement of the body, or the amount of food needed for energy, growth, and self-renewal, depends on the physical activity and age of the individual. A lumberjack may need 6,000 calories a day, the active mechanic 4,000, the letter carrier 3,000, and the sedentary worker 2,500. With advancing age physical activities decrease, the metabolism falls, and food requirements become less. A person leading a quiet, indoor life may get along on 2,200 calories, and most people over age seventy will find 1,500 to 1,800 calories sufficient.

Diet is, of course, a subject that should be thoroughly discussed with your physician, since much of the most significant work in the field of geriatrics concerns proper eating habits.

Unfortunately, appetite is more a result of habit than a response to the body's need for food. As we grow older and less active we require somewhat less food, but we are apt to continue eating the same amount we ate in our younger and more spirited days. Obesity results.

Excess weight in the later years is particularly undesirable from both the health and cosmetic viewpoint. The statistics of life-insurance companies have demonstrated conclusively that obesity is a very real hazard to life and frequently prepares the ground for illness and premature death.

At the first sight of gain in weight the diet should be adjusted so that a normal weight may be maintained. Radical starvation cures are rarely necessary, nor are they advisable. It is much better to acquire new eating habits, to diminish gradually the amount of food consumed, and to cut down particularly on starches and fats. Such a revamping of the dietary may cause some hunger and discomfort for the first few weeks, but the digestive system will quickly adjust itself to smaller quantities of food. Once this adjustment has taken place, the person will find that a return to the former larger scale of eating will bring prompt distress.

It is far better to take off a pound a week than to try to lose twenty to twenty-five pounds in a single month. Many overweight men and women, who find it difficult to cut down materially on their food, seek comfort in the idea that obesity is largely a glandular condition. Unfortunately this is not true, and they would be far wiser to recognize the fact that *obesity is almost always caused by a caloric intake greater than is needed by the body*. Few examples of obesity are due to glandular disturbance, and it is rarely necessary or desirable to take thyroid extract to induce weight reduction.

Overeating is often caused by a neurosis or anxiety state. This is frequently demonstrated in office workers who experience great hunger pains around eleven o'clock in the morning and can scarcely wait for their lunch hour to arrive. These same individuals on their days off are able to go all morning on nothing but a light breakfast and may forget about lunch until late in the afternoon. The difference in their eating pattern is due in large measure to the freedom from strain and nervous tension on the days when they are relaxing at home.

Those who find it difficult to control their diet might well check into their own emotional state to see if it is tension or anxiety that is causing them to experience hunger pains which can be allayed only by eating. They may need the help of psychotherapy to achieve weight reduction if the problem is a deep-seated one. Or it may be that their physician will prescribe benzedrine or dexedrine to help them dull their appetites. Such drugs tend to reduce the desire for food and at the same time reduce the sense of depression that sometimes accompanies feelings of hunger.

The diet should be well balanced at all times, and should include meat, fish, dairy products, vegetables, and fruits. A well-chosen diet contains plenty of vitamins, iron, and calcium, that important element which is so often lacking in the American dietary. The daily intake of calcium should be about one gram. This can be supplied by one quart of milk. Other good sources of calcium are green leafy vegetables and cheese, which can be substituted for some of the milk. Supplementary calcium, in the form of calcium lactate, can also be taken on the advice of a physician.

As we grow older we are apt to develop idiosyncrasies in eating. Some older persons believe that certain foodstuffs do not agree with them, and they gradually eliminate one after another until they are finally living on a very inadequate diet and one that is lacking in the essential vitamins. Others give up meat and eggs, in the false belief that such foods are bad for their high blood pressure on kidney trouble. Meat should be one of the *last* foods to be taken away from older people—not one of the first.

It is frequently found that patients with stomach ulcers have remained on very one-sided diets for years, and in such cases true vitamin deficiencies may develop. In such instances large doses of appropriate vitamins will be needed to correct the condition. Most persons, however, who eat a balanced diet do not need supplementary vitamins. The use of vitamins as "tonics" and "pep producers" is of more help to the pharmaceutical trade than it is to the patient. Indeed, it is rarely necessary to take vitamins except on the advice of a physician for some specific purpose. A balanced diet of well-prepared food gives the body all the building material and energy that it requires.

The use of tea and coffee in moderation is rarely harmful to the older person. These beverages are gentle stimulants to the circulation and to the kidneys. In some cases, of course, they may cause heartburn or sleeplessness, in which circumstances they should be omitted. The more we study the diet needs of older individuals, the clearer it becomes that men and women should not eliminate anything from their dietary that has agreed with them and induced pleasant reactions during their earlier years. In the past, one of the great drawbacks to growing older has been the general attitude that we should forego all the little pleasantries that have given warmth and color to our youth.

It has been suggested that coffee is upsetting to persons suffering from stomach ulcers, but most ulcer patients can take coffee in moderation, and should drink it if they enjoy it.

It has also become very popular to deny salt to older persons, particularly those with high blood pressure or with some forms of heart trouble. A strict salt-free diet is very valuable in certain instances, but the use of a salt-free diet is greatly overdone. It is true that an excess of salt should be avoided, but the normal amount may be used in the preparation of food unless your physician finds a specific reason for eliminating it. The same rule applies to sauces, condiments, and other special touches. We are not trying to prolong life at the sacrifice of all the little things which help make life interesting and worth prolonging. We have made the later years a barren waste for too many generations by clinging to the idea that anything older people enjoy must, of necessity, be injurious to them.

As is pointed out in greater detail elsewhere in this book, the preservation of teeth will go far to prevent many forms of indigestion and malnutrition. If teeth are lacking or are in poor condition, making it difficult to chew and assimilate a variety of foods, serious dietary deficiencies may result. Teeth should be repaired and preserved. They should not be extracted unless there is a compelling reason. The theory that teeth act as a focal point for infection and lead to arthritis, heart trouble, and other disorders has been pretty well exploded. Unless there is a definite apical abscess or a far-advanced pyorrhea, there is no reason for pulling out a tooth. Certainly any missing teeth should be replaced with comfortable, well-fitting dentures in order to permit the enjoyment and assimilation of a balanced diet.

The use of tobacco in moderation (fifteen to twenty cigarettes or a few cigars a day) is much less harmful than is generally supposed. There are some individuals who develop dizziness, headaches, palpitation, or chest pains from smoking, and such people should most certainly give up tobacco. It has been found, however, that many people with a heart disease, even with coronary artery disease, can smoke with impunity unless they develop such specific symptoms. Tobacco must be given up completely if the circulation of the legs is impaired by disease of the arteries of the lower extremities, for tobacco has a tendency to increase spasm of the peripheral blood vessels. It is also harmful to people with chronic bronchitis or chronic nasal catarrh associated with sinus infection. The local irritation from smoke encourages the condition and prevents healing.

The Importance of Sleep

There is a wide difference in the number of hours of sleep required by men and women in the later years. Some do well on six hours, while others feel the need for ten or more. Some people find that they need less sleep as they grow older, but there is no set rule. One should sleep long enough to awaken rested and refreshed. Certainly an older person should not deliberately try to cut down on his sleeping time in order to accomplish more work or to spend more time in recreation. An afternoon nap has great restorative value and should be indulged in freely if there is any feeling of fatigue. A nap of fifteen or twenty minutes is probably more helpful than a longer one, and we should all try to acquire the habit of taking advantage of any free time to restore our vitality in this way.

Insomnia is not an evitable part of growing older. Stubborn insomnia at any age is an indication of trouble somewhere along the mental or physical main line, and it calls for sound medical investigation. Don't succumb to the common and dangerous habit of taking sleeping pills and sedatives to mask this symptom. Make it a point to find out what is keeping you from sleeping.

If the lessened hours of sleep do not lead to weariness and sluggishness, they should be accepted as an accompaniment of aging, and the mode of living should be readjusted to make them tolerable or even useful. Frequently, lying awake but relaxed in bed will be as beneficial as sleep, since no strain is being placed on the body's machinery.

Older people are more susceptible to extremes of environmental temperature. They should avoid fatiguing activity when it is very hot, and should also avoid too great exposure to the sun. They do not easily tolerate cold and are most comfortable if the temperature of the house is about seventy-five degrees. When they go out in winter they should wear warm under and outer garments. Men past the age of fifty should not subject themselves to violent physical exertion in cold weather; they should not shovel snow too vigorously or attempt to push their car out of a snowdrift. Such exertion, particularly in the cold, may bring on a heart attack.

Periodic Health Examinations

Careful periodic examinations by a physician will serve to detect the onset of the chronic diseases of middle and later life and will guide the individual along the path of hygienic, healthful living. Periodic health examinations have long been advocated by workers in the field of public health, but it has been difficult to capture the interest of both the laity and the medical profession. Few people have the foresight to visit a doctor before they are ill, and many doctors, when asked to give a health examination, do so in rather a sketchy manner. Yet enough statistics have been accumulated, through mass surveys of selected groups in the population, to prove that by such means certain disease conditions can be discovered at an early stage when they are still amenable to treatment. Many cases of tuberculosis, diabetes, and cancer have been detected in this manner.

Every birthday anniversary should be the occasion for a thorough physical inventory. The patient should discuss with his physician his daily life, his habits, and any emotional problems he may have, as well as symptoms that may suggest some slight disorder of the body mechanism. The physical examination itself should be complete, including the eyes, ears, mouth, teeth, skin, heart, lungs, abdomen, the pelvic organs of women, the prostate gland of men, as well as the body weight and nutrition, and the condition of the joints, in particular the weight-bearing ones.

The hemoglobin should be checked. A simple blood test to determine the sedimentation rate of the red blood cells is useful, because an abnormal result indicates that there is some systemic disorder that requires further investigation. In people over the age of fifty, particularly men, it is desirable to take an electrocardiogram. How far one should go with special procedures depends on the time and money that is available. Routine X-ray studies of the stomach and intestines would be very costly, and test studies have shown that such routine examinations uncover an unsuspected cancer of the stomach in about only one out of a thousand cases. However, if there are any digestive symptoms or disorders in bowel function, X-ray studies definitely should be made.

Such a thorough health examination will take about an hour of the physician's time and necessitate the employment of several laboratory procedures. It is, therefore, relatively costly, and the expense alone will discourage vast numbers of people with modest incomes from setting aside a sum for such a "luxury" procedure. To overcome this hurdle, health officers today are working on methods by which large groups of people can be quickly and inexpensively screened to discover those harboring the most threatening diseases, such as tuberculosis, diabetes, heart diseases, and cancer.

Diseases of Later Life

There are few diseases that occur exclusively in the older age groups. Cancer, rheumatism, hardening of the arteries, and diabetes occur in young and old. However, these disorders are much more common among elderly people. The incidence of chronic disease rises rapidly with one's years. In the decade between ages twenty-five and thirty-four 159 persons per thousand have a chronic disease or permanent impairment. In the decade between fifty-five and sixty-four this rises to 273 per thousand and in the years sixty-five to seventy-four, to 467 per thousand, or nearly one half. The number who are actually invalided by their chronic disease is far lower: 5.6 per thousand for ages twenty-five to thirty-four, 15.7 per thousand for ages fifty-five to sixty-four, and 53.5 per thousand for ages sixty-five to seventy-four.

In the more advanced years it is common to find more than one disease condition in the same person. Thus patients with diabetes may have heart trouble as well. Those with coronary artery disease may also be afflicted with stomach ulcers, and so on. The aging body reacts differently to disease than does the young one. As a rule, it is less able to cope with the disabilities induced by disease, but there are some conditions much better tolerated by older persons. Thus high blood pressure and cancer, as a rule, run a much less harmful course in the elderly than they do in the young.

The observed frequency of different diseases among older people depends on the nature of the human material that is studied. The most common causes of death after age sixty, arranged in the order of their frequency, are: diseases of the heart, arteries, and kidneys, cancer, street accidents, influenza and pneumonia, diabetes, and tuberculosis. Many disorders cause invalidism without leading to early death. If we arrange the chronic diseases in the order of their frequency, we find them in the following sequence of importance:

Rheumatism
Heart diseases, arteriosclerosis, and high blood pressure
Hay fever and asthma
Hernia
Hemorrhoids and varicose veins
Chronic bronchitis
Kidney diseases
Nervous and mental diseases
Goiters
Cancer and other tumors
Diseases of the female organs
Tuberculosis
Diabetes
Diseases of the gall bladder and liver
Ulcer of the stomach and duodenum

Finally, if we inquire as to the nature of the diseases that lead patients to seek hospital treatment, we find the following order of conditions:

Heart and blood-vessel diseases
Cancer
Cerebral arteriosclerosis and hemorrhage
Fractures
Cataract
Diabetes
Bronchopneumonia
Arthritis
Tuberculosis
Lobar pneumonia
Appendicitis

Heart Diseases

Diseases of the heart are the disease conditions most frequently encountered in older people. Note that we say heart diseases, not heart disease, for there are several causes of cardiac disease, chief among which are rheumatic fever, syphilis, high blood pressure, and arteriosclerosis.

Rheumatic fever plays its chief role in childhood and youth, but there are many people who survive past the age of fifty with hearts damaged by a rheumatic infection in their younger years. Such people have scarred heart valves, which may be leaky or may obstruct one of the passages through the heart chambers. This makes the heart an inefficient pump, and to make up for this the heart enlarges and its muscle mass increases in size. In time this enlarged and stretched muscle is no longer equal to the task of maintaining the circulation by its pumping action, and heart failure occurs.

The direct cause of rheumatic fever remains unknown, but it appears that all acute attacks are initiated by an infection with a streptococcus. Early treatment of throat infections with penicillin greatly diminishes the probability of ensuing infection of the heart. It also seems that treatment of the acute rheumatic attack with cortisone or ACTH serves to minimize cardiac involvement. We may hope that in the near future rheumatic heart disease will be preventable. Its incidence has declined greatly in the past generation.

Syphilis affects the aorta—the great artery that conducts the blood from the left chamber of the heart—as well as the valve that guards its exit from the heart. As a result of the syphilitic inflammation the aorta may become greatly dilated and may actually form saclike outpouchings. The aortic valve may become leaky, or the openings of the coronary arteries, which leave the aorta just above the valve and supply blood to the heart muscle, may become narrowed or closed off. The valvular damage, as in rheumatic disease, leads to cardiac enlargement and strain. The narrowing of the mouths of the coronary arteries may induce symptoms identical with those of coronary artery disease. Syphilitic involvement of the aorta becomes manifest from five to twenty years after the original syphilitic infection. It can be absolutely prevented by the adequate treatment of early syphilis. Treatment at the time that symptoms become manifest prolongs life and often gives great relief.

High blood pressure or hypertension may give rise to disturbances of the heart, the brain, or the kidneys. At this point we shall refer only to its effect on the heart. The heart, compelled to pump against a much higher pressure than normal, in time increases in size, just as any other muscle tends to become enlarged from overuse. Eventually this adaptive mechanism is inadequate and the heart becomes unequal to its task, and heart failure results. Prolonged hypertension, too, hastens the development of arteriosclerosis, especially of the coronary arteries, so that people with hypertension often suffer from coronary artery disease as well as the familiar high blood pressure.

These several forms of heart disease—rheumatic, syphilitic, and hypertensive—have a significant common denominator. In each instance the heart is compelled to do an excessive amount of work, either because of damage to the valvular apparatus or because it must struggle against the constant load of a high pressure in the arterial system. For years it is able to adapt itself to this increased strain; it enlarges, and so is able to contract and pump more vigorously without the expenditure of too much energy. But a time comes when it reaches the limit of possible compensation for the heavy load it must carry. One can make an analogy with the behavior of a rubber band that is stretched. Up to a certain point it develops greater tension and more vigorous elastic recoil, but when it is over-stretched its elasticity is lost and it can no longer return to its original state. So it is with the heart. When finally it is dilated or overstretched beyond its capacity of efficient contraction, its pumping action becomes impaired and heart failure ensues. *It is significant that only the enlarged heart fails.*

The first symptom of heart weakness is shortness of breath. Not all labored breathing, however, is due to a heart ailment. Obesity is a common cause, and so is the loss of elasticity of the lungs, which is called pulmonary emphysema and which is usually associated with chronic bronchitis. Severe anemia, too, may induce shortness of breath. Shortness of breath due to heart failure appears at first only on great exertion, such as running or stair climbing, but gradually it is evoked more and more readily, and when heart weakness has progressed, it may be present when the patient is at rest. Blueness of the lips, face, and fingertips, and swelling of the liver and of the legs, are other evidences of heart disease. No one of these signs alone should be taken as definite evidence that the disease is present, but the appearance of any such symptoms calls for an immediate examination by a physician.

Much can be done to prevent and postpone the development of heart failure. The most important measure is not to overtax the heart, not to subject it to sudden intense strain. A person with an enlarged heart should not run or lift heavy objects. He can do a full day's work, unless it is a physically laborious occupation, but he must learn to act and move slowly and methodically rather than in fits and starts. The patient's symptoms, particularly the appearance of shortness of breath, are the best guides to activity. He should conduct himself so that shortness of breath will not appear. Stair climbing has become an unnecessary specter to patients with heart affections. Most such patients may climb stairs if they *take their time*. Again they should be guided by the symptoms that are provoked. This principle applies to all physical activities.

If the patient is stout, the diet should be adjusted to ensure a proper loss in weight. Unless there are symptoms of heart disease, no rigid or specific diet is indicated except that an excess of salt should be avoided. An absolutely salt-free diet is necessary only when symptoms of heart disease have actually appeared. Fluids may be taken freely if the salt intake is limited. Tea, coffee, and other stimulants are beneficial, and moderate smoking is harmless. The sexual life should be one of moderation but not of abstinence.

A patient with a damaged, enlarged heart should be under medical supervision. This does not necessarily mean frequent visits to the physician's office. But the doctor should guide the patient in the planning of his whole life and should set as his goal the maintenance of the patient as a happy, useful economic unit in society. When heart weakness has set in, closer regulation becomes necessary, and medication, such as digitalis to strengthen the heart and mercurial injections to stimulate the kidneys to greater excretion of urine, may be needed. But the outlook is usually hopeful, for with intelligent direction by the physician and faithful co-operation of the patient, the weakening heart can be restored to adequate function and the patient can lead a relatively normal life for many years.

Disease of the coronary arteries is the most common cause of cardiac disorders in the middle and later years of life. The coronary arteries furnish the heart muscle with its blood supply. Although the interior of the heart is constantly bathed in blood, its walls are so thick that the oxygen and food elements of the blood can reach the muscle mass only through the specialized coronary circulation. If the flow of blood through one of the coronary arteries is hindered or interrupted, the portion of heart muscle that receives an inadequate blood supply suffers from lack of nourishment. If the interference with blood flow is not permanent, the patient experiences only a particular type of heart pain called angina pectoris. With the appearance of such pain the person rests, circulatory balance in the coronary arteries is re-established, the pain disappears, and the heart muscle recovers from its momentary disturbance.

If the interruption of blood flow is prolonged or permanent, that portion of the heart muscle that has been deprived of blood dies, and is eventually replaced by scar tissue. This is what happens when a blood clot forms in a diseased coronary artery, giving rise to what is termed coronary thrombosis.

These disturbances of the coronary circulation are almost always due to arteriosclerosis or hardening of the arteries. Arteriosclerosis of the arteries of the heart is but one localization of a process which may involve any of the arteries of the body. Although arteriosclerosis is found with increasing frequency among the older age groups, it does not represent an inevitable aging process. It is apparently a metabolic disorder closely related to the metabolism of lipids (fatty substances) in the body.

The fatty substance that is most intimately concerned with arteriosclerosis is cholesterol. Children or young people who, because of some disease, have a high level of cholesterol in their blood develop arteriosclerosis. Diabetics who, in addition to their disturbed sugar metabolism, also have an abnormal fat metabolism are very prone to arteriosclerosis. The tendency to high concentrations of cholesterol in the blood runs in families, and in such families there is an exaggerated frequency of arteriosclerosis. Certain nationalities, such as the northern Chinese, who all their lives partake of no dairy food (the chief source of cholesterol in the diet) have low levels of cholesterol in the blood and rarely acquire arteriosclerosis. Arteriosclerosis, then, must be regarded as a disorder of metabolism, and there is every hope that the time is not too far off when we shall be able to prevent or treat successfully this major threat to longevity.

Coronary artery disease is much more common in men than in women. It is rare in women under the age of fifty unless they happen to have hypertension or diabetes. In both sexes these two diseases favor the development of arteriosclerosis. It is often said that coronary artery disease is due to the strain of the modern high-pressure city life. This does not appear to be the case. The disorder is encountered in all walks of life and in all communities; it is not more common among business executives than among other groups of the population.

The first evidence of coronary artery disease is pain in the region of the heart—the pain called angina pectoris. Not every chest pain is due to coronary artery disease; there are many forms of benign heart pain caused by conditions ranging from neuritis, irritation of the chest muscles, pleurisy, adhesions, and general sensitivity of the nervous system. Most persons are calm and little concerned about any pain in the right side of the chest, but as soon as a pain is localized on the left they become frightened by the thought that it may arise in the heart. Many become neurasthenic invalids, quite unnecessarily. The characteristic pain of angina pectoris is located under the breastbone or slightly to the left. It comes with exertion or excitement and promptly subsides as soon as the patient rests. The harmless type of heart pain does not bear this direct relationship to exertion and is often continuous.

Of course any chest pain calls for careful examination by a physician, and it is unwise for the patient to prejudge his own case. Frequently the examination of the heart, the blood pressure, and even the electrocardiogram are normal in persons with uncomplicated angina pectoris. The diagnosis must be made on the basis of a careful evaluation of the symptoms.

With every contraction the heart generates an electrical current. The electrocardiogram traces the pattern of the electrical phenomena which accompany each cardiac contraction. When the heart muscle is damaged, the pathway of the electrical current in the heart is distorted, and this can be recognized by a study of the electrocardiogram. An abnormal electrocardiogram gives evidence of heart-muscle damage, but it tells us nothing about the state of the coronary arteries. A normal electrocardiogram does not exclude the presence of coronary artery disease. An abnormal electrocardiogram shows that the coronary arteriosclerosis has progressed to the point where at least one artery has been obstructed, and has thus led to heart-muscle injury. The heart has great reserve power, and if the rest of the coronary circulation is sufficient, it can function undisturbed by closure of a coronary artery and consequent scarring of the heart muscle.

The course of coronary artery disease is extremely variable. In many instances the anginal pain remains unchanged for years, or it may abate and disappear. In other cases a coronary thrombosis (blood clot) may develop. This involves acute heart damage and is a serious and prostrating experience. However, most people recover from such an attack and within three months are restored to approximately their former condition. In other instances the symptoms are initiated by a coronary thrombosis, and after recovery the patient complains of angina pectoris. Many recover promptly from their coronary thrombosis and continue without symptoms for many years. In my experience, about three quarters of the people with coronary artery disease are able to do their usual work.

The core of treatment lies in regulating the patient's life so as to avoid anginal pain, which signalizes that the heart has been overtaxed. Some develop pain after walking one block, others after five blocks, and still others only after more strenuous exertion. The chief secret lies in disciplining oneself to an unhurried existence, to walk slowly and to avoid lifting and other physical strain. Cold weather favors the onset of anginal pain and should be avoided as much as possible. Steady, plodding activity is rarely harmful; it is the sudden, severe effort, such as running to catch a train or trying to push a car out of a ditch, that is apt to overtax the capacity of the narrowed coronary arteries and lead to inadequate circulation of blood to the heart muscle.

The diet should be adjusted to weight reduction if the patient is stout. It is important to eat lightly and not to overload the stomach. Evidence so far collected does not offer much hope of controlling the cholesterol level of the blood and thus improving the arteriosclerotic process by means of a diet low in cholesterol. Cholesterol is found chiefly in milk, cream, cheese, butter, eggs, and animal fat. A low cholesterol diet excludes all of these substances.

Smoking in moderation does not appear to be harmful to most people with coronary artery disease. If smoking induces chest pain, palpitation, or dizziness it should be given up.

By taking simple precautions the average patient with coronary artery disease can continue his accustomed mode of life. He must always remember, however, to live within the limitations set by his heart, which will promptly let him know if he is overstepping the bounds. Any sudden change in the character of the symptoms calls for immediate consultation with his physician.

Blood Pressure—High and Low

Blood pressure—that is, the pressure that the blood exerts on the walls of the arteries—is the result of a combination of forces: the efficiency of the heart, which pumps the blood into the arteries, the elasticity of the arteries that are the pipe lines for this blood, and the resistance to the flow of blood in the minute arteries in the organs, muscles, and other tissues of the body. The rate and strength of contraction of the heart and the caliber of the small arteries that maintain the peripheral resistance to the flow of blood are constantly varying in response to regulating nerve impulses and to changes in the concentration of chemical substances in the blood. The blood pressure, therefore, is not static or constant; it fluctuates from moment to moment, depending on the play of these several forces. During sleep, or in the resting, fasting state, it is at its lowest; with exercise, emotional stimulation, or after meals, it rises. This variability of the blood pressure is commonly observed in the doctor's office. At the first examination, particularly of a patient who is anxious, the pressure is apt to be elevated, only to drop to normal levels at subsequent visits. If a patient is allowed to lie in a comfortable, relaxed state, such a drop in blood pressure may be observed within five or ten minutes.

Rapid fluctuations in the level of the blood pressure are even more marked in people with high blood pressure. In them the pressure may rise or fall from thirty to fifty points within a few minutes, depending on their emotional state. That is why it is so difficult to judge the value of any particular drug or other technique in the treatment of high blood pressure.

The patient's faith in the therapy of the moment may in

itself suffice to bring the pressure down to materially lower levels. That is why so many drugs and so many procedures have had a passing popularity in the treatment of high blood pressure, and why in the course of time they all have been given up as useless.

Two phases of the blood pressure are commonly recorded— the systolic and the diastolic. The systolic pressure is taken at the time when blood is ejected into the arteries by the contracting heart; the diastolic pressure at the time when the heart is relaxed. The diastolic pressure measures chiefly the resistance in the peripheral arterioles, against which the heart has to pump the circulating blood; the systolic pressure has added to this the force of the cardiac contraction. The diastolic pressure is a measure of the resistance that the heart has to overcome and of the burden under which it is laboring, and is, therefore, the more significant of the two measurements.

The so-called "normal" blood pressure ranges from about 100 to 135 systolic and from 60 to 90 diastolic. Although it is true that many more people with pressures higher than these are found in the older age group than in the younger, the popular formula that the systolic blood pressure is 100 plus the age of the person is incorrect. Many individuals over seventy have systolic pressures of 120. With age the systolic pressure is apt to rise to 150 or 160 while the diastolic pressure remains unaltered. This involves no strain on the heart.

Low blood pressure, or hypotension, is not a disease. Many normal persons have systolic pressures of about 100. The blood pressure is apt to be low when a person is run-down, anemic, or emaciated. Low blood pressure is not, as a rule, evidence of weakness of the heart.

High blood pressure, or hypertension, also is not a disease; it is a symptom produced by various causes. It is a common accompaniment of inflammation of the kidneys or Bright's disease; it may occur in certain other disorders of the kidneys or of the adrenal glands.

In most instances of hypertension (high blood pressure) the blood pressure gradually begins to rise from no known cause and remains elevated thereafter. This, for want of a better term, is called essential hypertension. It is the condition that is responsible for most cases of high blood pressure. It is more common in women than in men, and tends to appear at earlier ages in women. There is a definite tendency for hypertension to occur in families, among brothers and sisters, parents, uncles, aunts, and grandparents of patients with hypertension.

In its early stages essential hypertension is characterized by a fluctuating blood pressure which tends to persist at levels over 150 systolic and 90 diastolic. Its presence ordinarily is discovered accidentally in the course of a routine examination. There are few, if any, accompanying symptoms. In the course of three, five, or ten years the blood pressure gradually rises and is maintained at higher levels, maybe 180/110. It is then that the systemic effects of the elevated pressure begin to develop.

These symptoms begin to show in the heart and in the arteries. The heart, constantly pumping against an elevated blood pressure, is overworked and adapts itself to the increased load by increasing its muscle mass. In the course of time—and this may be ten or twenty years—it begins to lag, and evidences of heart failure set in. Even then, with proper treatment, the overburdened heart can recover strength and continue to function satisfactorily for years. The arteries, too, subjected to a greater internal strain than that for which they were designed, gradually undergo structural alterations and are apt to develop the lesions of arteriosclerosis. This arterial damage gives rise to further trouble chiefly when it occurs in the arteries of the heart—the coronary arteries—the arteries of the brain, and those of the kidneys. Thus, in the late stages of hypertension patients are apt to develop heart weakness, symptoms of coronary artery disease, disturbances of the cerebral circulation and apoplexy, and impairment of kidney function.

By and large, the outlook for life, health, and working capacity of a person with hypertension is good. Most can continue at their occupations and live a relatively normal life with some common-sense modifications. Many survive long enough to succumb eventually to some altogether different disorder. There is, therefore, no reason to become panic-stricken if high blood pressure is discovered. Too many people invalid themselves at the first indication that their blood pressure is high. They become slaves to the blood-pressure apparatus and have their pressure measured at frequent intervals, rejoicing in a drop of a few points, downcast and worried if there is a slight rise. These slight variations have no significance; they are normal daily occurrences.

The successful management of hypertension is largely a matter of good common sense. Of course the patient should be under a doctor's supervision, but once he has been thoroughly checked and has worked out with his physician the necessary adjustments of his life and the line of treatment to be followed, a visit to the doctor twice a year is sufficient, unless new symptoms develop between visits.

There is no specific diet that will invariably control the blood pressure. The diet should be adjusted to enable the patient to achieve a normal weight. Meat and eggs may be eaten freely. There is no need for rigid restriction of salt intake except in rare cases of great severity, when such a salt-free diet should be carried out under strict medical supervision.

The rice diet is useful in some severe cases of high blood pressure. It is beneficial not because it consists largely of rice, but because it is a starvation diet that contains very little salt. It should be taken only under medical supervision.

Medication has no permanent effect on the blood pressure, and it is inadvisable to take drugs in an attempt to lower it. Sedatives are freely given, because many such patients are nervous and because calming the nerves has a salutary effect on the blood pressure.

Operations devised to lower the blood pressure by cutting the sympathetic nerves that control vascular tone have not lived up to their original promise. In many instances the blood pressure returns to its old level and the symptoms are not permanently relieved. The mild cases do well without any treatment, and the far-advanced cases do not do well with any form of treatment. In my opinion, operation should be reserved for rapidly progressing cases in young people that do not respond to other forms of therapy. Operations of this type are rarely indicated in persons past the age of fifty.

Cancer

Cancer, probably the most dreaded of illnesses, is second on the list of the most frequent causes of death. We know still less about its causes than we do about those of the heart diseases. For years mortality statistics have shown that cancer is on the increase. This increase is actually due to the fact that pneumonia, tuberculosis, and other infectious diseases that formerly caused many deaths have diminished to such an extent that we are living longer, and thus reaching an age at which cancer may strike.

The apparent increase in cancer results largely from the reduction in other preventable diseases and from the increasing average age of the population. If the cancer death rates are adjusted to make allowances for the aging of the population, there has actually been a *slight decrease* in the past decade. This is particularly noticeable in cancer that occurs in the so-called accessible sites—sites that are accessible to diagnosis, operation, and radiation. In ten years the reduction of the death rate from cancers in these parts of the body—chiefly the breast, uterus, skin, and mouth—has reached over ten per cent.

Cancer can be cured if it is discovered early and treated properly. That is the reason for the establishment of cancer detection clinics, which people are encouraged to visit annually, when they are in good health, for a complete checkup that may reveal an early lesion. The only drawback to these clinics, which are staffed by groups of specialists, is their high cost. If their cost is figured out per case of cancer that is detected, the expense of discovery of a single case becomes so high that it may run into several thousand dollars. So it is a technique that manifestly cannot be applied to the whole population. The early discovery of cancer is an added compelling reason for everyone to have an annual careful health examination.

In men, cancer of the stomach comprises one third of all cancers. Then come cancer of the intestines, the rectum, prostate, lungs, liver, mouth, bladder, and esophagus, in that order. In women, cancers of the uterus and of the breast are the most common, to be followed in order by cancers of the stomach, intestines, liver, ovaries, and rectum.

In their early stages cancers give rise to no symptoms. That is what makes their recognition difficult. Yet most cancers grow slowly, so if they are discovered in their earlier stages, the chances for cure are good. Cancer of the skin and mouth, regions which are accessible to examination, are easily discovered if every suspicious lesion is promptly shown to a physician. If in doubt, the physician will remove a small piece of the affected tissue for microscopic laboratory study. The newer technique of expert microscopic study of the nature of the cellular content of various bodily excretions and discharges—the vaginal secretions, the sputum, the stomach contents—is also a useful tool for early diagnosis.

Cancers of the stomach and intestines are the most difficult to diagnose because they usually give rise to few symptoms until they are far advanced. Furthermore, so many people have indigestion of some sort—a condition that is usually harmless and due to nervous tension and poor eating habits—that similar symptoms actually caused by a cancer are apt to be overlooked.

It should be an absolute rule for everyone over the age of fifty to be examined whenever new symptoms arise in the digestive tract. It may be just loss of appetite, some high abdominal oppression after meals, unusual accumulations of gas, or there may be a change in bowel habit: the sudden onset of constipation or of intermittent diarrhea. An examination should include careful X-ray studies by a physician specially trained in the field of gastrointestinal X ray. In appropriate cases physicians can use instruments that enable them to look into the stomach and into the rectum, and so make possible the visualization of a lesion. Early diagnosis of such cancers greatly increases the chances of real cure by operation.

Today, with the increasing use of the mass X-ray technique in an attempt to discover early cases of pulmonary tuberculosis, more and more early cancers of the lung are being discovered. Here again it is too late if one waits until cough and chest pains direct attention to the lungs. The spectacular development of lung surgery in the past decade makes operative removal of these early lesions quite feasible. Indeed, today chest surgeons are having recourse to exploratory operations on the chest when the diagnosis is in doubt, just as they have for years explored the abdomen for obscure abdominal conditions.

Recent studies suggest that there may be a relationship between cigarette smoking and lung cancer. Cancer of the lung appears to be more frequent among persons who have been heavy smokers for many years. This relationship is not an absolute one—many heavy smokers do not develop cancer—but undoubtedly it is wisest not to smoke, and certainly not to inhale, if any chest symptoms are present.

The facts about cancer of the breast have been so well publicized that it is hoped that every woman knows that as soon as a lump is discovered in the breast a small section should be removed for microscopic examination. Only by this method can the nature of the mass be definitely established. Cure is possible only by early diagnosis and operation. Statistics show that seventy-five per cent of patients who have been operated on for such early lesions are still free of any recurrence five years later. The early diagnosis of cancer of the womb depends on regular careful gynecological examination, with microscopic study of the cellular content of the secretions.

It is unnecessary to list the many different kinds of cancer. The lesson to be derived from this brief review is that by means of regular, careful physical examinations many cancers can be discovered at an early stage of development and at a time when operative or X-ray treatment offers a good chance of cure.

Rheumatism

Rheumatism is a term that is used very loosely to describe certain affections of the joints, muscles, and tendons. It is the most frequent cause of chronic disability, but it rarely kills. Most people are frightened at the thought of having rheumatism or arthritis, for they promptly visualize a far-advanced case with serious crippling from painful joint deformities.

The most common "rheumatic" disorder of the later years of life is called osteoarthritis. It is not an infection; it is not accompanied by fever or acute inflammation of the joints, or by constitutional symptoms such as anemia and loss in weight. It results, apparently, from a true degenerative process in the joints, due first to the aging process and secondly to the wear and tear resulting from the long-continued mechanical strains to which joints are subjected.

The earliest and the greatest changes are found in joints that are exposed to greatest pressure and stress, and the process is farthest advanced in those joint surfaces that undergo most strain. So, because of the erect posture of man, the joints of the knees, the hip, and the spine, and the sacroiliac joints, are most commonly involved. The process is hastened and exaggerated by obesity, which increases the burden of weight bearing, and by disturbances of bodily mechanics such as are occasioned by flat feet or by old fractures which bring about irregular weight bearing on the joint surfaces.

The patient complains of pain and difficulty in moving various joints. The affected joints are not acutely swollen or red. Pain and stiffness are the chief complaints, and creaking can often be felt in the joint. Symptoms vary a good deal, and there are periods of freedom from pain and disability. X-ray study of the joints reveals a characteristic picture. Curiously enough, the extent of the lesion as revealed by X-ray rarely parallels the intensity of the symptoms. Many persons whose X-ray pictures exhibit advanced joint changes have no symptoms, and others with slight changes on the X-ray film are quite incapacitated.

Patients with osteoarthritis can be helped a good deal, relieved of pain and enabled to continue their usual lives. The first indication is to give rest to the joints that are being damaged by the recurrent trauma of excessive use. If the knees are involved, stair climbing should be avoided; if it is the spine, there should be little bending and lifting.

Stout patients should lose weight and so lessen the load on the joints. Flat feet should be corrected by appropriate plates, and a sagging abdomen that drags on the spine should receive support. Various forms of physiotherapy, such as heat and massage, are helpful. Often the orthopedist should be called on for special treatment.

Rheumatoid arthritis is an infection of unknown cause that creates acute and chronic inflammation of the joints. It occurs most frequently among younger people, but may develop at any age. It is usually a prolonged, progressive illness which may eventually lead to joint deformities and great disability. During its periods of activity there may be fever, anemia, and wasting of the body. In the acuter stages patients with this disorder must be in bed. Neither sulfa drugs, penicillin, nor the other antibiotics influence its course. This is the disease that has been so spectacularly arrested and relieved by the new adrenal hormone, cortisone, and by the pituitary hormone, called ACTH for short, which stimulates the adrenal gland to produce its wonder-working internal secretion.

It still is too early to speak of cure, but it seems probable that this radical new approach to the treatment of this form of rheumatism will soon enable us to control not only this crippling rheumatoid arthritis but a number of other diseases which affect chiefly the connective tissues of the body—the tissues that give support to the specialized muscular and glandular structures and form the framework of the body.

Fibrositis is a term that includes a variety of conditions which the layman often calls muscular rheumatism. Lumbago is a good example. Also there are all sorts of aches and pains that many people develop in various tendons and fibrous structures. The symptoms may come on very acutely with severe pain and stiffness of the affected part, or they may be mild, with a constant nagging pain aggravated by movement. Pain commonly shifts from one region of the body to another. Change in weather, exposure to drafts or to cold and wet often bring on acute attacks. The cause of fibrositis is unknown and there is no specific curative treatment, but the pain and stiffness usually subside and there may be long periods of well-being. The condition never leads to crippling deformity. In the acute stage the affected part should be put at rest and should be covered to protect it against cold and drafts. As the sharp pain subsides, the application of heat and gentle massage hastens recovery. Aspirin is the drug that gives the best relief. In the more disabling cases certain local injections or treatment with X-ray may be useful.

Diabetes

The clinical and public-health aspects of diabetes have undergone a radical change during the past generation. In the pre-insulin days diabetes was a great hazard to life, particularly for young people, and was the cause of many premature deaths from acidosis (acid poisoning) and coma, induced by the disordered metabolism. Insulin has made it possible to avert acidosis and early death, and many young diabetics now live well into middle age or beyond. The incidence of diabetes rises steadily with advancing years, so that as a result of the aging of the population, the number of people with diabetes has greatly increased. One quarter of them are between fifty and sixty, and one half are over age sixty. In some manner that is not fully understood diabetes hastens the development of arterial disease—even in young people—and diabetics now die as a result of arteriosclerosis of the arteries of the heart, the brain, or the legs. For years the death rate from diabetes had steadily increased, but during the past decade there has been a twenty-five-per-cent drop in mortality for men between the ages of fifty-five and seventy-four and for women between fifty-five and sixty-four.

Diabetes has a strong familial trend, and it is unusual to encounter a patient who does not have at least one parent, grandparent, aunt, or uncle who also suffered from the disease. Obesity, too, predisposes to the development of diabetes. It is particularly important, therefore, that persons with family histories of diabetes maintain a normal weight and have themselves checked periodically to ascertain whether or not they excrete sugar in the urine or whether the blood-sugar level is too high. It is a simple matter to discover diabetes, but too often the condition is carelessly overlooked simply because a urine examination is not made. An annual urine test for sugar, and, in the case of members of diabetic families, a blood-sugar test, will uncover many cases in their early stages. Today there are thousands of unrecognized cases in the United States.

Fortunately, the diabetes that first develops in older persons is, as a rule, mild. Most cases can be controlled by diet alone, and only a few need insulin. If sensible dieting reduces a patient to his ideal weight, prevents the spilling over of sugar into the urine, and restores the blood-sugar level to normal, insulin is unnecessary. If the sugar in urine and blood cannot be controlled without a starvation diet that induces emaciation, or if diabetic acidosis develops readily, insulin injections become necessary.

Diabetics do not tolerate infections. These commonly aggravate the diabetes and induce acidosis. A sore throat, a fever, a small boil represent urgent indications to consult a doctor. Because of the great frequency with which arterio-sclerosis develops in diabetics, people with diabetes should be alert to recognize the first symptoms suggesting such a complication. Chest pain or shortness of breath should be called to the attention of the physician at once. Because of the frequency of arteriosclerosis of the arteries of the legs, which impairs the circulation of the lower extremities and may in turn lead to gangrene, diabetics should pay special attention to scrupulous cleanliness of the feet. They should not traumatize their toes by cutting corns or trimming their nails too short. The feet should be kept warm in cold weather.

To a large extent the diabetic has his health and his life in his own hands. If he carefully and persistently follows the rules of living laid out by his physician, he may expect to remain well and to live long. If he neglects himself, sooner or later he will have to pay the penalty for his carelessness.

The Climacteric, or the Change of Life

The climacteric occurs when the ovaries or testes atrophy and their secretion of the sex hormone becomes greatly diminished. The menopause begins before the age of fifty in all but twelve per cent of women. Its onset is gradual, and the symptoms that accompany it are extremely varied. Most women have little, if any, discomfort, while some suffer a great deal. Those with a nervous make-up experience the greatest distress. The many old wives' tales that embellish the popular concept of the change of life cause much unnecessary anxiety and contribute greatly to the development of symptoms. The fact that in many instances there are bodily changes such as shrinkage of the breasts and of the genitalia undoubtedly contributes to the emotional instability, the irritability, and the depression that so often accompanies the menopause. Severe symptoms occur in about only one fifth of all cases, and these can be readily controlled by the oral administration of the female sex hormone. Taking hormones by injection is now rarely necessary.

Still more important is a sane and sensible attitude toward this natural phenomenon, which is part of every woman's life, and the realization that the many fears that are so commonly entertained about the change of life are quite unfounded. It is customary to attribute almost every disability that develops in middle life to the impending menopause, or to the menopause itself, if it has already taken place. This false assumption often leads women to neglect warnings of disease and prevents them from seeking competent medical advice at a time when it would be most helpful. The menopause is not a cause of high blood pressure; the two conditions are quite independent but may happen to appear at about the same period of life. The menopause has no effect on the sexual drive or capacity of women, and many patients report far greater satisfaction in their marital life once the possibility of pregnancy is removed.

Men do not experience an abrupt climacteric as do women. But if they lose their testicular function as a result of disease or operation, they too exhibit hot flashes and psychic and constitutional symptoms similar to those of the female menopause. When such men lose their sexual potency, their symptoms can be relieved and their potency restored by the administration of male sex hormone. The great majority of men, however, do not experience a climacteric with accompanying symptoms. With the years they undergo a gradual reduction of sexual vigor and potency. Sexual potency does not depend alone on a normal hormonal state—psychogenic factors are of great importance—and men often find that they are only as old as they think they are. The treatment of sexual impotence and generalized weakness of aging men with injections of sex hormones is rarely indicated. It is usually ineffectual, and if it should succeed in occasional cases, it may do harm, for too vigorous sexual activity may injure the heart or other organs of the older body.

Aging is, after all, a universal occurrence which we should all recognize. It is marked by a *very gradual* reduction in the vitality of the body in its capacity to withstand stress and strain. A man or woman, healthy in body and mind, can adjust to such a gentle change without loss of joy or interest, especially if given the opportunity to continue economic and intellectual independence. Illness and disability in the later years of life are rarely due to the aging process alone; they are caused by superimposed disease. It is the task of doctor and patient, through co-operation, to avert and control these chronic diseases by preventive medicine. The problem has become one of great importance because of the ever-growing proportion of older people in the population.

The individual must understand the nature of his waning strength and co-operate with his physician in working out a schedule of living that will not overtax his powers. Society, through its changing attitudes, must make it possible for its aging members to live useful, independent lives and to obtain the health services which, unassisted, many are now unable to afford.

HOW TO LOOK AS GOOD AS YOU FEEL

by

JANET H. BAIRD

THE astute owner of a newsstand on a windy New York corner once changed a lagging business into a prosperous one by the simple expedient of hanging a mirror up in direct line with the vision of the passers-by. Prospective customers, who had previously rushed by with their heads lowered against the wind, now paused to straighten their ties, adjust their hats and veils, and pick up a copy of the latest edition. And the greater number of them, the happy newsman reported, were men!

Vanity, thy name is not so much woman as human. We all care, and care very deeply, about how we look. One of the greatest of all drawbacks to growing older has been the change which takes place in our appearance. So if we are to be truly grateful for what medical science has done to extend our stay on this planet, it behooves us to try to look as good as we feel.

Quite apart from the personal satisfaction of being able to glance into a mirror and say, "Not bad, not bad at all," is the very real obligation we owe to our fellow humans to keep ourselves as easy and pleasant to look upon as we can.

Up to now our world has been predominantly filled with young things, or fair-to-middling young things, who by their very youth and vitality have been pleasing to the eye. When we have occasionally encountered a shuffling, ungroomed, unhappy-looking older person, we have turned our eyes quickly away and forgotten the depressing sight as soon as possible. But think what could happen as we become a country of older people. Our immediate surroundings might become filled with men and women who go on living but do not care how they look! The prospect is appalling and all too imminent unless we realize our individual responsibilities to the collective scene. In the future we may all be called upon not only to brighten but to decorate the corner where we are!

The responsibility of "keeping ourselves up" is very like that of a property owner who buys on a street where each householder takes pride in the condition of his lawn and the freshness of the porch paint. If one or two of the new residents become indifferent to weeds and let the front steps fall into disrepair, the whole block will take on a run-down appearance and depreciation will set in fast.

So it is with human property. A few careless, untidy older people can render an entire group unattractive and uninviting. Just as no one enjoys visiting a slovenly house, no one enjoys association with an older person who has ceased to care about his appearance. In this obvious fact lies the answer to many an older person's complaint that "nobody comes to see me or pays any attention to me any more."

Far from feeling that "it's ridiculous to care about looks at my age," every man and woman should take an increasing interest in seeing just how spruce he can be. It has nothing to do with "silly vanity" or trying to "avoid being your age." It is entirely right and proper, and furthermore it is your solemn duty to your family and friends to keep yourself looking as attractive as you can.

In setting out to explore the easiest and most effective ways of keeping our looks on a par with our mind and our body for a vastly longer period than we have ever before thought possible, we should first decide what constitutes good looks in a mature person. It does not mean retaining the bloom of twenty-five or the athletic prowess of thirty. That is possible only for those whose professions require them to devote as much time and attention to their faces and figures as nurses and teachers, for instance, give to their careers. It can be done, of course, as the many glamorous stars of stage and screen have demonstrated time and time again. It is accomplished by a combination of careful diet, daily massage, and an all-abiding belief in their own physical loveliness. Great beauties remain youthful because they *think* of themselves as youthful, and the sureness of their own thoughts permeates their very being.

This kind of youthful thinking is not to be confused, however, with the empty-headed pretties who go simpering around at fifty the way they did at twenty. The successful lifelong beauty is the one who combines the charm of maturity with a fine skin and a well-groomed figure and thinks of herself as a beautiful woman of fifty and not as a perennial teen-ager.

For those who are interested in making a real project of this beauty business, let us quickly admit that the plastic surgeons are becoming ever more skillful at eradicating wrinkles and causing double chins and sagging muscles to disappear. Face lifting, however, is like hair dying: its greatest value lies in the lift that it gives to the individual's morale. It produces the feeling of having done something positive about looking younger. But for the average person such extreme measures are neither practical nor necessary. There are many ways of keeping your looks without having your face lifted or your midriff sliced away.

It isn't youth and beauty that we're striving for so much as grace, mellowness, and good grooming. A beautifully groomed woman of eighty is far more eye-catching than a pretty one of twenty-five. To have seen the elegant Lady Mendl enter a room in her wheel chair was always far more exciting than watching the pretty young things she invited to her parties come in after her.

Men who watch their figures are apt to improve with age too. It is very significant that those members of our male population who have been singled out for the designation "men of distinction" are seldom in the first flush of youth or even in the second.

Until now, however, the old masters have been about the only ones to recognize the richness of maturity. With their unfailing instinct for beauty and line, the great painters have often reproduced the wisdom and intricate patterns of older faces. The rest of us have appreciated the beauty of age in furniture and sculpture. We have handed down old silver and pewter and watched it grow more lovely with each generation, but we have been blind to the softly glowing patina that human beings can develop if they are given an opportunity.

Perhaps there is a lesson to be drawn from the "home-brew" era in this country, which anyone over forty can remember. Home-brew was never considered much of a drink as fine beers go, because its eager makers seldom let it set long enough for its full body and flavor to develop. It may be that human beings haven't had a chance to set long enough to realize their full possibilities either. They have been crippled by the thought that they were expected to be on the shelf at forty or that they might be conspicuous and silly if they showed an interest in looking alive at sixty-five. That is a very real mental handicap of which we must rid ourselves. We can now expect to remain hale and hearty for a long time, and good looks go right along with good health.

So let's throw out the old ideas about "getting to a point where we don't care about appearance any more," and find out just how good we really can look. After all, the lines of a

Hitchcock chair or a Grecian urn manage to hold up for a long, long time. Surely our human lines should do almost as well. The California redwoods, which have lived on this earth longer than anything else that is still alive, have improved and gained in beauty with their age. Therefore we humans, endowed with our "superior minds," should certainly try to add to and not detract from our surroundings as long as the life force is in us.

Breathing and Posture Come First

The first signpost along the road to good appearance is "elasticity." It is the key to the whole subject. Elasticity of muscle, elasticity of skin tissue, and, above all, elasticity of mind. Men and women who lose their elasticity, who sag into a set pattern and refuse to change with the times, look old, act old, and think old. For them there is little ahead to make the prospect of a longer life seem either pleasant or desirable.

The quality of elasticity gave an obscure Englishman of Shakespeare's time a lasting place in medical history and made the name of Thomas Parr familiar to every student of anatomy. For Tom Parr retained the elasticity of his tissues, particularly that of the muscles of his rib cage, to such a degree that he lived to the glorious age of 152! In performing an autopsy on his venerable body, to discover the secret of his long and healthy life, British surgeons came to the conclusion that the resilient quality of his rib cage indicated that he had used his breathing mechanism to the fullest. Tom Parr had kept his whole system in balance by giving it all the oxygen it needed for top operation, and had literally breathed himself into over a century and a half of life!

Breathing is such a simple thing that most of us fail to give it the attention it deserves. Yet in technical medical discussions of prevention of such apparently unrelated things as ulcers, indigestion, gall-bladder upsets, nervous tension, and illnesses of pregnancy, proper breathing is always stressed. From the standpoint of good posture, youthful appearance, and a sound healthy mental outlook, the importance of breathing cannot be too strongly emphasized! It's too bad so few of us know how to do it!

Like standing and walking, breathing is something we learn to do incorrectly when we are very young and keep on doing incorrectly all our lives. Animals have a great advantage over us in this respect, for many of them are born with the ability to stand and walk fully developed. It isn't something they learn to do a year or so later by trial and error, or by imitation of the poor example set by their elders. As a result, one rarely sees an animal with an unnatural or out-of-balance posture or an awkward carriage. They also know exactly how to get the maximum use out of their breathing equipment.

A graceful, completely balanced human being, on the other hand, who knows how to stand, move, and breathe properly, is a rare sight indeed. A free, easy, well-co-ordinated step will cause heads to turn and envious eyes to stare. In analyzing the movement of such a person you will find that the pleasant picture is produced by three basic and extremely simple factors: the person who stands and walks correctly is relaxed, the tone of the entire body is elastic, and the breathing mechanism is working properly. More encouraging still, you can do the same thing without resorting to a lot of strenuous and tiring exercises.

Doctors have been warning us for years that we should "slow down on exercise after we are forty." According to Albert Butler of New York, who has made a lifelong study of human engineering, or what makes us move like human beings, we can forget about strenuous exercise at any period of our lives and still keep our bodies elastic and looking their best.

In the Butler Studios—where Albert and Josephine Butler carry on their work and where many of Broadway's brightest stars come to get the kinks taken out of their posture and to learn to walk beautifully and easily before television's all-revealing eye—there are just two watchwords—*relax* and *breathe*.

Mr. Butler, originally a student of mechanical engineering, who has turned his knowledge of stresses, strains, and counterweights to the human body, maintains that most of us take better care of our cars than we do of ourselves. If our car wheels get out of alignment we have them adjusted, but we let our poor old spines get inches off center and then wonder why we feel tired and look droopy all the time!

Think of your body for a moment as a pile of children's blocks set one on top of another. The bottom block is your feet, the next one is your knees, then come your hips, your chest, and last of all your head. To build a good firm tower, each block must be set squarely over the one underneath. If any one of them gets out of line, the whole structure is weakened, and it is easy for such a wobbly tower to topple over if it has no outside support.

Now nature designed us to stand erect, just like that tower, and to stand that way without being propped up. One properly placed block balances the next all the way up to our head, which is the uppermost block. As soon as we begin to let any of the blocks get out of line we put unequal strains on our muscles, which must then develop tensions to keep us from falling over. Dowager's humps, potbellies, sagging chests, unsteady knees, sway-backs, and double chins are not signs of old age; they are actually the result of our bodies trying to compensate for the unnatural strains which have been put upon them all these years!

Stand in front of a mirror right now and check for yourself. If you are carrying your head too far forward (it should be held right above your shoulders), the chances are that your chest is caved in and your shoulders are rounding out toward the back. They have moved to this extreme rear position to counterbalance that too-forward position of your head. With your chest block so far to the rear, the stomach block immediately under it has had to move forward to maintain its load, and your body will have a slightly zigzag appearance instead of being in one lovely straight column. Naturally these unequal weights and strains tax all your joints and muscles, and it's no wonder they complain and let you down.

But enough about what's wrong—here are the simple things you can start to do right now to correct it. Fold a blanket two or three times lengthwise to make a long, narrow pad and place it on the floor. Roll up one end a little way to form a small pillow—but don't put your head on it! That pillow is for your poor, tired, abused feet! Now lie down on the blanket on your back. Bend your knees up in a comfortable position and place your feet on the rolled end of the blanket. You may place a small pillow at the nape of your neck if it makes you more comfortable than lying absolutely flat.

Next, *relax!* Think of yourself as a cake of ice that is just melting away into a flat puddle on the floor, or, as Josephine Butler tells her pupils, "Pretend you're pancake batter that is spreading out into one big pancake on a nice warm griddle."

You can think of yourself as anything you like, so long as you let your spine come down to a good, flat, relaxed position. Don't hurry yourself; give all those surrounding muscles plenty of time to ease up. It may have been years since you invited them to "let go" and assume the position that nature intended for them. Your backbone may have all but frozen into its off-balance position, so give each little segment time to loosen up and start functioning again.

Let the floor do the work. Don't ask your spine to do anything but relax and flatten out, and the flatter you can get it to the floor, the better it will be. With your feet elevated on the rolled end of the blanket, you should be able to feel the hollow at your waist begin to stretch out and come in contact with the floor. The too-tight feeling across your shoulders will begin to let go, and see how much better the muscles across your abdomen feel, now that they aren't being asked to carry weight that may be as much as ten inches too far forward to be over your natural center of gravity.

Wiggle your toes, rotate your feet at the ankles, but do it gently. This isn't meant to be exercise; it's just relaxation and gives your body structure and all your internal organs a chance to get back into place.

Now start breathing. Do so in little short sniffs, like a dog on the trail of a rabbit, or a camper who gets that first whiff of coffee and bacon in the morning. Never mind gulping great lungfuls of air, which we've always been told was "deep breathing." Breathe in little sniffs, but make the pull come not from your chest but from the diaphragm muscles *far below your waistline.* That is where you do your real "deep breathing"—down below your waistline and well back inside toward your spine! Singers know this because they have studied breathing as the foundation of tone production, but too many of the rest of us are "shallow breathers" all our lives. We never learn that those lower diaphragm muscles in the back of the abdomen should be doing the major part of the work instead of letting our chest heave up and down!

Next try a series of hisses—short, strong hisses—and feel the pull again deep in your abdomen. Say "ho" a few times. Say it as though you really meant it and you will feel the abdominal muscles pull in and back and force your chest up automatically. Inhale air in short sniffs, as though you were "trying to smell perfume from a closed bottle," to use another of the Butler word pictures, and then blow it out in one long, controlled breath, as though you were blowing out candles on a birthday cake.

Do this hissing and sniffing and "ho-ing" several times a day. You needn't lie down on the floor each time, although it's good to give your spine every opportunity to straighten out. The breathing can be done as you sit there reading, while you go about your daily chores or walk along a quiet street. It is the most exhilarating, and at the same time relaxing, thing you can do. Pull in that air in short, well-controlled sniffs and let it spread out through all the sinus cavities of the face. With a little practice you will be able to feel all the passages open up as the air and increased circulation moves through them. Close your eyes, smile a little as you sniff, think of something pleasant —perhaps you are sniffing violets beside a little mountain spring, or smelling lilies in a great cathedral, or frying trout beside a lake at sunset. Make up your own favorite sniff and think about it and enjoy it as you practice breathing and hissing.

The day you can hiss the whole tune of "Yankee Doodle," chorus and verse, without taking a second breath, you will know that you have come a long way toward using your breathing machinery correctly. Try it right now: take a deep breath and see how far you can hiss "Yankee Doodle" without taking another breath. Now keep it up until you can hiss the whole tune!

Think about how your body feels as you lie there on the floor. Remember you need to form new *habits* of posture, and habits are formed more quickly if you think about what you're doing. This is the way your body should be lined up when you are standing and walking and sitting, but you will have to work consciously against the habits of your life up to this time in order to establish new ones.

Practice lifting your head as high as you can without taking your shoulders off the floor. Hold your head in that position and then slowly return it to the pillow. Do this several times each day to strengthen those neck muscles whose job it is to hold your head up straight over your body instead of letting it fall forward in that drooping position so characteristic of dejected old age.

Another good way to encourage better head position is to sit and nod like a mandarin doll. You've seen those little Chinese dolls whose heads nod forward and backward at the touch of a finger. Well, try it, only be sure that your head, like theirs, is directly over your shoulders when you do it. Sit up straight, shoulders *back and down* (the pull on your shoulders should come from the small of your back). Again, to quote the Butlers, "Getting your shoulders into position is like fastening your suspenders in back: the pull is back and down to the waist." Now, with your head well back over your shoulders and your neck erect but not tense, let your head nod back and forth. See how easily it moves in this well-balanced position? See what happens to any suggestion of a double chin? Feel those too-tight muscles at the back of your neck and base of your skull let go? It's all so very simple, but it's so right! Poor position is largely a matter of poor habits, and you just have to give yourself better ones!

If you want to be a little more energetic you can try crawling on all fours, just the way a baby does. After all, it was from this position that you originally started off in the wrong direction, so it seeems plausible to go back to it and start over. Hold your head *up* as you crawl; don't let it fall forward or just hang down—you can't teach your neck muscles anything that way.

Keep your spine firm too; don't let it cave in like that of a sway-backed horse.

As you crawl notice that your hands and feet automatically *turn in*. This is the opposite of the *turned-out* position that characterizes arthritis. Sniff like an inquisitive puppy as you make the rounds of the room, and be sure to think about your sniffing as you do it, to check on those muscle pulls down along the spine below the diaphragm.

Like the deer in the forest and the fish in the sea, we were all meant to be beautiful, graceful creatures. Civilization has given us some unlovely posture habits, and aside from the unspoiled animals, we have few good examples around us to imitate. So the next time you step out on the street think of yourself as a fine, tall creature carrying your head erect to balance a handsome set of antlers. Your chest will come up and your shoulders will settle down in back, where they belong. If your imagination is equal to it, add a heavy peacock's tail dragging behind you, to give your hips that *tucked in and under* feeling they should have.

Now step out and walk with your whole spine. Start your steps from the center of your body—don't just shuffle one foot in front of the other in an "old man's gait."

The Butlers also ask their pupils to think of a squirrel when they sit down at the dinner table. Remember how straight a squirrel keeps his back and how he brings the nut up to his mouth instead of curving his spine over his food. Good posture is an excellent aid to good digestion, for an erect spine assures all the digestive organs enough room in which to function. Consider for a moment how cramped all our internal machinery gets when we habitually stand and sit in a stooped-over position. Both good digestion and the conservation of energy for protection against fatigue are directly related to how we stand, sit, and walk.

It is well known that pain cannot exist in a relaxed muscle. Most of the common medicines used to alleviate pain, such as aspirin, codeine, et cetera, are effective because they produce relaxation. Pain is caused by the tension and contortion of various parts of the body. When that part of the body is relaxed, the pain and congestion disappear. So start right now to learn relaxation in place of the tension and strain that you may have been teaching yourself all your life.

One of the many rewards of the harvest years is that relaxation seems to come more easily then, just as it is the natural attribute of the very young. Babies and older people are the best sleepers; they take naps more easily. However, we should all recapture our capacity for relaxing when we are awake.

The next time you are on the street or riding in a bus, take stock of the faces around you and see how few are blessed with a pleasant, relaxed expression. Tension and strain seem to have become such a constant part of modern living that many of us have forgotten what it feels like to be without them. The passage of time doesn't undermine our looks, our health, and our dispositions nearly so much as do the unnatural strains under which our looks, health, and dispositions are asked to operate. We wouldn't trust a bridge across a shallow stream that was as badly engineered as most of our bodies are, and yet we expect these delicate, complex structures to give us years of service when they are literally "all out of shape."

The "cat stretch" is another simple but extremely effective way of easing muscular tensions and promoting body flexibility. To do this you sit on your heels in your stockinged feet on a hard, flat surface. Now assume the "knee-chest" position by pulling the tip of your spine backward and downward onto your heels, while the upper part of your body stretches forward and downward. You should finish with your chest on your knees and your head on the floor. Keep your arms alongside your body or extend them forward beyond your head if that will help you to achieve a long, straight spine. Remain in this position as long as you are comfortable, for it gives the muscles, joints, and ligaments a residual stretch, which you will retain in some degree when you resume your regular posture.

Next we shall attack that too-often-neglected area of our bodies—the ankles. Loss of flexibility of the ankle and knee joints gives older men and women that creaky appearance. You don't want to get that look, so start right now to take a lesson from the natives, or from the babies of our own civilization. All babies and all primitive peoples know that squatting on the heels is the most restful way to sit. You've seen countless pictures of natives squatting along the roadside, resting from their heavy burdens. If you look carefully you will see that they are squatting with their *feet flat on the ground*. Sounds easy, but you'll find it's a neat trick if you can do it!

Take off your shoes before you start, and then, with your heels flat on the floor, bend your knees slowly until you are sitting on your heels. Keep your torso in a long, straight line and hang onto your knees with your clasped hands. (Unless you're far more flexible than the average person your age, you may find you have to hang onto something for support in order to attain this position.) Stay with it, however, even if it seems a little difficult at first, for it is a sure way to retain the elasticity of your ankles and knees and to prevent you from ever developing that stiff, shuffling gait that is so characteristic of old age.

This squatting position is also valuable for all who habitually carry their weight too far back on their heels—an almost universal fault—and particularly for women who have lost the flexibility of their ankle joints because of wearing high heels constantly.

If you want to be especially energetic you may want to try

some stretching exercises by hanging from an overhead bar. It's wonderful for your figure and your circulation, and there are gymnasium-type bars, designed to fit in doorways, that will support up to five hundred pounds. The late Douglas Fairbanks, who certainly knew as much as anyone about retaining elasticity and bounce, once said that if he had it to do over again, he would devote all his exercise time to stretching. When he was away from his elaborate home gymnasium he used to accomplish this by hanging from a heavy bath towel thrown over the top of a door. It's a good exercise, but you try it at your own risk—I recommend only the gentler ones!

Are Wrinkles Necessary?

Since the earliest days of recorded history mankind has been waging an intensive battle with nature on the subject of skin in general and wrinkles in particular. The Egyptian beauties of old knew that the skin tends to become dry with the passing years, and they combated it with a variety of oils and emollients surprisingly similar to the ones we use today. They may have been packaged in jars of rare and exquisite workmanship instead of polyethylene or thermosetting plastic, but their reaction on the skin was very much the same.

Creams and oils are valuable because the natural oils and fatty tissue of the face, neck, and hands tend to break down with the passage of time, leaving the skin dry and parchment-like unless their lubricating action is replaced from the outside. Creams, whether it be cold cream, cleansing cream, or the so-called "overnight" creams, have two great functions: they cleanse and they lubricate. They do not, however, *feed* the skin. Your skin gets its nourishment in exactly the same way as the rest of your body—from the food you eat, carried to it in the blood stream. Massage, at the time the cream is applied, stimulates the flow of blood to the skin of your face and neck, and that, of course, means healthier, cleaner, smoother, and more glowing skin.

Use whatever cream you prefer; select it for its lovely color, its delightful perfume, its seductive packaging, or go to the ten-cent store and get the large economy size of theatrical cleansing cream. They will all accomplish about the same result if you use them properly and regularly.

If you have given your skin reasonable care all through your life, you will undoubtedly reach the harvest years with a wonderful asset—a clear, smooth, unblemished complexion. If you've gone along on the hit-or-miss plan, and found yourself too tired at night to do much more than give your face a quick wash and fall into bed, you may have some rehabilitation work ahead to get your skin back on the credit side of the ledger.

Both dermatologists and geriatricians, the doctors who specialize in the care of the skin and in the patients of advancing years, are currently doing a number of interesting and highly scientific studies on skin and why it is so often the first part of our bodies to record the passage of time. They are formulating some interesting theories, which they set forth in impressive terms, but to date the best practical advance that they can give seems to be contained in the following simple rules:

1. Keep the skin clean with warm water and a mild soap, paying particular attention to the areas around the nose and chin, where clogged pores are so apt to turn into unsightly blackheads.

2. Use cream generously, working it upward from the neck. Pat gently or rub it in with a light upward motion. Don't give your skin any rough handling or do anything to encourage the underlying tissues to break down or sag.

3. Astringents may be used by women whose skin is not overly dry, but they are usually not so necessary in the later years as during early youth, when the oil glands may be extremely active. Mild astringents, especially when chilled, do have a stimulating effect which increases circulation, a thing greatly to be desired in nourishing and toning older skins.

4. Experiment with powder bases until you find the color and consistency that is best for your skin. It will probably be one with a cream base rather than the more drying type applied with a wet sponge. Select one that is just a tone darker than your skin. A shade lighter than your own flesh will give you that masklike appearance or even the fell-in-the-flour-barrel effect.

Before we get too far into the field of cosmetics, which is of interest only to women, let us consider some of the skin conditions which are equally important to men.

The thorough soaping that men's faces get in the process of shaving usually assures them of unclogged pores and a good circulation. The soap, however, has a drying action, and with the advance of years they might do well to dip into the least heavily scented of their wife's cold cream now and then.

They should also avoid disturbing any pigmented moles in the course of their shaving. Pigmented moles, which may be anywhere from light brown to almost black in color, and either flat or elevated above the surface of the skin, are common to almost everyone. It has been estimated that if all the moles in the world were added up and the total divided by the number of people on the globe, each one of us would average seventy-five moles! These moles are harmless enough as a rule, if they are not disturbed, but any constant source of irritation may cause a pigmented mole to burn, itch, become red and inflamed, and to increase in size. Such a condition demands expert medical attention, since they can rapidly develop into serious danger points. Attempts should not be made to remove unsightly moles by home methods. This is a job for a qualified medical man, since pigmented moles on the rampage can turn into a form of skin cancer.

This is true of many of the skin growths which tend to appear with age. These little wartlike growths answer to the medical name of keratoses, and the majority of them are harmless but far from pretty. In some cases an increase in vitamins A and D in the diet will cause them to disappear, but if they persist and become encrusted or ulcerated, they should be shown to a competent physician. Here again we find that regular physical checkups can do much to preserve our attractive appearance as well as our health.

On the subject of removing the freckles which often appear on arms and on the backs of hands, I could get little encouragement. Frequently called "liver spots," they actually have no connection with the liver, but their real cause and cure still remain to be discovered.

Perhaps we should say a word of caution about the prolonged use of argyrol and other silver preparations which are used as nose and eye drops. When used over a period of months, such preparations may tend to discolor the skin. Such deposits of silver in the skin cannot be removed, and older people, who sometimes go on using and reusing a favorite drug, should be on guard against overdoing it.

In discussing the care of older skin with several dermatologists, I was surprised to hear them say that we can even overdo the use of soap! Soap and detergents tend to defat the skin, and as we grow older we need all the natural skin oils we can produce. Some older skins are frankly allergic to soap, and many do much better when sulfonated oils are used in its place.

On the subject of the much-advertised hormone or estrogenic face creams the good doctors agreed that these estrogenic substances can be absorbed by the skin if they are in a cream base, but I could find little agreement on what they will accomplish once they are absorbed! Some patients reported near miracles in rejuvenation, while others had less spectacular results.

Certainly it will do no harm to try them; the extra lubrication and attention your skin will get in the process will be all to the good, and who knows, for you the cream may do everything that is promised on the label. At any rate, a new cosmetic or a new beauty ritual is as stimulating to a woman's over-all sense of well-being as a new hat, so try all the creams and lotions your purse will permit. Just be sure to keep your skin well oiled, absolutely clean; eat the balanced diet that you should, drink plenty of fluids, get sufficient rest, fill your mind and your heart with pleasant thoughts, and nature won't let you down in the matter of complexion.

Perhaps we should elaborate a little on the importance of the pleasant thoughts, since that appears to play a major part in the avoidance of skin disorders at all periods of life.

A navy dermatologist told me of a case of a young sailor who suffered from very painful hives. He had to be hospitalized for his condition, and it was soon noted that he always came in for treatment on Mondays. His skin would clear up in a few days and he would be returned to duty, only to break out again a few Mondays later. It didn't take the doctor long to discover that the week ends when the sailor and his wife visited his wife's mother always coincided with an attack. On being questioned, the young man readily admitted that he was frankly allergic to his mother-in-law and being around her upset him to such a point that he actually broke out in hives!

This may seem an extreme case to the average reader, but skin specialists' files are filled with cases equally or even more dramatic. Our mental and emotional condition has a profound effect on the condition of both our skin and our hair, and the sagging lines and deep creases which appear in some older faces are the end result of a lifetime of sagging thoughts and deeply creased personality patterns.

There is a big difference between laugh lines and scowl lines, although both could be technically classified as wrinkles. Laugh lines have an upward sweep, and the deeper they get, the better the face looks. The downward lines do nothing for anybody, and right now is the time to erase them or at least change their direction.

Keep your skin as supple as possible with generous applications of cream, and mold your facial contours with both your hands and your thoughts. Don't forget your eyelids in the creaming process, and put some cream around and behind your ears as well. But, most important of all, be sure that the eyes behind the well-greased eyelids have a lively, friendly expression in them!

Books and books have been written on the subject of make-up and cosmetics, and by this time you have undoubtedly found brands which suit you very well. However, it may be time now to alter your make-up to match your richer, more mature personality, so take a second look at the colors you are using. Do they really blend with your skin tones as well as they did ten years ago, or would you be better advised to use a little softer shade of lipstick and a rouge with a lighter touch? Make the most of your eyes and be sure to use a dab of cream on your lashes to prevent that dry, parched look that comes when the natural oil glands decrease their function. Don't be afraid to be daring and glamorous; just remember to be so with the sure touch of an experienced, sophisticated woman, don't be kittenish about it.

Senator Thomas C. Desmond of New York, who has long

been interested in finding solutions to the situations which face us as we grow older, frequently points out the difference between making the most of life at every age and trying to cling to youth forever. He tells a story about a woman who resorted to all manner of artifice to hold back the clock, believing that her dyed hair, plastic surgery, and extravagant make-up really gave her the appearance of youth. The end of her dream came the day a sweet young girl got up on a crowded bus to give this poor old soul a seat!

The truth of the matter is that so few of us have lived to attain a really vigorous and healthy old age that the doctors themselves can't say for sure what the older man or woman of the future will actually look like! But we may be certain that the ideal of physical beauty at sixty or seventy will be different from that of twenty and thirty, and we already know that we defeat our own purpose when we confuse the two and try to make them measure up on the same yardstick.

Can You Save Your Hair?

Your hair—the amount you have, its texture, color, and how long you will hang on to it—depends in large measure upon your choice of parents! One does not need to be a very scientific observer to notice that baldness and premature grayness appear to run in some families while the members of others retain the youthful vigor and color of their hair when well advanced in years.

Since hair plays so important a part in a person's over-all appearance, it is encouraging to know that it is the most indestructible tissue of the human body and the last one to break down. If such were not the case, it is doubtful that we civilized humans would have enough hair left at this date in our history to make it worth considering how best to preserve it.

The depressing fact is that baldness appears to be a man-made condition and is rarely found among native peoples living an out-of-doors and hatless existence. Baldness is a thing that civilized man has brought on himself, and it would take generations of carefully selected breeding to eliminate the tendency toward baldness from our pattern of heredity. However, we shall leave to the future such a long-range project and tackle the problem at the place where we now stand, surrounded by an amazing amount of carelessness and mis-information about the best ways to make the most of the hair we have.

There are about 1,000 hairs to the square inch on the average healthy scalp, or a total count of about 120,000. Blondes tend to have a higher count than brunettes, averaging a total of about 140,000, while redheads drop to about 90,000 and make up for it in texture and arresting color. Hair grows at an average rate of three quarters of an inch a month from birth until the middle years. It tends to slow up around the age of sixty, and new hair that grows in after that is apt to remain rather short. Because heat stimulates growth, hair grows a little faster in the summer than in winter, but there is no truth in the widely ac-cepted idea that hair continues to grow after death. Shrinkage of the skin tissue around the hair makes it project farther and gives it the appearance of growth.

The health of your hair depends upon the general health of the rest of your body, for your hair is not a separate entity. It is more like a continuation of your skin, and any condition which affects your body as a whole will be reflected in your hair. Like all rapidly growing tissue that is constantly replacing itself, the hair and scalp need a plentiful supply of nourishment. Anything that impedes circulation and cuts off this nourish-ment will cause your hair to lose its luster, or may even cause you to lose your hair! Tight hatbands come immediately to mind as a hazard to the hair, but it should be borne in mind that nervous tension is far more frequently the villain! Tension of any kind causes the scalp to contract and become tight to the skull. This tightness cuts down on the blood supply just as effectively as a band tied around the head. Daily massage is the second-best way to counteract this; relaxation is, of course, the first and best way!

Put your hand to your head right now as you read and test how relaxed and flexible your scalp is. It should respond readily to a little pressure and move freely in all directions. If it seems tight and resists the pressure of your fingers, begin right now to loosen it gently.

Start at the temples and work upward and backward. Then place your fingers at the base of your skull and move your scalp up and down, working gradually to the top of your head. Don't be discouraged if the skin seems determined to adhere to your skull; remember you've let it get a real head start through all these years. A few minutes of massage a day will loosen the scalp, and the increased circulation will be as welcome to the roots of your hair as water is to a plant that has been trying to struggle along in dry, tightly packed soil.

Get the habit of pulling your hair away from the scalp. Take hold of it in bunches and give it strong, firm tugs. A few hairs may come out in your hand, but you may be sure that they were dead anyway, and you have just saved yourself the trouble of picking them off your shoulders later. Keep working on your scalp to relax it as we consider rule two, which is— keep your hair clean!

You would be amazed and perhaps a little chagrined at what a microscopic examination of your hair and scalp might reveal. No other part of the body gets quite so dirty or is washed so infrequently! This is due in part to the popular fallacy that too much shampooing isn't good for the hair.

Nothing could be farther from the truth, and if you don't believe it, ask Mary Martin, who has washed her hair three times a night and six times on matinee days during the lengthy run of the musical play *South Pacific*. Your hair is just as much a part of you as your hands, face, or teeth, and you never hear anyone express any doubts about washing them as often as necessary.

It is true that excessively oily hair does appear to take a turn for the worse when shampooed twice a week or more. But that is only at the beginning. Much of such excess oiliness is caused by enlargement of the openings of the sebaceous glands at the roots of the hair, which become clogged with dirt, dandruff, and the hardened oil itself. Frequent cleansing, together with vigorous massage, will work all this foreign matter to the surface, where it can be rinsed away. The oil will flow more freely until the tissues have time to shrink back to a normal, healthy condition, and repeated washing is particularly important during this trying period. Tincture of green soap, which has a slightly drying reaction, is excellent to use on over-oily hair. In addition to its drying qualities it has the advantage of being inexpensive and places no premium on daily shampoos, if these are needed to get your hair and scalp back into top condition.

One of the many pleasant facets of living a longer life is that oily hair tends to become less and less a problem with the passing years. The scalp, along with the skin, leans toward dryness in the later years, a condition that is easily corrected by rubbing in a little pomade or olive oil. A shampoo with an oil base should be used on dry scalps rather than tincture of green soap. Dry or oily, however, we should never forget that our hair is exposed to more dust and dirt than the rest of our body and that it will collect and retain this dirt. Wash it frequently and give it daily brushings and massage.

We are all aware that we lose a few hairs every day. This is a continual process of loss and replacement which is quite normal. It is when hair starts "coming out in bunches" that we become alarmed, especially if, upon examination, it appears to be "coming out by the roots." Actually the little colorless ball which is often seen at the end of a hair is not the root at all. It is only the bulb that rests on the papilla at the base of the hair follicle, or the pocket out of which each hair grows. The appearance of the little bulb at the root end of the hair does *not* mean that the hair is gone for good and will not replace itself. Only when the circulation of blood to the papilla is cut off, or something happens to permanently damage the follicle, does a new hair fail to grow.

If your hair appears to be coming out in abnormal quantities, you may want to use a simple test devised by a European dermatologist to see if you have any cause for alarm. Collect all the hair that comes out on your comb for the next three days. Divide these hairs carefully into two groups: those that are at least six inches long or longer and those that are less than six inches long. If the short hairs number only about one third of the total of all the hairs that have come out, the shedding is nothing to worry about. The long hairs have lived their normal life and are being replaced by shorter ones, which of course are healthy new hairs.

For men, who may not have a hair six inches long on their entire heads, the test should be made by separating the hairs with blunt, cut ends from those which taper to a point. In this case the cut hairs should far outnumber the pointed ones, to show that it is old hair and not new hair that is being lost.

What causes baldness and what can be done to prevent it has claimed man's attention for many generations without producing any spectacular remedies or preventive measures. In addition to the hereditary factors, it is known that baldness can be the result of worry and nervous tension, local infections of the scalp, and diseases of the body, such as typhoid, erysipelas, pneumonia, influenza, diabetes, tuberculosis, kidney disease, gout, rheumatism, and syphilis.

In many cases baldness disappears when the contributing factor is removed. This is often true of the type of temporary baldness, which afflicts women as well as men, in which the hair comes out in small round patches. This type of sudden baldness appears to be associated most frequently with severe nervous strain or shock, and if the scalp is in otherwise healthy condition, the tendency is for the hair to grow back again, although it may be softer in texture and lighter in color than the original growth.

In their book, *Your Hair and Its Care,* Dr. Oscar L. Levin and Dr. Howard T. Behrman emphasize that frequent shampooing is one of the best preventive measures against the premature loss of hair. It is their belief that the baldness we associate with old age is most often caused by, or at least hastened by, seborrheic dandruff, a condition that proper cleansing can do much to alleviate. Dandruff is a warning signal of a diseased scalp, and it is a warning that far too many men and women fail to heed. Dandruff is not a trifle to be taken lightly, especially if it is associated with a tight, itching scalp.

A certain amount of the loose scales, which we often consider dandruff, is normal to all scalps, since the process of shedding the scales of our skin goes on continually all over our bodies. The scales of the head are more noticeable because they are trapped by the hair and combine readily with loose dust and dirt which is also present. These scales, readily removed by brushing, are not to be confused with dandruff, which is an indication of a diseased scalp.

Dandruff frequently begins early in life and becomes increasingly serious with the years. The sebaceous glands become diseased and throw off an excessive amount of oil, which collects with the normal scales and cakes to the scalp. Crusts and scales become apparent over the entire head and are accompanied by a considerable amount of itching. Although the scales are dry and fall readily to the shoulders, the dandruff material feels greasy to the touch. If the condition is not checked by proper treatment and frequent shampoos, inflamed spots, covered with greasy yellow crusts and grayish-white scales, will appear. Moist, raw spots may develop under these crusts; the loss of hair becomes greater, and the individual is in real danger of having the infection spread to other parts of the body.

As the infection progresses, flat, wartlike growths appear on the scalp, and if the fallen dandruff is allowed to accumulate in the folds of the face and neck or behind the ears, spots will appear there which in time will take on a flat, smooth, or protruding warty appearance. These growths may be red or pink, black or brown in color, and covered with either dry or greasy scales. Constant irritation, such as the rubbing of a tight collar, or the habit of scratching at these hardened spots, encourages their development, and if allowed to remain, there is a possibility that they may turn into cancers of the skin.

No attempt should be made to treat these keratoses (warts) without the supervision of a physician. Under no condition should they be allowed to ulcerate and form crusts, which tend to break down and ulcerate again and again. All such growths, including those which may appear on the backs of the hands in later years, deserve prompt medical attention. Treatment in the early stages is a simple procedure, but they should not be permitted to go unattended until they have assumed serious proportions.

The time to start saving your hair is now, just as now is the time to preserve your skin. The danger signals to watch for, the little things which indicate that your hair and scalp are in need of prompt attention, are:

Excessive oiliness of the hair and scalp.
Excessive dryness of the hair and scalp.
Scaliness on the scalp and the development of dandruff in sufficient quantity to be apparent on clothing.
Itching of the scalp.
Formation of crusts and raw spots on the scalp.
Abnormal shedding of hair.
Tenderness of the scalp.
Thinning of the hair so that the scalp shows through.

If the customs of our civilization were such that women could wash their hair often and set it becomingly without a time-and-money-consuming trip to the hairdresser, and if men were not given to wearing tight, unventilated hats which limit the blood supply and create a moist, unwholesome atmosphere for the scalp and hair, dandruff might cease to be the common disease that it undoubtedly is. Lacking such an ideal situation, however, the best we can do is to give our hair plenty of brushing, frequent washing, exposure to sunlight and fresh air, and, above all, to make it a habit to massage and loosen the scalp on the head several times a day.

Silver Threads among the Gold

Watching our hair turn gray is a common enough sight, but one that is little understood. We all know that it happens, but how it happens remains something of a mystery to everyone but the experts.

To understand what causes hair to lose its color, it is important to know how an individual hair is constructed. A normal hair has three parts; one part is the outer layer of flat, transparent cells, which are arranged in an overlapping pattern, somewhat like shingles on a roof. Under this outer protective layer is the cortex, made up of elongated cells which give the hair its flexibility and hold the oil in which the coloring matter is suspended. This color, mixed with oil and air, shows through the outside layer of transparent cells. The center of the hair is not hollow, as many persons imagine, but is made up of two rows of lengthwise cells placed side by side to make up the marrow. In very fine, weak hairs this central part is missing.

From this it is easy to see that the color of the hair is governed by the second layer, or cortex, where minute granules of pigment are mixed with oil and air and distributed along the length of the hair. Surprisingly enough, these granules appear to come in only two colors—reddish yellow and sepia brown. All of the wide variation in hair shades is produced by different concentrations of these particles of color or by various mixtures of the two. Blond hair is produced by the sepia particles widely diffused with air. Black hair is the result of the same pigment appearing in dense concentration, with little or no air present in the cortex.

Hair begins to change color when the oil glands start to dry up and the particles of pigment are no longer carried up into the elongated cells. The hair at first may appear to be turning light yellow—the blond straw color produced by the presence of oil and air in the cells with a minimum amount of pigment. As the pigment decreases and more air takes its place, the hair turns gray, and when there is an even greater amount of air in relation to oil in the hair shaft, it becomes the much-admired and extremely flattering snowy white!

In some individuals this process begins at a very early age, and in some families the tendency to premature grayness is so well established that children will find their hair losing its pigmentation at almost the identical age at which their parents' hair began to change color.

Until very recently our attitude toward age, and the gray hair we associated with it, has been so negative that many men and women have gone to great lengths to conceal the fact that their hair lost its color early in life. In spite of the flattering softness of gray hair in combination with a young face, they have covered it with dye even though the artificial result was not half so complimentary or distinguished.

With our changing attitudes and the wider recognition that gray hair is the result of the action of the oil glands of our scalps and may have little or no connection with chronological age, the practice of dying prematurely gray hair may disappear and we shall discover more distinguished-looking younger people among us.

Skin specialists as a group are inclined to take a dim view of hair dyes and color retouching. Some hair-coloring preparations are injurious to hair and scalp and others contain ingredients to which individuals may be allergic. No bleach or coloring agent should ever be used on a sensitive scalp or on one on which there are any irritations or raw spots. In the hands of experts, hair dyes can sometimes produce a result that looks almost as good as nature's own, but for the most part dyed hair looks like what it is—dyed hair—and its owner might be far more attractive if nature were allowed to have its way.

This point was brought home rather forcefully not long ago when my young daughter and I happened to meet the headmistress of the nursery school where my daughter had begun her education several years before. We had never been particularly attracted to the woman, and I had been forced to agree with the children that she was a cold and rather brittle specimen of female educator. She seemed an ageless person, her hair dyed a hard, uncompromising black, so out of key with her skin tone that the effect was almost frightening. When we met her again after the passage of years we were both impressed with her warmth and charm and quite enjoyed our little sidewalk chat. As we walked away my daughter expressed her surprise that the woman was not at all as she remembered her, and we mused about it for a block or more before it occurred to us that it was her soft, undyed gray hair that made the difference! In allowing her hair to revert to its natural color, the woman's whole personality had undergone a change. She, too, had softened and become more easy and relaxed. She had lost some of that fierce determination to appear to be other than what she was, and I'm sure the children no longer find her terrifying as she makes her rounds to supervise the excellent school she operates.

The role of vitamins and other preparations in restoring hair to its original color has received considerable publicity of late, but so far science has not found any reliable way to replace the oil and pigment within the hair shaft, which must be done if the graying process is to be reversed. It is quite possible that science will find ways to prevent hair from losing its color, just as it may someday be possible to keep the scalp from losing its hair, but that day is still in the future. Right now the best plan is to maintain your over-all health, eat a well-balanced diet, keep your hair and scalp as clean and relaxed as possible, and don't worry about your hair—or anything else, if you can help it!

While we are on the subject of gray hair, it might be well to add that scientific investigation has not borne out the often-repeated story of men and women whose "hair turned white overnight from grief or shock." Severe emotional experiences might so affect the scalp that the oil supply to the hair would

be cut off and hair growing out after such an event would be
noticeably lighter in color, but nothing could affect the hair
that was already grown or cause the pigment to be drained
out of it.

Glasses Give Glamour

Back in the days when only Granny was supposed to wear
glasses, any sort of help in reading fine print was considered a
mark of the passing years. It's very different now that our
schools are giving children routine eye tests, for it has been
found that a surprising number of youngsters need glasses to
correct their vision and that poor eyesight can no longer be
thought of solely in terms of age. High-school and college
students painted their newly discovered aids to better sight
with fingernail polish in vivid hues, and from then on eye
glasses lost their austere, unlovely appearance.

Today glasses are worn by men and women of all ages as a
smart and complimentary accessory as well as a very real comfort in seeing the world in proper focus. They are made in an
endless number of flattering shapes and colors, and the materials that are employed verge on the fantastic. In a brief hour
of spectacle shopping I tried on frames made to resemble Scotch
plaid, candy stripes, dotted Swiss, handmade lace, cornflowers,
glittering jewel-set masks, and a combination of tortoise-shell
and gold on which the wearer's zodiac sign was emblazoned.
There was one frame mounted with golden turtles, and still
another on which a pair of brilliant butterflies had apparently
come to light. For a few brief seconds I had a pair of solid gold
spectacles that retail for four hundred dollars perched on my
nose! Fancy misplacing that particular pair!

Some designers make the glasses so large that they all but

obscure the wearer's face, while others make them so small that they fit into a case as compact as a lipstick, to carry in one's handbag or dangle like a charm from a bracelet.

Lorgnettes, so long associated with dowagers, and more often with professional snobs, are now being used as the very real convenience that they are. Available in very practical, pencil-slim plastic frames, they fold neatly to fit into a purse or hang from a chain or lapel pin, and are instantly available for reading menus, telephone books, and price tags when shopping.

Rimless glasses, so popular a generation ago, now seem to be disappearing. Only the most conservative of the older men and women cling to them in preference to the more flattering newer designs. The popularity of rimless glasses, which are more subject to breakage than those with frames, is based on a negative philosophy. In the evolution of eyeglasses from their unlovely steel-framed predecessors, it was believed that they were less conspicuous and gave the wearer an ostrichlike sense of other people not noticing that he wore them.

Rimless glasses, of course, fooled no one, and today the whole idea is to make the most of the glasses themselves and have them add color and interest to your appearance while they add comfort and ease to your vision.

No set rules can be laid down for selecting frames which will do the most for you, but the general practice is for individuals with sharp features to wear frames with rounded lines, while those with round faces should choose the more angular shapes. Be sure that the lines of the frames sweep upward and give your face the appearance of being lifted rather than drawn down.

Unless you can afford several pairs to compliment various outfits, it is best to avoid the overelaborate and too-glittering frames. These are designed primarily for evening wear and are beautiful when worn with the proper costume. Some of the rhinestone-set glasses seen at the theater and opera in recent seasons are delightful, but they would look sadly out of place on the street at high noon. Think about the predominating colors in your wardrobe when you purchase frames, and if you decide on a bold, brave red, be sure it is a shade that blends well with your lipstick color.

You might like to experiment, too, with softly tinted lenses to get away from the too-glaring quality of clear, uncolored ones. The tints are very soft pink, blue, and lavender, just enough color to take away that cold, hard, glassy look.

Men's glasses are so well designed now that a prominent New York optician, who makes a point of giving glasses "specs appeal," made up several pairs with plain ordinary glass for a man who has excellent vision but who looks more distinguished with glasses than without! Certainly the newer types, with broad, straight temple pieces, are far more comfortable than the old-fashioned metal ones that curve behind the ears, and busy men, who do not need to wear glasses constantly, find them much easier to slide on and off.

Contact lenses, the glasses which are worn directly over the eyeball itself, without frames of any kind, have been vastly improved in recent years. Much smaller and more comfortable now than the original ones, they can be worn by some people for as long as eighteen hours at a time. For the most part, however, such lenses are recommended for younger men and women and are particularly useful to stage and television performers, athletes, and others prominent in public life. The ability to wear them successfully is a highly individual matter and should be discussed with qualified medical and professional consultants.

Our eyes are extremely precious possessions, and ones from which we now expect longer service than ever before. They should be examined regularly, and the adoption of glasses shouldn't be postponed if eyes need help in performing their work. Get flattering ones, and wear them with the same style and assurance that you would any other smart accessory. Just be a little careful about the selection of your hats; you may find you need a slightly different brim line when you are wearing glasses.

Aids for the Hard-of-Hearing

Whereas eyeglasses have become more and more dramatic and spectacular, aids for the hard-of-hearing have been progressing just as fast in the opposite direction. Ingenious designers have succeeded in making them all but invisible. They are so far removed from the unlovely ear trumpets of a few generations ago that it is hard to believe that they were created for the same purpose.

Much of this progress has followed World War II, with its greatly increased use of electronics and sound transmission, coupled with the demand for hearing aids for veterans. These young men needed lightweight, efficient, inconspicuous earphones which would permit them to enter fully into normal living. Sound engineers and designers had at their disposal all the vast new technical knowledge as well as newly developed lightweight plastics and other synthetics. The results are the finest, most attractive, efficiently operating hearing aids that man has ever known. Today many of the fifteen million Americans who need help in hearing are enjoying the products of modern sound engineering, and at least some of the three million children with impaired hearing are being fitted with aids so that they may grow up with the world clearly audible around them. The number being helped, however, is still far too small in proportion to those who could and should be benefiting from these new developments.

Hearing aids are no longer associated with old age, any more than are glasses. They are for anyone at any age who wants to be sure he or she isn't missing a thing!

Because we are concerned in this chapter with appearances, we shall skip any discussion of the physical conditions which can cause the loss of hearing with the passing years. It is interesting to note, however, that repeated studies have shown that some impaired hearing in older people can be attributed to a loss of interest in things outside themselves rather than to any real loss of function in their hearing mechanism. There is a great deal of truth in that often-repeated observation that deaf people sometimes manage to hear what they want to hear, while that which doesn't interest them appears to pass unnoticed. This is not the place, however, to discuss deafness as a psychological withdrawal from the world, although it is easy enough to see what a ready-made alibi it is for those who no longer want to participate in family or community affairs.

We are concerned here with the men and women who want very much to keep abreast of the world and all its doings. We are concerned with the men and women who want to hear what's going on around them and who are interested in looking as attractive as possible while they are listening.

It is for them that the new hearing aids have been created. Powered with electric batteries to amplify the sounds and transmit voices directly to the ear, these aids have been available for many years. Until recently, however, they were large and bulky, both uncomfortable and unsightly to wear. Now better materials and improved knowledge of sound conduction have made it possible to create efficient hearing aids that take up little more room in a pocket than a fountain pen.

Men will be particularly interested in the advances which

have been made in invisible ear molds, since they have never been able to conceal this part of their hearing apparatus under their hair, as women can. New designs have made it possible for the entire receiver to fit behind the ear or beneath the collar, instead of projecting like a large button on the outside of the head. The clear plastic is molded to fit the individual ear, and an inconspicuous plastic tube goes snugly over the top of the ear and drops down behind to disappear inside the collar.

The "single pack" hearing aid has done away with the need for a separate battery unit, which used to be worn strapped on the inside of the leg, while the microphone was concealed under the dress or shirt front. Now the entire assembly can be clipped like a fountain pen in a man's coat pocket, or a separate microphone unit can be worn as a handsome jeweled lapel pin on a woman's suit or dress front. Placement of the sound pickup equipment on the outside has the added advantage of eliminating the constant "clothing noises" caused by garments rubbing across the sensitive microphone when the aid is concealed beneath wearing apparel.

While women have always been able to camouflage inconspicuous earpieces by skillful arrangement of their hair, it is now possible to purchase hearing aids in the form of specially designed earrings which can be worn with the smartest "upsweep."

In the past many men and women whose lives could have been greatly enriched by the use of a hearing aid have avoided getting one. This was due in some measure to a natural disinclination to admit publicly that their hearing was impaired, plus the fact that some of their acquaintances who did have hearing aids complained that they couldn't use them with any degree of pleasure or satisfaction.

Now pride is a fine, healthy, wholesome thing and something we all need in adequate amounts. But when natural pride turns to foolish pride it's time to do something about it. You aren't fooling anyone but yourself if you need a hearing aid and refuse to get one. You aren't making yourself appear any younger as you strain to catch what is going on around you and constantly ask to have the important parts of conversation repeated. The tension shows in your face and posture and will be reflected quickly in your disposition. You may become belligerent and snap at your associates because of the annoyance of not hearing what is being said, or you may become unsure of yourself and withdraw more and more from what is going on around you. In either case you are doing yourself and your family and friends a great injustice. You are making it unnecessarily difficult for others to communicate with you, and it won't be long before they give up trying. As a friend of mine said not long ago, "I'm not going to ask that couple over for an evening again until the husband gets a hearing aid. Maybe his wife doesn't mind shouting at him all the time, but I'm not going to do it or ask my other guests to do it either!"

Don't wait for your loss of hearing to become acute before getting good medical advice about it and inquiring into the best type of hearing aid for your individual needs. There is a wide choice both in price and design, and once you have learned to live with a good hearing aid you will find that it adds years of vastly improved living.

There is a tendency on the part of some individuals to wear their aids only for special occasions. This is all right if their hearing impairment is slight and they need help only in theaters or at large gatherings. In the case of others, however, it implies that their everyday associates are not apt to say anything worth hearing, and it also does the owner of the hearing aid a great disservice. A hearing aid should be worn most of the time if it is to fulfill its best function.

Those who are wearing an aid for the first time should get

used to their new hearing partner in the quiet of their own homes. It should be worn for only an hour or so at a time, in order to come to terms with it before setting out for an all-day session. Both the wearer and the aid have limitations, and it is important to find out what they are. Finding out will take some patient experimenting, but the end result of hearing adequately is worth all the trials and errors that seem to be part of the initial process.

Since all sounds are amplified, the wearer may find himself listening to incidentals which he is not the least interested in hearing, or he may find that these unwanted sounds drown out the things he is trying to hear. Volume adjustment is a highly individual thing, but the right level can be found, and patient training will enable the individual to ignore the unwelcome sounds just as city dwellers learn not to hear the traffic noises that sound like thunder to their country cousins.

Once you have been fitted with the aid best suited to your purpose, don't devote too much energy to trying to conceal the fact that you have one. It is a rather common experience to find that the person who worked hard for years trying to cover up the fact that he was hard of hearing will spend just as much energy trying to disguise the fact that he is now using a hearing aid. Wear your aid with pride and rejoice in the fact that you are living in the electronic age that makes such efficient help possible. Suppose the best you could get was an ear trumpet—how would you feel then?

In addition to wearing a hearing aid, you will do much for your own peace of mind and add immeasurably to your social graces if you make a study of lip reading. Certain letters—namely, *f, v, sh, p, b,* and *m*—are easily read on the lips, even though they are often difficult to distinguish by sound. Lip reading is a fascinating study in itself and has the added advantage of forcing the lip reader to concentrate his attention on the person with whom he is talking. Since deafness tends to make a person withdraw and keep more and more to himself, lip reading is one of the best ways to retain an outgoing personality.

Further proof that impaired hearing need not limit the enjoyment of life is found in the many special features which large manufacturing companies are now building into sound equipment. Telephones are available with bells adjusted to a more audible pitch and with a volume control which amplifies the voice for the hard-of-hearing but which can be turned down for the other members of the family who do not need it. Many movie theaters have seats equipped with headphones which bring the sound track directly to the viewer's ears, and the same is true of radio, television, and record players for the home. These are now being marketed with special headphones and volume control for the hard-of-hearing, while the balance of the family listens to the loud-speaker set at normal. This one piece of home equipment should do much to eliminate the friction that may be caused by some members of the family wanting the radio playing quietly while others may need it blaring in order to hear it at all.

Information on all this special equipment, together with booklets on hearing aids and the study of lip reading, can be secured from the New York League For The Hard Of Hearing, a non-profit organization operated for the express purpose of keeping those with impaired hearing active in normal life. The League's address is 480 Lexington Avenue, New York 17, New York, and it will gladly put you in touch with similar groups which may be operating in your community.

Clothes Can Do a Lot

Good packaging, as any smart merchandiser knows, can make any product look more attractive and increase sales. As it is with perfume and kitchen soap, so it is with us humans, and the clothes in which we package ourselves can have the same attention-arresting and magnetic effect.

No self-respecting person is ever too old to care about appearance, and as we add to our years we also add to our authority and individuality in expressing ourselves through our clothes. When we are very young, the need to conform and to be like everyone else is very important, but with the years we can afford to dress in the way that best suits our needs and enhances our personalities.

Far from adopting drab, monotonous colors, we should let our harvest years be as rich and gay as the autumn which they so truly represent. Dignity need not always be clothed in black, nor maturity encased in awkward, unlovely lines.

It has been rightly pointed out that as our physical attractions lose some of their force we should give more attention to presenting ourselves as handsomely as possible. Instead of letting our clothes become less colorful as we grow older, we should do quite the reverse.

I recently encountered a handsome, beautifully groomed man of perhaps seventy-five striding along Fifth Avenue in a well-tailored suit and a tattersall vest! He was by far the most pleasing and eye-catching person on the block.

A few days later I was almost tempted to get off the bus to question a woman, who might have been anywhere from fifty-five to seventy-five, who had had her pure white hair dyed a magnificent robin's-egg blue. This blue is not to be confused with the light rinses of blue or lavender that are so frequently used on white hair. This hair was a vibrant, carefree, I'm-having-a-wonderful-time-out-of-life blue, and with it she wore an orange-red coat and a small black velvet hat! Her skin was firm and her face was made up in a careful, quiet way, so as not to compete with the triumph of her hair. Not everyone would want bright blue hair, but the point is that if you do, and it will make you feel happier and more confident to have it, now is the time to indulge yourself. You're old enough to be able to dress as you please, and you shouldn't limit yourself to the "old-lady colors and styles" that used to be prescribed for the "middle-aged woman."

On the other hand, don't make the mistake of selecting girlish things when what you really want are beautiful, gracious dresses and suits with that knowing, experienced air. The woman with the bright blue hair wasn't trying to pretend that her hair hadn't turned gray; what she was saying was, "My hair has finally turned gray and I'm having a lot of fun with it."

Don't let yourself be talked into poorly cut garments that do nothing for your figure or colors that don't flatter your skin. You may find that you are now ready for a completely different range of colors than you have previously worn, or for different shades or tints of your lifetime favorites.

The cut and color are more important now than they ever have been, and you should make your selections carefully, since clothes tend to last longer as we curtail our activities, and there is no excuse and certainly no satisfaction in owning a dress or coat that doesn't give you a sense of pleasure and well-being every time you put it on.

Hats become more important with every year you live, and the height of a crown or the line of a brim can make all the difference in the world. Necklines are equally important and deserve careful study to find which do the most for you.

Perhaps our perfumes should tend more to the light floral scents as we go along, leaving the headier things for the younger thirty to fifty crowd, but we should never forego perfume and cologne completely.

In fact, we should add to and not take away from the many little things which give us pleasure as we go through the years. Life should become richer and more meaningful and filled with the little pleasures of day-to-day living.

More and more men and women are marrying at forty and fifty and sixty than ever before in our human history, and the statistics in the field are bound to rise steadily. Remember the sensation that was created a generation ago by that play called *Only 38*, in which an attractive widow with full-grown children actually fell in love and married a very personable man of her own age! Only thirty-eight, indeed! Practically a child bride by tomorrow's standards, for both medical and human science has demonstrated that we never outgrow our need for love and affection and a sense of sharing our lives with someone else.

Women are beginning to learn that the menopause does not mean the end of sexual attraction or sexual desire; it is simply a time that frees sex of uneasiness about pregnancy. Modern hormone therapy has relieved this period of life of physical and mental discomfort, so that a woman at this time can now appear at her most desirable and tranquil best. With her children grown, she is free to devote herself to a myriad of other interests, particularly to developing her own personality and making the most of her own potentials.

Modern women know that life after the menopause, far from being something to dread, can hold much physical and emotional interest. In fact, one progressive dress manufacturer is already designing a line for the "mature bride"!

It is to be hoped that the "mature groom" will be equally resplendent!

DENTAL HEALTH

by

SIDNEY EPSTEIN, D.D.S.

The American people are noted for their good teeth—or more accurately, for their interest in the health and preservation of their teeth. The high standards of American dentistry have, of course, encouraged and supported this interest.

The average American who has cared for his teeth throughout childhood and young adulthood will probably reach the age of forty or fifty with a complete set of natural teeth (twenty-eight plus four wisdom teeth, for a total of thirty-two). At this point, however, he will be faced with somewhat different problems if he is to continue to maintain the health of his original dentition. The dental problems at this time of life are apt to be unlike those of the earlier periods.

If you have your teeth at mid-life, it may be taken as a good indication that you will continue to have them for many years to come. There is no age level, however, at which you are ever free from the possibility of dental caries (tooth decay) or of developing cavities.

At the age of twenty-five the rate of tooth decay usually shows a marked drop. Fewer cavities develop, because the most susceptible areas have already been attacked and filled and also because with the years the nutritional requirements decrease and show considerable change. Older people have a much smaller need or desire for sugars and starches—foods which are closely related to the process of tooth decay. It has been found that "decay and failure of teeth in modern man is probably more a matter of nutrition and other accidents of living than due to the rapid ticking of the hereditary time clock."

Teeth that have been filled and repaired in earlier years will require constant observation as the years go by. All filling materials—whether of gold, silver, amalgam, porcelain, or plastics—are a poor substitute at best for the enamel and dentine of a sound tooth. All fillings have a limited life and will deteriorate and perhaps need to be replaced. How long they will last is determined by the original skill of the dentist and the care you have given them.

Teeth that have large fillings and crowns should be X-rayed periodically to check any breakdown in its early stages. The edges of fillings should be kept smooth and polished by the dentist in order to reduce the rate of breakdown and leakage.

Fillings which are worn and fractured so that they permit foodstuffs to wedge between the teeth and irritate the gum tissue by packing between the teeth should be replaced. This condition is not only painful and annoying, but the continued irritation and destructive process may cause infection which can result in the breaking down and loosening of the supporting gums and bones. With care, a filling can be removed from the original cavity and replaced, without involving much additional sacrifice of sound tooth structure and without increasing the size of the restoration. Needless to say, the protection and preservation of the gum tissue is equally as important as the preservation of the teeth.

Pyorrhea, the common destroyer of the gums, is a disease as old as the human race. Old as it is, though, we still have much to learn about what causes it and how it can best be eradicated. For some peculiar reason there is an antagonistic relationship between pyorrhea and tooth decay. One is seldom found in the presence of the other. Tooth decay is most destructive during youth and young adulthood. With age, tooth decay decreases and the diseases of the gums become increasingly prevalent. Older individuals may have less tooth decay. However, the person of forty or fifty with a full set of sound natural teeth may, for some unexplained reason, be faced with the possibility of losing his sound teeth because of the breakdown of the supporting tissues.

Generally speaking, where there is extensive tooth decay there may be little loss or change in gums and bone. On the other hand, where the teeth are sound, well formed, and in good position, there may be a rapid breakdown of the investing tissues of the teeth. This condition may be related to changes disturbing the endocrine balance, which may mean an interference with the body's ability to assimilate calcium and phosphorus salts needed to maintain and to build bone. It may also have some relationship to disturbance of important enzymes that cause chemical transformations in living-tissue mechanisms.

Other factors responsible for the loosening of teeth in the bone are premature loss of teeth, with subsequent drifting of adjacent teeth producing spaces that allow for food impaction; poor fillings, bridges, and crowns that irritate the supporting tissues of the teeth and permit accumulations; poor habits of oral hygiene, such as incorrect toothbrush habits; the use of toothpicks; careless use of dental floss, which causes unnecessary or undue irritation.

Improperly designed and ill-fitting removable bridges and partial dentures place an abnormal amount of stress upon the supporting teeth. When there are irregular positions of the teeth in the jaws, undue force is received by a tooth or teeth in masticating. Thus, under the stress of constant pounding, the supporting tissues drift away from the teeth just as earth will shift away from a post that is constantly rocked in the ground. Vitamin and food deficiencies and metabolic diseases, such as diabetes and parathyroid disturbances, will also cause initial changes in the soft tissues.

Vincent's infection—or trench mouth, as it is more popularly known—is an acute ulcerative disease of the soft tissues of the mouth. The gums, tongue, and throat become painful and the gums tend to bleed readily. Patches of grayish membrane appear, and the patient usually experiences a general lack of well-being.

Like many infectious diseases, Vincent's infection is most often associated with decreased physical resistance. While it is moderately contagious, it has been found that a person who receives balanced nutrition and sufficient rest and who observes good mouth hygiene will not be too susceptible to it.

Diagnosis of the condition should be made by a physician or dentist, and home treatment should be limited to careful attention to a good diet particularly high in vitamins B and C, adequate rest, and mouth hygiene. During the acute stage use of tobacco, alcohol, and highly seasoned foods should be discontinued.

Only the medication prescribed by dentist or physician should be used. In the absence of professional advice, nothing but a saline solution (one-half teaspoon of table salt in a glass of warm water) should be used as a vigorous mouthwash.

Brush the *gums* and teeth thoroughly, in spite of bleeding and tenderness. This should be done three to five times a day, and the brushing continued for five minutes by the clock. A mild, unscented, non-medicated toilet soap is the only dentifrice that should be used during the period of infection.

Normally, throughout life, the teeth continue to erupt slightly to compensate for the wear of the biting surface and to maintain the correct tooth-jaw height. As the tooth moves up from its supporting bed, the gum tissue will move down from the neck of the tooth to produce areas that are slightly sensitive. Usually these areas will disappear with the exposure of the tooth to the fluids of the mouth and the passage of time. Painful areas may be desensitized by the dentist.

Too enthusiastic use of a toothbrush can be responsible for much gum damage. The person who scrubs his teeth in a vigorous back-and-forth motion or in a rotary motion on the teeth themselves does irreparable harm to the teeth as well as to the supporting tissues. In enthusiastic but unwise use of the toothbrush, the gum tissue is irritated so that it will recede downward as a result of constant laceration. A combination of rigorous toothbrushing with an abrasive dentifrice wears away the thin enamel near the gum line and later the covering on the root itself. In such areas of recession deep wedge-shaped or saucer-shaped cuts are produced by the abrasive action of the toothbrush and dentifrice. This condition is often further aggravated by the frequent use of acid beverages, candy, and mouthwashes. Individuals who routinely start their day with lemon juice, or lemon juice in hot water, are apt to cause the minerals in the teeth to dissolve and also soften the teeth so that they wear away more rapidly. Where these areas of toothbrush destruction have occurred, it is frequently necessary to replace the missing tooth structure with filling material to prevent the possibility of tooth decay as well as continued abrasion.

How to Select and Use a Toothbrush

It would be well to consider what constitutes good mouth hygiene. First, of course, is the correct selection of a toothbrush. A toothbrush should not be considered as a gadget. It should have certain very definite requirements. For most people a toothbrush should have a straight handle that is reinforced just back of the bristles. The bristles of the toothbrush should be *straight,* with no convexity or concavity. The brush should be no more than three rows of bristles in width or more than six rows of bristles in length. Animal-bristle brushes are preferable to the synthetic plastic bristles. Good toothbrushes have bristles that are stiff, flexible, durable, and dry quickly. Two toothbrushes should be in routine use, so that the brush used in the morning has twenty-four hours in which to dry out.

Teeth, if brushed correctly, can be brushed as frequently as one desires. However, one should brush his teeth at least twice a day—after breakfast, the first meal of the day, and, if possible, immediately after the evening meal, or certainly before retiring. The teeth should be brushed for a sufficient length of time.

Time is the most important thing one can put on the toothbrush. Most of us have no concept of time values, therefore a clock or watch should be used until one learns how to time an interval of three to five minutes when using a toothbrush.

The toothbrush should be used with a sweeping motion. It would be well to think of the toothbrush as a tooth *broom.* The ends of the bristles of the brush are directed up toward the gum tissue on the upper jaw or down toward the gum tissue on the lower jaw. Pressure is exerted on the sides of the bristles that sweep from the gums into the spaces between the teeth and over the surface of the teeth. The only place the brush might be used in a scrubbing motion would be on the biting surface of the teeth, in order to get into any pits or fissures. The toothbrush should be worked in and about the surfaces of teeth where there are spaces caused by missing teeth, particularly if the teeth are supporting members for artificial appliances.

The toothbrush should also be used to clean thoroughly in and about fixed bridgework. If one has a removable restoration, it should be cleansed thoroughly, either with the toothbrush or with a brush specially designed for the bars and retaining clasps. The decomposition of accumulated debris of foodstuff about the attachment teeth and around the retainers of removable restorations causes the supporting teeth to decay. *Do not* use scouring powders on artificial teeth or on appliances. Use either a mild, unscented toilet soap or tooth paste.

There are small rubber points made for attaching to the handle of a toothbrush—or some come on an independent handle—which may be used for getting into the interdental spaces to remove additional debris and to stimulate the tissue to keep it healthy.

The routine use of dental floss should be condemned. The reasons necessitating the use of dental floss should be corrected. If there are areas that require the use of some kind of floss or tape, it would be well to substitute thin rubber bands. The forcing down of dental floss or tape on the gum tissue produces additional irritation and laceration. The rubber band will do the same work and yield when it strikes the soft underlying tissues. Toothpicks also should be used with care. A toothpick should never be used to dig into a deep pocket between teeth or used in a manner that will produce abrasion and wear.

How to Choose a Dentifrice

Most paste and powder dentifrices are relatively safe. In choosing a dentifrice it is well to use one that contains either some natural or synthetic soap and a limited degree of abrasive action. Dentifrices, in the light of present research knowledge, must still be considered primarily as cosmetics and as an adjunct to the toothbrush. New chemicals are now being added that may make them an effective means for reducing tooth decay. There are no known drugs that can be added to dentifrices to make them effective means for treating gum or mouth infections. Some of the new antibiotics are being used experimentally. Claims of manufacturers should be viewed with caution. Special preparations should be used only by prescription or recommendation of a physician or dentist.

In brushing the teeth, attention should be given to cleansing the teeth as well as to massaging and cleansing the gum tissues. It may be necessary to divide the procedure into distinct phases, with effort directed toward both areas. It is advisable to use a smaller toothbrush to reach areas that are especially difficult.

Thorough rinsing after toothbrushing is an important phase of oral hygiene. A warm saline solution, made of a half teaspoon of salt in a glass of warm water, is an excellent mouthwash. It should be churned vigorously about the mouth and in between the teeth, using the lips and tongue to develop agitating force. Other aromatic and medicated mouthwashes have no particular healing value. They merely provide a pleasant taste to cover up another that is less pleasant or less desirable.

Too much emphasis cannot be placed upon the necessity for good mouth hygiene. As indicated earlier, while, with the years, there is less tooth decay, pyorrhea and related gum infections become more and more prevalent and serious. The accumulation of food material and hard deposits on the teeth is a constant irritant that produces permanent and irreparable damage. This material must be removed as thoroughly and as often as possible. Frequent periodic visits to the dentist are necessary to overcome the inadequacies of home care.

The Importance of Replacements

The question is often asked, "Why replace missing teeth with artificial substitutes, such as fixed (non-removable) bridges, or with partial restorations, such as removable bridges?" In the instance of even a single missing tooth, if it is in the front part of the mouth, there is the factor of appearance. A pleasant smile and a full complement of teeth are important to a pleasing personality. There is nothing quite so unsightly as a smile broken by jagged, discolored, or missing teeth. In the back part of the mouth the loss of a tooth or teeth causes interference with function and the beginning of breakdown of the whole dental pattern.

The creation of a space by the loss of a tooth causes the drifting of the adjacent teeth in a natural effort to close the gap. The opposing teeth may become elongated as they, too, try to fill in the vacant space. The replacement of a single tooth or teeth helps to maintain the remaining teeth in their correct relationship in the dental arch.

There are definite alterations in the size and shape of the face as we grow older, due, to some extent, to changes in the upper and lower jaws as a result of a decrease in the jaw distance after the loss of several or all of the teeth. This is also accompanied by alterations in size and shape of the maxillary antrum (sinuses). With the changes in the shape of the lower jaw, particularly at the angle, there is a tendency to revert toward the original condition seen in the infant's jaw. However, this change can be prevented and the original adult form maintained by establishing correct jaw relationships with properly constructed and adapted dentures or other restorations. Partial dentures which replace several of the back teeth on either one or both sides are important because the back teeth have the responsibility of maintaining correct jaw relationship.

If the lower jaw is not kept in its correct relationship to the upper jaw, the hinge joint of the lower jaw, which is just in front of and below the opening of the ear, is allowed to move in an abnormal manner. With the loss of the back teeth or the drifting of teeth, and the change in support, the jaw will move upward, backward, and to one side and press upon the structures in and about the ear. It will be responsible for many painful and unpleasant symptoms. These symptoms frequently are stuffiness, popping sounds, ringing in the ears, a crackling sound in the hinge joint, dizziness (frequently after eating), a radiating pain up along the side of the head and above the eyes. It may even cause involvement of the nerve fibers of the tongue, and when these are interfered with there may be a burning sensation along the side of the tongue. There may also be changes in hearing, although decrease in hearing ability may be due to other causes, and it is not always possible for changes in hearing ability to be altered by dental restorations.

When these symptoms develop, it is important to replace the teeth, using some form of restoration that will re-establish the structures in their correct relationship to each other. Likewise it is important for those individuals who are already wearing partial restorations to have their dental appliances maintained at correct biting height and relationship to the supporting tissues. Undue shrinkage of tissues or wear of the artificial teeth may cause similar displacement.

Partial dentures should be kept scrupulously clean. They should be cleansed every time the supporting teeth are cleansed, because there is a tendency for food to adhere to them more readily than to the tooth structure. If the inner surfaces that contact the natural teeth are not kept clean, the supporting teeth will decay rapidly. If the appliances are not adjusted at frequent intervals to compensate for tissue shrinkage, there will be undue force exerted upon the supporting teeth and they will be pulled out of their normal position in the arch and ultimately lost.

What to Expect of Dentures

The subject of full dentures can be discussed from many aspects. It will be limited here to a few essential points. What should one expect from dentures? At best, dentures are only a substitute for the original teeth. They have definite limitations as to aesthetics, function, and comfort. The age at which one first begins with full upper and lower dentures is important. A young person adapts himself very readily to their use. The later in life that one has the misfortune of losing all his teeth and requiring full dentures, the more difficult it is to make the adjustments necessary to learn to use them.

Dental science, which makes use of plastic materials and translucent porcelain, plus the artistry and skill of the individual dentist, makes it possible for dental restorations to duplicate the original natural dentition in all important details and individual characteristics. It is possible to make almost any kind of change in the physical appearance of the teeth to eliminate the false or artificial character. The denture base— that is, the material that forms the base in which the teeth are set to hold them in the mouth—can also be camouflaged so that no one but the wearer need know that the teeth are not nature's own.

Denture techniques permit the dentist to prepare accurate records readily and easily and to establish and determine jaw relationships and forms necessary for making the denture. It is the factors that the dentist cannot control or influence that may add to the patient's difficulty in using dentures. Age and temperament are extremely important. The general physical condition and well-being of the individual, as well as the health and contour of the oral tissues, are also significant. Tissues that are thin and tender, bony ridges that are spiny and sharp, will make it difficult to use dentures comfortably. Tongues that are large, muscles that are weak, mouths that are dry, abnormal muscle attachments, excess tissue, will all add to individual difficulties with "new teeth."

It is important to realize that the so-called denture base is for all practical purposes permanent. Because the mouth and tissues change constantly, dentures may require frequent adjustment and replacement to compensate for the shrinkage of the ridges as well as for other changes in the mouth. Loose, ill-fitting dentures irritate the supporting tissues and cause an increased amount of inflammatory tissue to develop. They cause the bone to shrink away from the denture base at an abnormally fast rate.

Loose dentures are responsible also for gagging and loss of ability to masticate the food. Dentures that have rough or broken teeth, cracks, broken edges, should be corrected and repaired. The jagged, rough edges may be sufficiently irritating to be responsible for the development of an oral cancer.

No one should expect even the best-fitting denture to be as efficient as the original teeth, although it may vastly improve the individual's appearance. With natural teeth one can exert biting forces of approximately one hundred and fifty pounds per square inch. With artificial teeth the efficiency drops down to about fifteen to thirty pounds per square inch. This means that one must put smaller quantities of food into the mouth and chew for a longer period of time. The consistency of foods has something to do with the ease with which the patient can masticate them. Foods that are thin and tough are difficult. A dry crust of bread often is much easier to chew up than is a thin, pliable lettuce leaf.

How to Use Dentures to Advantage

In using dentures, do not bite with the front teeth. When eating a piece of bread or sandwich, bite with the canine teeth and the teeth at the corner of the mouth. Grasp the mass of food, tear it by biting into it, and at the same time pull in an upward and backward direction against the upper denture. This procedure will prevent the upper denture from being displaced and will not dislodge the lower denture. Do not develop the habit of eating and chewing with the front teeth. The back teeth are grinding teeth. After a morsel of food has been placed in the mouth, the natural process of chewing and swallowing is for the tongue to move the food back onto the grinding surface of the molar teeth, where it is crushed, broken up, mixed with saliva, and ready to be swallowed.

Some individuals who wear dentures say that for them food has no taste. If they would carry the morsel of food onto the back teeth and chew it there, the food would be in contact with the back and sides of the tongue, where the taste buds are located. The pleasurable sensation from food therefore would be increased.

When eating food that requires shearing action, such as biting an apple or eating kernels off an ear of corn, the lower teeth are used for the incising action instead of the upper. In other words, when eating an ear of corn, if the corncob is rotated against the lower front teeth and pressed against the upper denture at the same time, the lower teeth will be forced tightly onto their base and the upper denture will not be dislodged. In this manner it is possible to enjoy an ear of corn right down to its last kernel.

The tendency of upper dentures to loosen or drop after considerable conversation or passage of time may be caused by unusual dryness of the mouth. This condition can be corrected by taking a mouthful of water to moisten the gums, palate, and the denture. It will help to increase the amount of suction and stability.

Denture sores and areas of irritation usually require treatment by the dentist. No attempt should ever be made to treat oneself. However, it is well for the patient to learn to recognize the conditions that cause areas of denture irritation. When there is a change in general physical state and well-being, it is reflected in the oral tissues, which become oversensitive and more readily irritated. Overindulgence in food or alcohol, which may lower resistance, and eating foods that require much chewing and grinding are also responsible for irritation.

It is important that the artificial denture help to maintain the muscles of the face and the jaws in correct relationship. However, one should not seek the services of the dentist for denture corrections for the sole purpose of using them to compensate for the changes of years and for the normal changes in muscle and tissue tone. Within limits, it is possible to make certain cosmetic corrections in face form and contour, but it is not possible for dentures to plump out areas where tissues have shrunken away after long illness or dieting or to smooth out the lines and wrinkles that come with external tissue change.

Dentures must be kept clean. Scrub them as often as possible during the day with a suitable denture brush and a mild soap or dentifrice. Consult a dentist about using any of the so-called deodorants for dentures. Do not use undue amounts of denture adhesives to retain or stabilize the denture. Do not use "reline"

pastes to correct denture fit. These preparations are irritating
to the tissues and may cause chemical burns. The denture may
require other more important adjustments. One who wears
dentures must not neglect periodic dental examination. Dentures are no more permanent than eyeglasses.

Although at the age of seventy about 80 per cent of women
and 70 per cent of men have lost all their teeth, this condition
is not inevitable and preventive measures at an earlier age
would do much to change this picture. We cannot yet state
positively whether or not the loss of teeth should be considered
a normal and voluntary change. But we do feel that the loss of
teeth should not begin before the age of sixty. Of course the
loss of teeth due to old age is different from that due to caries,
pyorrhea, abscess, et cetera. However, even without these
pathological changes the teeth eventually would undergo the
regular changes of age.

Your Diet and Your Teeth

The frequent and casual disregard of proper chewing function in elderly people appears to have its origin in the common
assumption that they need very little food and that an adequate
diet for them requires the use of few, if any, teeth. There is no
evidence that older people require any less food than they did
during the rest of their maturity. They may require less caloric
intake than they did during their more active years, but it is
obvious that proper nutrition should be maintained even for
those living very quiet lives. This does not mean a diet judged
by older standards, but rather a nutritional status in terms of
our present knowledge.

The immediate and long-range effects of poor mastication
were not considered important in the days when food was

simply food and the calorie was the sole yardstick of nutrition. Proper food choices are now of greater significance, and any factor that limits the individual's diet is considered a matter of some concern. The loss of even a few teeth will markedly lower chewing efficiency.

Choices of food are determined not only by taste and individual economic status, but by the loss of teeth, painful chewing, poorly fitting dentures, and any other factors which make the process of eating either uncomfortable or prolonged.

People without their natural teeth are sometimes severely handicapped in their eating habits, and this may exaggerate the pathological changes of the later years. Patients with poorly fitting dentures will often refuse to eat anything but the softer, starchy carbohydrate foods, and the poorly masticated food will, in turn, result in improper digestion and irritation of the colon.

All people, regardless of age, should have dentition adequate for enjoying a varied diet. The enjoyment of food is important in all periods of our lives, and authorities agree that the lack of teeth or a set of poorly fitting teeth can be a major cause of digestive upsets in older patients.

Empty spaces, unfilled by dentures, are objectionable, as thorough mastication is impossible without sufficient grinding surfaces. Because the carbohydrate foods are more easily chewed, it is natural that they should occupy too large a place in the diet of those who lack the ability to chew their food. For this reason older people frequently suffer from protein deficiencies. They avoid eating the meat which they so greatly need, and marked improvement in their physical condition is often noted when this important part of their diet is restored.

Unfortunately, many people are much too casual in their willingness to give up their teeth. Good artificial teeth at best have all the inadequacies of any man-made substitute, and it has been said that "it is a wise physician who retains the teeth of the patient as long as possible, albeit scanty and diseased unless absolutely convinced they cause disease elsewhere, for in the elderly the fitting of plates is often difficult or impossible and it is poor consolation to the patient to know that he no longer harbors potential foci of infection if he may no longer chew and must perforce live on pap."

There is ample justification for the foregoing warning. It is nothing short of brutal to deprive older people of their teeth on the basis of a general and ill-founded assumption that they will invariably find relief from their symptoms of systemic disease or disorder. The problem of extracting teeth is far more complex in an older patient than in a young one, and careful diagnosis and planning are necessary before reaching the decision to remove all of the existing teeth.

The subject of nutrition as it relates to dental problems warrants some consideration. The kinds of food eaten during the formative period of tooth development are important in determining the future physical condition of the teeth as well as their resistance to tooth decay. In later life the maintenance of the health of the teeth and the gums may also be related to dietary habit. Adequacy of diet and the building in of certain trace mineral elements into teeth during the period of tooth development prior to eruption are important factors. The diet in later life may not influence the physical character of the teeth, because after teeth have erupted they undergo no other changes of growth and development. The consumption of large quantities of milk or dairy products, which would provide the maximum quantities of mineral elements, may have little bearing on the tooth's over-all resistance. However, abnormal consumption of carbohydrate material, which readily breaks down to produce acid products, may hasten the rate of tooth decay.

Although calcium and phosphorus are among the most prominent elements in the tooth structure and must be regarded among the major nutritional factors concerned in the building of good teeth, they are not of prime importance after the tooth has developed. Once they have been built into the tooth structure they are not readily withdrawn by the circulation or by any metabolic change in the body. This is also true of vitamins A and D, which are essential during formation of the tooth but later lose their particular significance as it relates to the tooth structure itself. Vitamin C and its related compounds are of particular importance to the well-being of the gum tissues. This vitamin—which is found mostly in citrus fruits, berries, and fresh green leafy vegetables—helps to maintain the strength of the fine blood-vessel walls in the gum tissues. When these blood-vessel walls are weakened, the gum tissues swell and bleed readily. Where there is severe and prolonged vitamin C deficiency, a condition known as scurvy exists. This may be a precursor to the more violent condition of pyorrhea.

Research has demonstrated conclusively that the character of the general development of the teeth and jaws has been greatly influenced by diet. If we were to switch to an all-meat diet, which would be impractical or impossible in most countries, tooth decay would disappear. It appears that wherever we find a low-sugar, high-protein type of diet, such as is prescribed for the diabetic patient, we can expect a prompt and marked reduction in caries. This type of diet is impractical in many countries, as fats and proteins are often more expensive to produce than are sugars and starches.

Vitamin B deficiency often manifests itself about the mouth and on the oral tissues. In riboflavin deficiency there are ulcerating lesions present on the upper and lower lips, with deep transverse fissures at the angles of the mouth. This condition is sometimes confused with a condition of closed bite caused by ill-fitting dentures. Also the tongue may be very red and the patient will complain of a burning sensation. The gums are dry and swollen. In the case of nicotinic acid deficiency the symptoms are similar. The membranes are involved and inflamed, and the gum margins are covered with a grayish material which resembles a trench-mouth infection (Vincent's angina).

There are many diseases of the tissues in and about the mouth which may be of local origin or due to disturbances elsewhere in the body. Systemic diseases which have oral manifestations will be recognized by the dentist or physician if the patient goes for a consultation as soon as the condition appears. Changes in color and character of the tissue, unusual smoothness or roughness, the appearance of patches, swelling membranes, or areas of peculiar sensation—in short, any deviation from apparently normal conditions—should serve as a warning to seek professional aid. Enlargement of the tongue and swelling of the glands of the neck below the border of the lower jaw may be indications of infection or more serious complications. In no instance should you indulge in self-diagnosis or self-treatment.

Many serious and fatal systemic diseases present their first visible evidence in the mouth. The dentist is often the first to be consulted by patients who are suffering from such generalized diseases as pernicious anemia, agranulocytosis, and leukemia, because of the oral manifestations which accompany these disorders.

Certain drugs also may give rise to oral lesions in people who are sensitized to them. The most common of these are mercury, bismuth, arsphenamine, amidopyrine, barbital, salicylates, sulfonamides, and penicillin.

Specific diseases which may have attendant oral lesions include tuberculosis of the mouth tissues, syphilis, and the yeast infections, the most common of which is thrush or "white mouth." Tumors of the oral tissue may be either harmless or the beginning of cancer of the mouth. In the latter case the importance of removing all irritating factors such as smoking, correcting ill-fitting dentures, and overcoming poor mouth hygiene cannot be overemphasized.

Lesions of the mouth tissues which arise from constant irritation, such as broken teeth, rough filling margins, or over-indulgence in tobacco in its several forms, should be examined frequently to preclude the possibility of developing malignant lesions. Those who use tobacco in unusual or excessive quantities should have the tissues of their mouths and throats checked at regular intervals. Heavy white patched areas (leucoplakia), which are the result of heat and tobacco, as well as other forms of irritation, should also be watched as possible danger signals.

Good oral hygiene should be started early in life and continued up to and including the harvest years. In colonial days no one was expected to preserve his own teeth past the age of thirty. Many of our early citizens had full sets of uncomfortable and inefficient dentures by the time they were twenty-five. Today, with the proper care and a good diet, we know that our teeth can and should last as long as the rest of our bodies.

REFERENCES

BECKS, H., and MORGAN, A. F. "Tooth Decay and Pyorrhea." *Science Supplement,* November 1941.

BURKET, LESTER W. *Oral Medicine.* Lippincott, 1946.

CARLSON, A. J. "Physiology of Aging." *Northwest Medicine,* February 1943.

HOWARTH, WILLARD A. *Pennsylvania Dental Journal,* December 1947.

McCOLLUM, E. V., and SIMMONDS, NINA. *The Newer Knowledge of Nutrition.* The Macmillan Company, 1939.

MANLY, R. S., and SHIERE, F. R. "The Effect of Dental Deficiency on Mastication and Food Preference." *Oral Surgery, Oral Medicine and Oral Pathology,* May 1950.

O'ROURKE, J. T. "Dental Care for Children in Relation to Geriatrics." *Journal of the American Dental Association,* May 1947

SHERMAN, H. C., and LANFORD, CAROLINE S. *Essentials of Nutrition* The Macmillan Company, 1943.

THOMAS, B. O. A. *Gerodontology,* "The Study and Changes in Oral Tissues Associated with Aging." *Journal of the American Dental Association,* February 1946.

WARTHIN, A. S. *Old Age, the Major Involution.* Paul B. Hoeber Inc., 1929.

FINANCING THE LATER YEARS

by

HENRY W. STEINHAUS, Ph.D.

THE leisure afforded by financial security is what makes possible the varied and delightful pleasures of the harvest years. Whether you are twenty-five, forty-five, or sixty-five, the time for you to plan for that financial security is *now*. The following is a realistic report on what problems you may face and what means you may take advantage of in solving them.

YOUR BUDGET

Budgeting is advisable at every stage of life, but it is an absolute necessity for those who wish to plan intelligently for the financing of their retirement. Your own ideas should, of course, govern the main features of the budget. Your place of residence, your physical and cultural needs, your family status and resources will produce numerous variations. We can, however, outline the main factors in a budget and discuss what items may be anticipated during our working years and what items require continuous cash outlay and therefore income. The budget for a mature couple has been described as one "providing the goods and services necessary for a healthful, self-respecting mode of living, allowing normal participation in the life of the community in accordance with current

American standards." The budget which we will call the "minimum" is supposed to provide such a modest but adequate living standard. Those who desire more detail on budget items may wish to consult memorandum No. 67 of the Social Security Administration, issued March 1948, and supplemented May 16, 1949, entitled *A Budget for an Elderly Couple.*

Housing

Since housing presents the largest item in the budget for the aged, and since it is the most interesting one from the point of view of financing, let us review it first. The monthly rent outlay for a two- or three-room unfurnished apartment, inclusive of heating fuel, electricity, and gas, averages some $42 in seven larger cities used in the investigation. This figure is about at prewar level, held there by rent control. To the bare rent item should be added the cost of repairs and replacements of household furnishings and equipment, household textiles, household services, such as laundry, cleaning, and telephone (assumed to be available in about half the families), and the cost of other miscellaneous household commodities, such as laundry soap, flakes, or powder. The addition of these items brings the monthly average to $55. We will use this figure, although we should keep in mind that the rent is bound to rise as controls are relinquished.

It is apparent that expenditures for rent are bound to be a strain on our retirement income. Therefore our first and most important conclusion is that a home free of obligations is a necessity for a successfully financed later life. A survey of Social Security pensioners actually reveals that about half of them own their own homes, usually mortgage-free. Moreover, experience in other countries reveals that possession of a mortgage-free home not only takes care of the rent budget (real-estate taxes excepted) but offers in many instances income-producing possibilities.

In vacation sections it might be possible to sublet your home while you spend some time with your children. In industrial sections you might have permanent renters or tourist accommodations. In any case there could be some income to help offset tax and upkeep expenses which do require cash. But the most interesting part of this picture of "your own home" is that it is an inflationproof investment, which can be acquired over a long number of years and in relatively small installments which on the whole should compare favorably with normal rent expenditures. In purchasing a house for such purposes, one should consider the sturdiness of construction and be sure that the house meets standards, as to floor plan, state of repair, and location, which would fulfill the needs of older people. Moreover, the location should be convenient to churches, shops, and relatives, the water supply should be pure and plentiful, and the house should not have steep stairways.

Perhaps the heating problem needs special consideration. In our northern states fuel consumption is quite large, in our southern states negligible. Similar considerations apply to cost of clothing. If you are free to choose, your budget would certainly appreciate a southern location, particularly if you think of renting your home for "the season." But if your family, social, and cultural requirements are such that you want to remain in the locality where you now live and work, you must plan accordingly.

It is no secret that in the older age group two can live cheaper than one and one. As a matter of fact, it appears that the standard of living elderly people can afford rises in proportion to the number of people who combine their resources. An example may illustrate what group planning can accomplish. Three families in the lower-income brackets, who used to meet regularly during their annual vacations devoted to fishing, found that equality in ages, hobbies, interests, and customs made them quite a congenial group. These families raised the question of planning for retirement, but being members of the "white-collar" fixed-income group, they had little left to save for this eventuality. As a matter of fact, the annual vacation trip was about the only luxury they allowed themselves.

These three families decided that if they were to pool the amounts usually spent for hotel expenses they could purchase a modest summer residence. The families could use the summer residence during their vacation periods—in succession, of course—and their annual savings on hotel expenses, plus such rental income as they would obtain during the intervening months, could make the place mortgage-free before long. Residential expenses would then be limited to upkeep and taxes, which were quite low and which should be kept low in all such projects. The summer house was of the one-floor type, and while it was not big enough to accommodate at one time all three families with their children, there was enough room to accommodate three older couples as well as one additional person for permanent help. It should be noted that joint occupancy by three couples may more easily permit the luxury of help or a nurse, if required.

While the families do not meet any more during vacations, as they used to, they find they meet even more often in between, as the planning goes on. The latest project is the joint purchase of a fishing boat, which will not only substitute capital acquisition for the usual boat rental but will serve to reduce the meal budget as well. In addition, one member of the group plans to hire himself out as a guide, if customers can be found

–which is quite likely, particularly on week ends during the ishing season.

Another illustration of joint planning, involving housing articularly, comes from a midwestern university, where a roup of teachers and administrators are planning the erection of a club center for elderly couples who are retired members of the university staff. The place will be like an apartment hotel in which each couple will have a private apartment. There will be a general living room, a library, a social center, and laundry rooms (with automatic equipment, of course). The land is to be granted by the university, which will in turn benefit by the continued presence of people with wide business and professional experience. How far the planning of such a group can go may be surmised from the plans of some of these retired members who want to conduct real-estate-brokerage or farm-management operations, management services, legal and economic consulting and other services, in order to supplement their retirement pay. Others hope that more universities will develop such settlements and that an exchange can take place, between California and Chicago, or between New York and Florida, whereby a member of one center may exchange quarters for a number of months with a member of another center. Another illustration comes from Germany, where there formerly existed, and presumably still exist, large groups of retired civil-service employees who have purchased or built residences in the neighborhood of the numerous small universities, where they serve the students by providing housing and even meal requirements and at the same time enjoy the cultural associations of a college community. The student's rent pays for the pensioner's home, which leaves the small pension for the other items of the budget, which we will analyze now.

Food

The next largest item in the budget is food, requiring an average of roughly $40 a month. This is evidently a low-cost budget, with little room for an occasional guest or an occasional meal out. Food expenses require cash—cash of adequate purchasing power, since food prices are quite sensitive to inflationary price rises. Very little can be done to anticipate food expenses in planning retirement. Of course group arrangements will facilitate group purchase of food and its use on a more economical basis, but other difficulties arise in the case of special diets and preferences, which on the whole appear to offset the advantages of community dining.

There is another possibility of anticipating such expenditures which might be explored, particularly by corporations engaged in the manufacture and distribution of canned foods. An investment in stocks of such companies payable in merchandise might be a method of financing some food expenditures in advance. An individual financially able to invest in stock might therefore consider such an investment, in the expectation that returns would be closely related to the cost of the product.

Incidentals

Other items in the budget are clothing, requiring about $10 a month; normal medical and dental care, requiring another $10 a month; items of personal care, such as barber- and beauty-shop expenditures, soap, tooth paste, and shaving cream, requiring roughly $3 a month; and, finally, books, magazines, and newspapers, tobacco, transportation, gifts, contributions, radio and television, movies and other recreation, requiring about $12 a month. Precautions would normally be taken by people close to retirement, who face a considerable reduction in their incomes, to see to it that necessary items such as linens are plentiful and in good condition. It is also likely that careful planning will extend such precautions to other items, such as clothing, but even a minimum budget does not fail to allow a new hat for the lady of the house at least once every two years.

The cost of medical care is unpredictable, and no suggestion has as yet come to the author's attention which would permit continuation of health insurance to the older groups. Blue Cross hospitalization coverage can be continued individually after retirement, and Blue Cross administrators even permit transfer of a member from one location to another. Needy people (particularly those eligible for old-age assistance) will receive proper treatment free of charge, but for others illnesses of old age appear uninsurable.

Again precautions can be taken to anticipate some expenditures, such as reading glasses, and extra sets of false teeth can be provided, but cash and savings are necessary in any event. To some extent a safety margin exists in that expenses for entertainment and recreation can be curtailed if special medical expenses arise, and since it is important to have such a margin, the proposed "luxury" items cannot be considered too liberal.

This budget does not assume an income tax. Under the current federal law an elderly couple, both of whom are sixty-five years or over, have a total exemption of $2,400. Exemption under State Income Tax laws are also of the same order—for instance, $2,500 in New York State. Additional allowances are permitted for medical-care expenditures in excess of five per cent of income. Furthermore, Social Security benefits are not taxable, and special tax provisions apply to annuity returns, as we will see later. There is the question of real-estate taxes, but much of that is a matter of location and therefore free choice, and such taxes often represent a fair value for the services rendered by the community.

Summary

Nationally speaking, an elderly couple requires a monthly minimum of about $55 for housing, light, fuel, et cetera, $40 for food, and $35 for all other items—a monthly total of $130, or $1,560 annually. Walter P. Reuther, speaking for the automobile workers, made a statement before the Senate Finance Committee (*Hearings,* March 15, 1950, p. 1837) suggesting a budget of $2,089.49 for an elderly couple, applicable to conditions in the city of Detroit. This budget, admittedly not a minimum, provided better food at home at a monthly average of $57, compared with our average of $40; rent, et cetera, was set at $60, compared with our $55, and other expenses, including cost of a car for one third of the families, at $45 instead of $35. On that basis he asked for pensions of $125 a month and expects to increase this to $200 a month within ten years.

YOUR RETIREMENT INCOME

Out of the minimum of $130 a month, you can anticipate and prepare for cost of living quarters, which would be about $40. The remainder of $90 takes care of the cash expenditures. Therefore, to plan the financing of a cash income of at least $90 a month, examine various methods of increasing this amount and finally explore other financing or income possibilities to add something which would take these pensions out of the bare subsistence class.

The first step in financing monthly cash requirements is an investigation of the amount of life income that is available. In addition to privately purchased annuities, there are Social Security old-age pensions, civil-service, state, and municipal retirement pensions, railroad retirement pensions, military-service pensions, and pensions provided by non-governmental employers. All these pensions are payable for the lifetime of an individual and, therefore, form the basic security for retirement. Let us now, in somewhat greater detail, determine our rights, if any, under the Social Security Act.

Federal Retirement Systems

Social Security Act. The Social Security Act Amendments of 1950 made major revisions in coverage and benefits which were effective with respect to benefits in September 1950 and with respect to coverage on January 1, 1951.

First let us review the extent of coverage. If you are now covered by the Act, you will of course remain covered, but if you are not now under the Act, you may be covered beginning with 1951. The following classes of employees will be covered:

1. Farm workers, domestic servants, and employees performing casual labor not in the course of an employer's trade or business. These employees must be regularly employed by *one* employer, and receive, in *cash,* at least $50 in a calendar quarter (hereinafter called "quarter"). A farm *worker* is regularly employed in a quarter in which he had sixty full days of work if he had continuous employment with the same employer during a preceding three-month period. A domestic servant or casual laborer is regularly employed in a quarter in which

he worked on some twenty-four days for the same employer. A domestic servant on a farm operated for profit is classified as farm worker.

2. Federal civilian employees not covered by a retirement system, with certain exceptions; employees of national farm loan associations, production credit associations, federal credit unions, Federal Reserve Banks, post exchanges and similar organizations under the National Defense establishment, and state, county, and community committees under the Production and Marketing Administration.

3. Employees not covered by a retirement system of state and local governments which elect to have Social Security coverage for their employees; in certain cases services rendered by employees of a public transportation system operated by a state or a political subdivision.

4. Employees of non-profit organizations with the concurrence of the employer and at least two thirds of employees.

5. American employees of American employers outside of the United States; employees in the Virgin Islands, and in Puerto Rico after a specified date.

The taxes payable are going to be determined by future Congresses, but the new law proposes to increase employee taxes to 3¼ per cent of earnings by 1970, the employer to match the employee's contributions. The self-employed will be taxed at a rate 50 per cent greater than that of the employees. The maximum taxable annual salary is raised to $3,600.

If a person is covered by the Social Security Act, the pension is not paid automatically upon attainment of age sixty-five. In order to be entitled to a pension, the individual who is to receive his pensions or on whose account a pension is payable must have been under the Act for a minimum number of calendar quarters and must file an application. There are actually three kinds of retirement pensions. First there is the regular one, payable to a person who has reached age sixty-five.

This pension may be increased by 50 per cent if the individual has a wife sixty-five years of age or over or an unmarried dependent child under eighteen. The second type of retirement pension is paid to the widow of an individual covered by the Act when she reaches age sixty-five, and the third type is paid to a dependent sixty-five-year-old parent of a deceased individual, provided there is no widow or child eligible for benefits under the Act.

In order to be entitled to any one of these three types of old-age benefits, the person on whose account pensions would be payable must be a fully insured individual. In order to be fully insured, an individual must have been under the Act for forty quarters, or must be under the Act about half of the time between 1950 and the day he attains age sixty-five or dies. For example, an individual who will be sixty-five in 1960 needs about five years of coverage. There must have been at least six calendar quarters of coverage, but quarters of coverage earned before 1951 would count in establishing the minimum of six quarters. A quarter of coverage does not necessarily mean a full calendar quarter spent under the Act; all that is necessary is that an employee earned at least $50 ($100 in the case of a self-employed person) in such a quarter. If he earns the maximum taxable salary in any part of a calendar year, all quarters in such year are quarters of coverage.

The monthly pension for an individual is based on average monthly income as defined in the Act and is not subject to income taxes. If the average monthly income is $35 to $100, the monthly pension will be 50 per cent of such average income, but not less than $25. For example, if average monthly wages were $90, the monthly pension would be $45. If the average monthly income is over $100, the monthly pension is $35 plus 15 per cent of average monthly income, but not more than $80. For instance, if the monthly wage averages $200, the monthly pension would be $65 ($35 plus 15 per cent of $200). This pension is increased by 50 per cent if the pensioner has a wife at least sixty-five years of age. If the pensioner has a dependent unmarried child under eighteen years of age, the pension is increased by 50 per cent because of the child, and if he has both a wife sixty-five years old and a child under eighteen (which may be adopted), the pension is increased by 100 per cent; but on such family benefits there is also a maximum limit of $150 a month, or 80 per cent of average monthly income, whichever is the least.

It is of considerable importance in any retirement planning to realize that old-age benefits paid to a pensioner under seventy-five years of age will cease for any month in which the individual earns more than $50 in employment covered by the Act. If a pensioner under seventy-five has a net income of more than $600 annually from self-employment covered by the Act, he will also lose one month's pension for each additional $50 earned. There is no restriction in respect to employment or self-employment of the type not covered by the Act. For instance, employment as a farmer or gardener will not impair Social Security pension rights.

We can conclude that a couple, both of whom are sixty-five years or over, will be able to obtain from Social Security our minimum of $90 a month if the man's earnings were steady and averaged about $160 a month. Of course if the wife has acquired the right to larger benefits because of her own employment, she will receive those. But there is no chance, even under the revised plan, that Social Security pensions will reach $130, since the maximum pension is only slightly more than $100 monthly for people continuously earning the maximum credit. Moreover, since the wife is generally younger than the husband, there will be a few years after the husband's retirement when the 50 per cent additional will not be payable.

Railroad Retirement Act. If you are not eligible for an old-age pension under the Social Security Act, you may be eligible for a similar pension. There is the Railroad Retirement Act, under which pensions are paid to railroad employees and employees of associations owned or controlled by railroads. Pensions now being paid average $67.50 monthly. About 1,600,000 persons are covered, and 180,000 are already drawing pensions.

Civil Service Retirement Systems. The Civil Service retirement systems involve military services, lighthouse service, coast and geodetic survey services, public health services, foreign services, and the following services: in the Canal Zone; as a federal judge; as a member of Congress; with federal banks; with the Tennessee Valley Authority; and with the Bureau of the Comptroller of Currency. There are about 85,000 pensioners now under all these federal retirement systems. Those desiring more details are referred to Bureau Report No. 15, *Outline of Federal Retirement Systems,* published by the Federal Security Agency.

State and Local Retirement Plans. There are numerous state and local government employee-retirement systems, which pay about $77 monthly average pensions to some 140,000 pensioners. There are also veteran's pensions paid to some 150,000 war veterans over sixty-five years of age. For instance, some 112,000 Spanish American War veterans receive $70 monthly. The question might be raised as to whether old-age pensions may become payable to veterans of World War I or II, but it is this observer's opinion that any pensions that may be granted would be in replacement of Social Security pensions or other governmental pensions rather than in addition thereto.

None of these pensions involve additional payments because of a wife, but since 1940 Civil Service employees may elect an annuity under which payments are continued to a survivor (a joint and survivor annuity). The same applies to the Congressional Plan, to Canal Zone workers, to Federal Reserve Bank employees, to TVA employees, and to a few other federal employees. The cost of the pension continuation to a widow is provided either by increased employer contribution or by a reduced employee annuity, depending on the plan chosen.

These pensions naturally play the same part in providing a basic retirement income as do Social Security pensions. As a matter of fact, were it not for the existence of these plans, the employees involved would probably have been covered by the Social Security Act. As it is, there is now already a reciprocity arrangement between services covered by the Social Security Act and by the Railroad Retirement Act. It is also true that these pensions are, on the whole, more liberal than those under the Social Security Act. This was by design, since these pensions were supposed to provide enough income for subsistence, whereas Social Security pensions are not necessarily in that class. But the average figures indicate that only a small number of the pensioners draw enough to cover our minimum rate. Of some 100,000 retired Civil Service employees, only 7,000 pensioners receive more than $130 a month; some additional 17,000 annuitants receive $125 monthly, but only because Congress increased their pension by $25 on February 28, 1948. Some 60,000 pensioners receive less than $90 a month.

Therefore, if governmental pensions represent your only guaranteed income, you had better make sure that you are at least not obligated for rent and that you have some savings to tide you over the years during which no benefits are payable on behalf of your wife. Social Security pensions currently paid under the old Act average only $25 monthly, and the maximum that would be paid is about $45 to an individual and $67.50 to a couple sixty-five years of age or over. The change in the Social Security Act increases these benefits, but not quite to the same level as the benefits payable to those retiring in the near future. If in the past few years you had relied for your daily bread on these benefits you would have been quite disappointed. If further price rises take place, it is quite likely that there will again be a lag of a few years until the benefits are adjusted to the new price level. It is therefore better for your peace of mind to obtain some additional income guarantees, just in case. In view of this situation, we shall review the possibility of increasing your monthly income by investments and with annuities.

Investments

When people begin thinking about retirement they usually ask, very hopefully, if they can invest their money and then live off the interest. For those people this report is going to be frankly discouraging. So that you won't become too despondent, let me tell you in advance that the prospect of private annuities, discussed below, is much more encouraging.

Only about 10 per cent of people sixty-five and over are apparently able to finance necessary retirement income from investments. If you, dear reader, wish to join this selected group, you will have to invest a lot more money than they did. When the generations now retired were active, income taxes were negligible and a top-grade bond paid 4 per cent or more. Nowadays the government first takes a good slice of your income, then grants its bondholders a magnificent interest return of $2\frac{1}{2}$ per cent, then takes an income tax out of that. Moreover, there is no assurance that you will be able to reinvest your funds at maturity at even that rate; neither do you know what the money will buy when you get it back. However, for illustrative purposes, let us assume that you can count on a yearly income of 2½ per cent of your total investment. In order to have $90 cash minimum a month, you need a capital of $43,200, and if you wanted $130 a month, you need a capital of $62,400. To carry this illustration a little further, let us assume that you will be able to save 5 per cent of your net income after taxes, toward $43,200, and that you have twenty-five years in which to do it. You will have to save $100 a month in order to reach your goal, and if this represents 5 per cent of your net income after taxes, you would have to have an annual net income of $24,000—or, under current taxation, a gross income of some $50,000. It is quite obvious that an accumulation of funds of such magnitude to produce just the minimum cash is quite a waste. Furthermore, a person commanding a $50,000 gross income would be quite unable to cut his income to such a level.

Annuities

Those who cannot live on interest income alone will have to use a part of their capital to supplement what would otherwise be too meager a return. At this point insurance science enters the picture, because the individual would not know what amounts he could safely withdraw each year without exhausting his capital before his death. This is how an annuity operates. It is the exact reverse of a life-insurance policy. An ordinary life-insurance contract provides that the individual pay an annual premium to the insurance company, which in turn pays a single sum to the insured's beneficiary when death occurs. An ordinary life annuity provides that the individual make a single cash payment to the insurance company and that the insurance company in turn pay a fixed annual amount to the insured until death.

As with life insurance, there are several kinds of annuities.

An annuity may be purchased which provides for a minimum number of annual payments. For example, five, ten, or twenty annual payments may be guaranteed, even though the recipient may die before the end of the guaranteed minimum period. An annuity may also be purchased by installments, rather than by a single sum, in which event it is called an "annual premium deferred annuity." An annuity may also be payable to more than one person, say a husband and wife, with the stipulation that the income is paid while both live and continues to be paid to a survivor in the same or a smaller amount. To complete the illustration, if a couple, both of whom are sixty-five, wish the annuity to guarantee a monthly payment of $90 (our budget minimum), they require not $43,200, as in the case of the investment, but only $20,000. It is true that the annuity uses up the capital whereas interest payments do not, but we are here concerned with the problem of financing retirement and not with the problem of maintaining capital for the benefit of survivors.

The cost of annuities is high. It has risen in the last few years and may rise even further. For a fuller understanding of the retirement problem it is worth while to review briefly the reasons for this increasing cost. One of the things everyone knows is that our life expectancy has been increasing. Not only do our own funds have to last longer after our retirement, because the tremendous medical advances of the past decades have added years to our lives, but, by the same token, the insurance company has to obtain more funds to retire a person at a given age. Since an individual has to part with a large amount of money in return for an indefinite number of payments, you may be sure that the individual buying an annuity believes himself to be in excellent health. The insurance company's statistics reflects the fact that it is usually individuals with better-than-average health prospects who join their circle of annuitants, and this experience in turn is necessarily reflected in higher charges.

Furthermore, the general decline in interest rates not only makes it difficult for an individual to accumulate funds but also makes it difficult for the insurance company to invest the funds profitably; and this affects the cost. On the average, pension costs rise by about 25 per cent for each 1 per cent decrease in the rate of interest earned. Finally, taxes and other expenses have increased. The states are raising taxes on annuity premiums, federal taxes on investment income are rising, and administrative expenses have also risen in line with the general trend. The uncertainty of future developments, in respect to further medical advances, still lower interest rates, and still higher operating expenses and taxes, requires reserves for such contingencies. For all these reasons, it costs a man aged sixty-five between $150 and $160 for each $1 monthly annuity payable for life, and since women generally live longer, it costs a woman aged sixty-five between $180 and $200 for each dollar of monthly life income. Insurance companies charging the lower rate usually state that no dividends are payable. Insurance companies showing the higher rate expect to return some of the premiums in the form of refunds.

If your funds do not permit you to buy as much pension security as you need at age sixty-five, you may find that by delaying the starting date of such a life annuity to a later age you may be able to get the amount you need. If a man waits until age seventy-five to start collecting on an annuity, he needs only $100 for each dollar of monthly life annuity payable thereafter. Three thousand dollars invested in this way would guarantee at least $30 to supplement Social Security pensions. If that is not enough, you may be one of the farsighted and thrifty people who have in force a life-insurance policy issued some years back, when annuity payments were based on what then appeared to be conservative assumptions as to length of life, interest rates, and operating costs. Life-insurance policies quite generally permit the insured to elect having the proceeds of the insurance policy paid in various ways, one of which is a life-income option. If your policy was issued in 1932 or thereabouts, you would find that it costs only $130 for each dollar of monthly annuity at age sixty-five. Moreover, this amount is the same for men and women and is guaranteed for at least five years regardless of death. If you wait until age seventy, the cost for each dollar of monthly annuity is reduced to $113, and at age seventy-five to $96.

Annuities and life-income provisions have a much greater flexibility than do government pensions. Social Security payments begin at sixty-five, and if you do not retire until later, the pension is still the same. Furthermore, if you work between sixty-five and seventy-five and earn more than $50 a month, you lose your pension for any such month. The retirement date under an individual annuity or life-insurance income option is determined by you and there are no restrictions as to earnings. On the other hand, of course, Social Security pensions cost little (based on current charges) and are not taxable as income, whereas private pensions are expensive and are partially taxable as income.[1]

Employer-Employee Retirement Plans

We should take note of the differences existing between annuities purchased by an individual and pensions provided by an employer under a retirement system. The choice of retire-

[1]Under current law such pensions are taxable as income to the extent of 3 per cent of your own payments for it. The remainder of the pension is income-tax-exempt until the total amount so exempted equals the total of your own payments.

ment age is not often yours in the latter case, and the pension then is likely to begin at a predetermined age without your having a chance to delay it and thereby increase the value of the retirement benefit. Or, even if your retirement is delayed, the pension is either paid out in place of a corresponding part of salary or is withheld and paid back to the fund or the trustees; but by continuing to work, you conserve and even add to your resources and you reduce the number of years during which your resources must last—in other words, delay of retirement reduces the span of life spent in retirement. Furthermore, if you cannot increase your retirement pension by deferring the starting date, you can achieve about the same effect by reinvesting the pensions paid to you for additional life annuities.

If you look forward to retiring at an age earlier than sixty-five, most retirement plans permit this to be arranged. Of course, if the pension begins earlier, it is materially reduced, partly because you are likely to draw it for a much longer period and partly because you and your employer made a smaller number of contributions. At age fifty-five the annuity for a man is about half of what it would have been at sixty-five, a little higher on that part of the pension purchased by your money, a little lower on that part purchased by your employer's money.

If your wife's health is excellent, and you wish to provide that the income continue to her in full after your death, you will find in most plans that this is possible by means of another option—that of selecting a joint and survivor annuity, mentioned above. If you decide to include your wife under such a pension, the pension is reduced by about one third if your wife is five years younger and you retire at sixty-five. If your wife is the same age as you, the reduction is less than 30 per cent. These same percentages hold true if you are seventy years of age. The reductions are smaller if the pension is continued in a smaller amount after the death of one of the two persons. Since expenses decrease after the death of one, the survivor may be able to get along by continuing only two thirds of the pension.

Most of the pensioners under private retirement plans are also eligible for Social Security pensions, and if these pensions are raised, the total of the two pensions would average about $130. It is of interest to note what employers have been doing recently when they found that the pensions provided under private plans plus the meager Social Security pensions were inadequate. Recent surveys showed that nearly 80 per cent of the employers permitted employees to defer retirement. Where this was not possible, or where the employee had already re-tired, supplementary payments were made by the employer in about one third of the cases. Again the preferred method of adjustment for insufficient pension is deferment of retirement. In these instances additional resources are obtained because of the longer employment. Before reviewing some suggestions for financing deferment of the start of a guaranteed pension by means other than continued employment, we will discuss briefly the role of life insurance during retirement.

Life Insurance

The first question that may be raised is whether a retired individual should provide for a dependent wife by means of a joint annuity or by means of life insurance. While it was not mentioned specifically, it is obvious that the budget of older people is not constructed to include payment of life-insurance premiums. This is a type of expense that can be anticipated and probably eliminated. One method is to limit the period of premium payments to twenty or thirty years, so that the policy is paid up at retirment. If your current policy requires continuing premium payments, you may wish to choose one of two ways to terminate payments. If you do not need the entire amount of insurance, investigate what reductions in your insurance would take place if it were changed to a paid-up policy. Or, if you need the entire amount for only a limited number of years, investigate for how many years the insurance can be carried in full, without any premium payments, as "extended death benefit." As a rule, your insurance plans will fill either one of these types, because the need for insurance decreases as you grow older—as your parents and elderly relatives die and as your children become independent. Furthermore, you will find that a retirement program can often cover your insurance needs as well as, if not better than, life insurance. For instance, it would be difficult to leave your wife a definite annual pension until her death with life insurance, because if you insure a definite amount, the payments to your wife will depend on her age at the time of your death, and the older she is when the pension begins, the higher the pension will be. Under a joint annuity, however, the amounts payable will always be the same.

Similarly, provision can be made by insurance for a dependent child; but again, if such a child is going to be dependent for only a few years, it might be simpler to adopt an annuity under which payments are made to a surviving child for a specified number of years. For instance, if your child is sixteen and you wish payments continued, in case of your prior death, until his twenty-sixth birthday, a ten-year certain annuity can be adopted to accomplish this.

As far as possible, the values in existing life insurance should be used for retirement purposes, after the life-insurance purposes have been taken care of. The "extended death benefit," mentioned before, uses up all values in the policy, which expires after a stated period, and is therefore not the recommended procedure. There is a lesson in the value of retirement benefits included in life-insurance policies, particularly to those who are interested only in term insurance (temporary insurance without any reserves), and that is that the reserves in regular policies build up retirement values. The higher-premium types of life insurance, such as endowment insurance, require, if taken out at younger ages, only a few dollars more premiums per $1,000 of insurance than the less expensive ordinary life-insurance contracts, but for every dollar so added, retirement values are increased 15 to 20 per cent.

In addition to group pension plans of the type discussed before, some employers have adopted group life-insurance or profit-sharing plans for the benefit of their employees, and many of these plans have retirement values. The fundamental thought is that the mass accumulation and the mass administration make possible more liberal benefits and options. Groups that are not employer-employee groups, such as professional societies, may arrange to become eligible for similar benefits. There are many European examples of groups organized to take advantage of collective-insurance methods. A county medical society has arranged that medical fees from the Health Insurance system be paid through them. From such funds regular deductions are taken for insurance and retirement purposes, with all tax advantages inherent in such a system, tax advantages which an individual cannot obtain. Similar examples exist for other professional groups, retail merchants associations, and others.

In this country group annuity plans for associations of savings banks, manufacturers, and accounting firms are known. Such plans permit many small groups to form a larger group and obtain not only the expense savings available to large groups but also the tax advantages that qualified plans have: namely, employer contributions to such plans are not considered taxable income to the employees. Again, it is joint planning that can bring about better financial retirement security.

Mutual Investment Trusts

While few people deny the necessity of securing the lifelong guarantees inherent in annuity contracts issued by insurance companies, the question is often raised as to whether the individual would not be wiser to invest funds in securities which tend to rise during an inflationary period. In this way they hope that when the time comes to purchase an annuity, the money invested will have risen in proportion to the inflation, and the annuity purchased with these increased funds will have an element of inflationproofing.

The usual arguments pro and con on this subject refer to the inability of an individual investor to find secure investments, particularly if the investment is to be a modest one. For such small investors the open-end investment trusts (so-called mutual funds) have had increased recognition, and the experience of these groups would seem to indicate that the argument against small investments is no longer a valid one. Incidentally, there is an element of joint planning and investment in the operation of these funds which has contributed to their rapid growth and popularity.[2]

A second argument is that an individual is not so likely to accumulate regularly if he is not forced to do so by the necessity

[2] Those interested in the subject of open-end trusts are referred to a study by William D. Carter, entitled "Mutual Investment Funds," in the *Harvard Business Review,* November 1946, and to the "Quarterly Index Figures of Mutual Investment Companies," by Henry Ansbacher Long, in *Trusts and Estates,* May 1950.

of keeping up a contract. This is still an important factor, but an even more deciding one is the fact, frequently overlooked, that the guarantee of an income under an annuity contract is obtainable only when the contract is purchased. Therefore the individual, in deferring the purchase of a contract, would not know what guarantee, if any, would be obtainable at the time of actual retirement.

During the past twenty years the cost of annuities has risen considerably. In 1930 the payment of $1,000 for an annuity beginning at age sixty-five would have brought a guarantee of about $107 a year for male pensioners and $95 a year for female pensioners. More recently, a payment of $1,000 would have brought a guarantee of $78 a year for men and $66 a year for women. In order to offset the increased cost of annuities alone, the funds in addition to interest accumulation would have to rise some 30 per cent in capital value.

When one compares the experience of mutual investment companies during the same period, the average increase in capital value was some 40 per cent. Therefore very little would have been gained by the use of mutual investment companies even during a period of sustained increases in the value of the underlying securities.

It would seem to me that it is more important to obtain a fixed guarantee, particularly where a minimum requirement is needed, than to take a chance on the possibility that the cost of the annuity may outrun the appreciation of the funds. There is also the risk that the annuity guarantees, in part or in whole, may not be obtainable at all if their purchase is put off until the future.

The foregoing discussion may have been somewhat technical, but we trust it also brings out the important point that problems of this nature are individual and require tailor-made solutions. We have tried to give general directions and review the main points while arriving at some major conclusions. Individual problems, however, require the attention of special- ists. You do have to keep in mind, though, the theme of this outline—namely, the importance of providing a guaranty of income in the later years of life when you cannot work and when there are no other resources. It is expensive enough to provide a lifelong guaranty for one or two persons after age seventy or seventy-five. What should be done to finance the period between retirement and the beginning of the "assured" security?

BRIDGING THE GULF BETWEEN RETIREMENT AND ASSURED SECURITY

Living with Your Children

We have touched only once on the role of children in plan- ning for the retirement of their parents. But of all the aged in this nation, not even a quarter depend on their children. It seems to me that if children had to make a choice, they would prefer a larger obligation for a limited number of years to a smaller obligation of a permanent nature. Grown children should be taken into full confidence in respect to both the retirement budget and the means of financing it.

We did mention that parents who wish to rent their home during "the season" might wish to visit with children during such a period. Beyond that, children might consider the value of furnishing assistance for a number of years immediately following retirement, until the resources of the parents have grown to a point where the parents can be independent, rather than having parents first use up accumulated resources to maintain their independence, only to have to make bitter adjustments still later in life when the resources are gone. Again much depends on individual situations, health of parents, and so on, and all we can do here is to touch on this point.

Unemployment Compensation

Individual planning for the in-between period after retirement can take into account several additional factors. Employed persons are generally eligible for unemployment-compensation payments. Provided they are not disabled and are able to do some work, they can apply for unemployment benefits, and unless work can be found, they will draw benefits, the number of weeks and the amount dependent on past earnings and other provisions of the state law. If work can be found, most older people prefer this method of implementing their resources. Even if they are disabled they may qualify for payments under an applicable State Disability Compensation Law, such as those which already exist in California, New York, New Jersey, and Rhode Island, and which are planned for a number of other states. Such payments, often made for twenty-six weeks in a year, will help to conserve savings.

Living Abroad

Another factor that might be explored is the possibility of combining pleasure with necessity, and that is to move, at least temporarily, to another country where living expenses are low in terms of dollar income. Foreign-born people may consider living for a few years in their native country, and while some prefer to live there for the rest of their lives, most appear to wish to return to this country, particularly those whose families are here. Of course if American dollars allow a princely living abroad, a beggarly living here, conflicts will arise.

Native-born citizens might explore the situation in Mexico. I know a couple who sold their business and went to live in Mexico, on the Pacific Coast. They reported living expenses seventy per cent less than in the United States. Similar reports have come from Italy and from some South American countries. Such conditions may change, and probably will, as the standard of living in these countries improves, but we would be neglecting a source of improved financing of the later years if we did not mention this. Currently no restrictions exist on the use of American funds abroad; even Social Security old-age pensions are paid to qualified individuals who reside abroad. While we are fortunate that there are no currency-transfer restrictions in this country, there is no guarantee that this will continue, and again it is better to plan for a minimum according to American standards.

Hobbies and Unusual Skills

Another factor to be taken into account is the possibility of income from unusual hobbies or skills instead of from a regular job. Again it stands to reason that an individual may be able to earn some funds here and there in the first few years after retirement, whereas this naturally becomes more difficult as these people reach their seventies. As mentioned before, earnings up to $600 annually, earnings of individuals over seventy-five, and earnings in employment not covered by the Act do not impair Social Security pensions.

A great deal has been written about the use of hobbies, but

new ideas appear all the time and much can still be learned from the old countries, where an aging population, because of the financial bankruptcy brought about by inflation, had to attempt to raise all skills to income-producing levels. Restoring antique furniture, pictures, photographs, and clocks; dealing in stamps or coins; repairing sports equipment, radios, or other electrical gadgets; applying the knowledge of foreign languages for tutoring, translating, or teaching; short-story or textbook writing; music teaching; dog breeding or boarding; dressmaking; piecework manufacturing of jewelry; and, currently, baby-sitting, are only a few of the innumerable examples.

Opportunities for Employment

Still another factor to be taken into consideration is that it is easier to employ an older person if part of the salary is paid in the form of maintenance or in merchandise. Domestic service, hotel or boardinghouse management, and building service involve maintenance as part of the earnings, and such maintenance can be taken into account while planning. Each individual's judgment and abilities, with such compromises as joint planning requires, must govern the final decisions.

If this chapter brings about a greater awareness of methods for financing retirement by long-range and skillful planning, it will have worked toward the solution of a tremendous social and political problem faced by our nation in leading the lives of the growing number of older people into happier channels.

WHAT YOUR COMMUNITY CAN DO TO HELP

by

OLLIE A. RANDALL

What Is a Community?

THE word "community" has become so familiar to us in the impersonal terms of community welfare, community activities, and community service that we are sometimes apt to lose sight of the fact that any group of human beings living in a single geographical area and sharing in common institutions and services forms a community. It may be a village, town, city, county, state, or nation, with very closely knit civic organization. It may be a small rural community in which the ties are loose. But in either case it is the environment in which the individual moves and in which his personality will either thrive or wither.

In the middle of our twentieth century no community, large or small, can be either self-sufficient or self-determining. National and international forces have become potent factors in the life of every community and, in turn, in the lives of every human being included in these groups. The strength of the combination of these forces cannot be exactly measured. At times these forces are in real or apparent conflict with the existing patterns of the community's organization, and the individual who is caught up in the sweep of events may be the ast to benefit from the remarkable scientific and revolutionary changes that are going on around us.

The Aging Population

One of these powerful forces which until very recently has been given little thought and has had even less understanding is the aging of the population in this and in many other countries. The age composition of the population of practically every community in our land is shifting and reflects this trend. Almost no community has prepared to cope with the problem. Worse than that, very few individuals in any community are prepared in any way to deal with its meaning for themselves, let alone work constructively on a collective basis for the common good.

Since almost every person or family is faced with one or more problems which stem from the fact that more and more people are living longer than ever before in modern civilization, it is easy to see that every community is also faced with problems of the same origin. Fortunately the American people have a genius for solving problems, and even more fortunately there is a quality in the national character that rejects the idea of defeat in any matter that is capable of human solution. Herein lies the hope both for the community and for the older people in it. The health and wealth of any community is, in the last analysis, dependent on the state of well-being of its component member citizens.

Citizens' Committee

The unique and compelling need in every community today —whether local, national, or international—is for a large, informed group of citizens to concern themselves directly with the needs of older people and those who will be older people tomorrow or day after tomorrow. That, of course, includes all of us. These needs can be divided into two groups, and each calls for a different approach. First there is the immediate need to remedy present conditions—to improve the lot of a large and growing segment of our population who have been "caught short" by both their own unpreparedness and the general lack of realization of the advances which science has made without pointing out how we can make the best use of them. The world's scientists have given us greater health and longer life, but the science of applying these gifts for ourselves and for those who live about us has not been well worked out.

Secondly there is the urgent need to study our present situation of unpreparedness, so that we can prevent its continuation or recurrence. Now is the time to establish the better pattern for those who will soon be following in our footsteps. Such a pattern should not favor the older members of the community at the expense of the other age groups, for such a situation would be as unfair to the younger elements as our present attitude has been to the older ones. Thorough study is needed now in order to strike a balance and reconcile the interests of all age groups if the community is to function dynamically. Special privileges for older individuals on a planned basis at the expense of others will not permanently improve our attitude toward the status of older members of the community but will only replace the present bad situation with an untenable one.

Individual's Responsibility for Self

In addition to the need for an enlightened group of citizens to study the needs and find the most workable solutions for living longer and more rewarding lives, there is the need for every individual to become aware of what this new order of life means to himself and to his family. Living a longer life is a real challenge to us all, a challenge we must face but can enjoy only if we are prepared to make the most of it.

If we had a "Middletown," a typical American community in which both the individual's and the community's responsibility could be worked out in detail as an active demonstration, society would benefit immeasurably. In such a "Middletown" we could all see how to put our added years to the most productive use, how to prepare for a life of deeper, richer meaning, and how to put our family and community relationships on a more enduring basis. Since there is no such model community, we must for the present rely upon more comprehensive and less easily observed personal and community efforts.

We all know, of course, that the individual relates himself to his community in many ways and through many institutions, but first and foremost through his family. The family has been said to be the single most important unit of society for maintaining mental health and stability, because the family has changed less in its essential character than any other man-made unit throughout history. Even so, the impact upon the family of our changing social values, of the rapid movement from a rural to an urban society, from an agricultural to an industrialized economy, has been great. It has in turn been reflected in the internal strain upon family relationships. This has been particularly evident in frictions which develop between adult generations (of which the average family now has two, if not three) and in the pressures which such frictions exert upon the family unity.

The suffering which results from such frictions is made even greater by the sharp conflict between our culture, which belittles age, and the avowed Christian principles which demand that we honor our father and mother. All too often it is impossible or impractical for young adults to "honor" their parents by maintaining them in one household and under the same roof with themselves.

This is particularly true when there is not enough money or space to accommodate the old folks and the younger people without deprivation to one or the other, or in all probability both! Lowering everyone's standard of living is only part of the price that is paid—far greater is the irreparable break in the family circle, the loss of love and respect that is due every member of the group. This destruction of family values, and family structure itself, will not be avoided unless the community at large understands and insists that the family must not subject its individual members to indignities caused by the frictions of too-intimate living.

These frictions occur when the strains of daily life break down the intangible bonds of kinship and undermine the love and affection which everyone yearns to receive from his "own." Some way must be found to hold the older persons beloved by the family group, so that they, too, may have their share in keeping their families a cohesive force in the life of the community. None of us like to feel that we are of little or no value —none of us can endure the position of being "excess baggage."

Work During the Later Years

The older person is particularly interested in relating himself to both his family and his community through his work. Here again society has failed to prepare itself for the present reality. The lack of opportunity either to continue at work or to be assigned different work with the passing years is a genuine threat to the stability of the individual and to the economy of which he is a part. Work for hire is the respectable way of maintaining oneself in the world. In this industrial age the difficulty has been that for a large portion of the population such work has been difficult to find or to keep. In the twenties and thirties, in prosperity and depression the effect of this present business practice was pronounced and large-scale programs were started to cope with it. But the WPA and other "make-work" projects, as well as the assistance programs, have signally failed to satisfy, except on a temporary emergency basis, either the people concerned or the communities in which they lived. Such programs, useful in their way, should not be the *only* employment available to older workers.

So far there has been little general appreciation of the problem which unemployed older individuals are becoming and the size of the burden they promise to be in a few short years unless more drastic measures are adopted to make them an economic asset instead of a liability. We are wasting a precious resource in maturity, knowledge, experienced judgment, and wisdom when we fail to give older persons an active part in community life. If the people of every town and city could be aroused to the extravagance of wasting human energies and skill, as they are to the dumping of potatoes and other "surplus" goods, the problems could be eased. Dependency is not an enviable status for any human being, especially if he is adult and capable of work. Yet that is the status to which this country has legislatively and socially consigned a large number of mature men and women who would infinitely prefer to be self-supporting and independent.

Education in the Later Years

If there has been scant attention paid to the economic and social changes that are taking place around us, there are some encouraging signs that educational groups here and there have sensed the trend and have started to devise ways to be of help and service. Education, in its real meaning, is a process which aids human beings to adapt to other human beings and to the demands of society. Up to this time education has been used primarily in the formal school systems to prepare youth for adulthood. The use of education in a less formal way, to help adults adjust to the changing pattern of their environment and to their continued growth as individuals, is literally an unexplored frontier. But enough is already known about adult education to assure us that great changes can be made in a person's vocational, avocational, and cultural equipment through the right methods. Certainly as the horizons widen, and the knowledge we already have is put to more general use, a brighter tomorrow for the community seems assured.

The Older Person and the Church

The Church, too, is beginning to set its ministerial and social sights with the lengthening of the span of earthly life in mind, for older people have an even greater need for spiritual strength and moral support than ever before. Church ties have a way of becoming tenuous as life grows more complex, and as it spins out to greater length, the desire to understand its meaning, here and hereafter, intensifies and deepens. It would appear that the Church has, through its older members and through older people in the community who may not be numbered

n its membership, a rare chance to regain lost ground and to
ecapture the place it once held in the day-to-day, humble life
»f our people. This can be accomplished through its pastoral
ervices and its religious teachings, together with the op-
»ortunity it offers for association and intercourse with like-
ninded fellow beings.

Other Institutions

The Church, however, is only one of the many institutions
nd services of a community upon which the aging of the
»opulation exercises its pressures and which must expand to
over new needs. Business and industry, real estate and hous-
ng, schools, social-service agencies, settlements, group-work
gencies such as the young men's and young women's associa-
ions, health and medical-care services, the courts, fraternal
nd service associations, men's and women's clubs, voluntary
gencies, recreational activities, governmental services, includ-
ng those which affect the national security—all these and
»thers, too, will find that their character and services must be
nodified by the gradual aging of their membership and those
vhom they serve. In the merchandising of material goods
here are indications that this shift is recognized and plans are
»eing made to meet it. But what about the people themselves
ind the services which have been created to meet their needs?
Here the lag between changing demand and plans to meet it
s great. Unfortunately it seems to be growing greater.

The Older Person and His Needs

What are the needs of any human being in any community
—no matter what his age? The Society of Friends has defined

these for older people quite simply as "Somewhere to live, something to do, and someone to care." These hold good for everyone, but for individuals the order of importance may differ. The need of younger people for a place to live is satisfied by their parents or their elders, and therefore is seldom consciously felt in youth. "Something to do" is essential for each person who realizes his needs, but the place and the reason for doing something change in different stages of life. "Someone to care" is a universal need, and also variable at different periods of life.

The community, as a rule, has organized itself to meet these three needs for infants and young children. If it does not always meet these needs, it is at least working to remedy shortcomings in the system to provide for a sound, well-rounded childhood and youth. Young adults in most cases have the energy and will to satisfy these needs for themselves. But society is in default in providing for the needs of the middle-aged and of those who are living into later maturity. Here we find the economic and social machinery creaking badly. The mounting scrap pile of unused human potential resulting from this signal neglect should spur united action in our own interest and, equally important, in that of our fellows.

Need for Understanding

Reducing all the personal needs of individuals may help to bring one's plans for preparation for later years into focus. But to do this it is obvious that there must first of all be understanding of the reason for any preparation at all—and of conditions which in the long run may mean that plans will have to be revised or given up for others at almost any point along the way. This must not lead to discouragement or to the attitude which is held to be common—the "why bother" attitude when there's a chance that plans cannot be carried out. Certainly the reply to that is that if there are *no* plans, and no *habit* of making plans, the future will be even more unpredictable than if there were a definite goal which seemed worth striving for. The understanding must be twofold: it must reckon with what happens subjectively to the inner being as the aging process continues; and it must reckon equally with the external factors—the environment in which the process occurs and by which it is modified. This *understanding* can lead to the conviction that maturity is *not* a static period of life; that it can be fruitful and enjoyable; that it can be healthy and productive; that it can be useful and an important part of the whole life scheme. It is the only means at hand which will succeed in finally uprooting and eliminating the stereotyped concept of age as a period of stagnation.

A Positive Philosophy

Each one of us must learn to look at later maturity as it *can* be, in a modern world, and cease to judge it by values set upon it in a past era. We must realize that much of the misery of old age which surrounds us today is the consequence of ignorance or of neglect, both of which can be remedied. All our attitudes are colored by this outworn dictum. None of us look squarely at the potentialities of later life without prejudice. Most of us, if we look at it at all, cast sneaking glances at it, as though we had caught ourselves looking at the new moon over our right shoulder! Apprehension and even fear that this can happen to us in its familiar role almost make it impossible to be sensible and plan well. Understanding, based on the knowledge of the facts which are coming to light with startling rapidity, is the only antidote to this pessimism. Now there is new reason for optimism and for pleasurable anticipation, even eagerness. Old wives' tales, and the disturbing evidence of things and people we have seen, can be tossed aside if we make intelligent use of what is already known. For the whole community there is every reason to believe that the days ahead are propitious for a harvest time which can round out life with a measure of satisfaction hitherto experienced only by a few. Each of us must carry his full share toward reaching this goal, and to do so each of us must have a *personality reserve* which will see us through with that content which ideally has been associated with the eventide of life.

The Principal Foes of the Older Person

Once we have the will and the wish to understand, understanding itself cannot be far behind. Then comes the query: What can one person do, with such difficult natural and man-made problems to combat? No one can foretell with any degree of accuracy how long any one of us will live—but the average for all people supplies estimates in which one can have some confidence. A long life is more or less assured to us through the advances of science, but "a long life and a happy one" depends upon ourselves as well as upon the community.

Financial security has always been regarded as the primary essential for a happy later life, but even this traditional belief is yielding before broader experience. As individuals, there rests upon each of us a heavy responsibility to do what we can to provide for ourselves. At the same time we must take into consideration the difference between personal failure in this direction and the failure of the society in which we have lived and worked.

Up to the present perhaps fewer than a third of the people who survived to retirement time have remained completely independent, with the other two thirds either partially or wholly dependent on relatives, friends, or public or private sources of financial assistance. Only a very small fraction of those unable to maintain themselves have expected to be dependent or have accepted that status gracefully.

One of the most painful adjustments which older people have had to make is this shift from independence to dependency. It has been even more painful because the rest of the community has accepted it as logical and inevitable and has congratulated itself upon the huge programs of public assistance and social insurance (with benefits as yet barely sufficient to assure independence) which have removed older workers as serious competitors in a loose labor market.

And what about health—or ill-health, which is such a bugaboo at any time during life but which so often accompanies old age as we now know it? The conquest of acute diseases and the controls of some of the communicable diseases have left a distressing aftermath of chronic disease and chronic invalidism. This is a genuine "double-header" for the community; there are the diseases themselves to overcome and to treat, and the problem of providing care for the individuals suffering from their long-term ailments or crippled by them. This is demanding a reorganization of health and medical care services and has created a new set of problems for older people themselves as well as for their families, their employers, the professions, and even the city planners.

In the realm of mental health in later life, which is still the hinterland of medical and psychiatric knowledge, there are danger zones for everyone, but even in these areas shrouded by our ignorance and our superstitions there is room for

encouragement and optimism. Recent experiments and obser-
vations seem to indicate that if normal associations and relationships can be kept vital and meaningful, senility may be
deferred if not prevented. It is hoped that studies now being
made will substantiate these reporis with dependable findings.
If so, then individuals, families, and the community will have
sound reason for adopting cultural, educational, occupational,
and recreational activities as a desirable compromise for the
present method of admitting to state hospitals for mental illness old people who are forgetful, lost, or without clear personal identity in their own minds.

The Community's Response to the Problem—Its Activities and Services

In each community the pattern of organized effort on behalf
of its elderly citizens will be, and should be, quite different. In
many of them the local council of social agencies will have a
committee of lay and professional workers from public and
voluntary agencies who are charged with the task of planning
and of stimulating necessary action. In many instances these
committees have not been regarded as dealing with a major
socio-economic problem. They have been subcommittees of
the more firmly entrenched social-work groups. These old-line
agencies have shared the general public opinion that they were
engaged in a sentimental movement which had to do with
people to whom it was fine to be kind but for whom little
in a constructive way could be done. This situation is gradually
changing. "Committees on the Aging" are appearing and are
acquiring the stature which the size and importance of the
problem deserve. In some cities the mayor or the planning
commission is examining how the city can avoid further crises

which arise from lack of knowledge of facts and from lack of planning in the light of those which are known.

In rural communities, or in those in which there are no such councils, in small cities, towns, and counties, citizens' committees and the public health and welfare departments are taking the leadership. In smaller communities it is more difficult to plan for organized effort. However, there are at hand in the local grange, in the churches with their auxiliary societies, and in the county farm and extension bureaus, resources which can be used in the interest of the older people.

On the state level, there are in several states special departments and departmental committees, most commonly in the health and welfare departments, which are devoting considerable attention to this new crop of problems. There are also movements which indicate that soon there will be citizens' councils to co-operate with the state legislatures and state departments in dealing with the situation. In at least one state, New York, there is a very active legislative committee studying state and local programs of business and industry, health, education, and recreation, with a view to encouraging the development of opportunities for older people.

On the national level, there are major assistance, insurance, and health services which are the essential underpinning of state, local, and personal plans for old age. There are also, in both public and voluntary agencies, committees devoting their attention to the issues which are confronting the nation. The recent National Conference on Aging called by the Administrator of the Federal Security Agency at the behest of the President of the United States is strong evidence of the serious implications of an aging population and their importance in national planning.

Information and Referral Services

In those communities in which there are councils of social agencies or welfare councils there is usually a general information service which gives what is known as a "referral service." The function of the personnel of these services is to receive inquiries and to make available information about established facts and existing services. When a request is made which requires more than a factual reply about existing services, and when it seems apparent that either more information or more service is needed by the inquirer, then referral is made to the appropriate agency or agencies. This is a service for the public to which any person in the community is entitled to apply although it is generally maintained through voluntary contributions given for this specific purpose. In practically all of these services today there is a growing volume of information as to what is being done, or not being done, for older people and what individuals and what agencies are best equipped to follow through on the original information. It is also true that these information services can secure additional data from national groups which co-ordinate and bring together material from other parts of the country for exchange with other communities.

Information services are also widely used by professional and lay workers in agencies in a community to supplement their own knowledge and the services of their own agencies which may not wholly meet the demands of the individual or family seeking advice or help.

Therefore any person or family in a community in which there exists a council will find it a saving of money and disposition to consult such an information service. Since one of its aims is to prevent needless shopping around from place to place for help, it makes it possible for the individual to avoid much frustration.

In communities where there is no such council there is usually a public-welfare or health department which should have information on community agencies available for older people. While it is true that most of the workers in these departments are overburdened, inquiry at the main office or at the local branch office will give helpful leads. If the county office cannot help, then inquiry to the state office, especially if the programs for health and welfare are administered by the state rather than by the locality, should produce information of a helpful nature.

All of this sounds dull and routine, but if more people and more families would learn to consult existing agencies which are organized for the single purpose of rendering service, and would not hesitate to call upon the public servants in charge of the publicly supported agencies which are also organized for the same purpose, many of the mishaps and delays in sound planning for individuals would be avoided. While there are directories which give the essential analysis of services which different agencies render, it is usually well to have the judgment of someone accustomed to the use of these directories in making a decision as to which one to visit for help in the particular situation.

Individual Counseling

To seek sound counseling on all the aspects of growing older, and to expect to find advice which will be so comprehensive and all-inclusive that one can feel confident that one's over-all personal planning has been accomplished, will only lead to disappointment at the start. There is as yet no single place in which aging and its psychological, emotional, economic, and social consequences have been adequately explored and understood. The problem must still be tackled piecemeal, and this may be true for some time to come. We are hearing much these days about such individual counseling, and some of it can give genuine guidance for total planning. To expect anything beyond that is unwise. There are those who have given much time, thought, and study to different phases of aging, but they are still few in number and the most thoughtful of them recognize the limitations of their knowledge and experience.

For a better understanding of one's personal needs, as well as of one's family situation, it seems good judgment to seek out the local family service agency, in which the workers are trained in the skill of helping people, both as individuals and as members of a family. While they have been somewhat dilatory in recognizing that older people respond to what is known as "case-work" skill, these agencies and the social-service workers who make up their staffs and the professional consultants upon whom they can call are keenly aware that people who come to them are looking for help in time of trouble, which may be real or imaginary, great or small. But in any event they are there as the expression of the conscience of the community to try to give that help, if people are willing to ask for it.

In many agencies this service is now rendered on a fee basis for those who are able and willing to pay, which again represents a long stride in the social-service field away from the time when such agencies were sought out only by the "poor" in time of financial distress.

Financial help is supplied only infrequently by voluntary or privately supported agencies, and then usually on an emergency basis. Financial support is the task which has been assumed in the community by the public tax-supported agencies. These administer the public-assistance programs for people in need. They also administer the Old Age and Survivors' Insurance program—known popularly as "Social Security." Information about these can be secured at information centers, at private agencies, at the local, state, or regional offices of the federal government, and at the offices of the public agencies. Since these form the major program of the nation for preventing economic need in later years, an understanding of them and eligibility for them is a practical necessity for everyone. Dependency is no respecter of persons or of a person's former financial status.

If there is no local family agency, supported from voluntary contributions, then there may be a public agency whose major function is to give financial help. Occasionally, too, there is a chapter of the American Red Cross which will supplement the public agency's program by service which does not come within the province of the public service.

Family Counseling

Very few families, large or small, rich or poor, are free from problems. Practically everyone now has complications which have their roots in relationships between older and younger generations. Young parents and their children sometimes find the going hard, but when the young parents are torn between responsibility for their children and for their elders, there is apt to be agonizing trouble. We know that public opinion maintains that young folks are trying to dodge their responsibilities to their elders and expect the community, or the public, to take over. The fact of the matter is that it is not at present economically possible for all surviving generations to be supported in every single family unit. This is not understood by the community or by the people who are affected by this state of affairs. Hence family relationships and family status the country over are being undermined. The tensions created find expression in so many ways that it is seldom simple to analyze their primary cause. It is of the greatest importance, therefore, that families, whatever their social or economic status, should turn to their local agencies for the real assistance which the skills of the social workers can give to them. The objective yet sympathetic approach of such workers can do much to straighten out tangled emotions and lives more surely than can the more personal approach of those too closely involved with the problems. Failing a family agency, the minister and the public-agency worker can often combine to find an answer to the seemingly unanswerable. Everyone has problems—almost everyone needs help in solving them.

Even without seeking consultation of this kind for ourselves, each of us can make a distinct contribution to community opinion if we refrain from making judgment as to whether or not people are carrying their full share of family responsibility, especially when we may not know all the facts. Examination of our own problems, about which others cannot possibly know enough to sit in judgment on our methods of solving them, should warn us of the futility of being the one to cast the stone of criticism. In this day of specialization it might be the better part of wisdom to let the case rest with the specialist —the family worker whose objective is to preserve, not to destroy, family life.

Job Counseling

Having "something to do," preferably for profit, is a leading motif in American culture. This holds true for most men and women for some period of their lives. Playboys and ladies of leisure are suspect in a social order which has no use for "drones." The paradox for the older worker is that this is the role which has been established by legislation for him, when he reaches the age of sixty-five, and even earlier when the economy reduces its production so that there is competition for a job between the older and the younger worker. The tragedy of this is that in most instances the individual worker is inclined to accuse himself of personal failure—whether or not such accusation is deserved.

Job counseling for the older worker is a relatively new field of interest for the vocational counselor, and one in which he will almost inevitably feel handicapped and helpless. There are few standards available to help in evaluating the older worker for the job, or the job for the worker. Many decisions are made on the basis of preconceived notions and on favorable or unfavorable prejudice. The bogeys of a higher accident rate, absenteeism, and the tendency to errors on the part of older workers have all been laid low by the actual experience during World War II. But, although disproved, they still warp our decisions when the requirements for personnel are fewer and there are younger people ready and waiting for every vacancy.

It is, however, encouraging to note that the federal and state government employment services are studying the needs of older workers who still consider themselves eligible for the labor market, the opportunities which are open to them in the normal line of business activity, and the reasons why such opportunities are not more readily available. Their findings, to-gether with those of voluntary employment agencies which have entered upon special campaigns to help the older worker, will be of great help to the individual who is looking for work or who is anxious to keep his job. It will pay, if one is under the necessity of looking for work, to try to find a counselor in either a public or private employment office who is sympathetic and who understands that rejection after rejection can kill any eagerness to make the rounds of employment offices. There are more of them each month and each year. It will also pay to look to one's own experience and attitude to try to discover how much of the problem is inherent in oneself.

No worker—man or woman—can place upon an employer the entire responsibility for employment. There is no escape from the fact that once the opportunity has been given a worker, the major responsibility for employability rests with the employee. Also older workers can easily fortify themselves in a job with their own skills, experience, tenure, and seniority. The world is moving fast. Unless individual workers move just as fast, they may be left behind and become liabilities to their employers without realizing it. Therefore it is essential for workers who wish to remain useful employees to keep on the alert—vocationally and avocationally—watching for signs which may mean a speeding up or a slowing down and being willing to accept either. It is no longer possible to rest on the laurels of a single kind of job well done—for new methods and new ideas come along at a breathless pace and may soon outmode even the best of work.

The facilities of vocational-training programs—through adult education and special extension programs—as well as those which may be offered by one's employer, mean that one's job need not remain static but can be an absorbing pursuit. Avocational interests tend to give balance as well, in these days of more leisure time. The habit of spending some time in educational activity—whether vocational, avocational, or cultural—will pay huge dividends throughout one's working life, but even greater dividends will be accumulated for the days when retirement from gainful employment is advisable.

For women, especially those who leave work to take up the role of wife and mother, there is a special point of interest in this whole pattern of business and professional life which finds little use for the older worker. Most women are outliving the time when their children reach adulthood, and many of them are outliving their husbands, so that when idleness becomes irksome or economic need becomes pressing there is the urge to return to work. Few of them have kept up the skills which they had prior to marriage, and even fewer have taken the pains to acquire new ones, except as they may have been needed in the discharge of their family duties. True, many middle-aged women can afford to enter the professional world or the civic community as volunteers when time hangs heavy on their hands and they no longer feel themselves important in the lives of the other members of their families. But for many it is desirable, either psychologically or materially, that there be a pay check for whatever work is undertaken. For that reason it would pay most women to keep in touch with developments in their special fields or in those in which they have a hope of someday being engaged. Otherwise the penalty may be work of a kind which does not in any way use fully the educational or professional ability which the person may have.

The number of middle-aged and older women who are looking for positions as companions—and only occasionally as companion-housekeeper (for lack of planning for anything else)—is so much greater than the number of positions open that this situation should be a warning. And the middle-aged "receptionist" who dreams of successful competition with the young thing who can also offer typing or can operate a switchboard, at the same time providing decoration to the outer office, is not being sensible. The older women one sees at the outer desk are usually those who have been transferred there from more important posts in the company.

Health Counseling

With ill-health, invalidism, or handicap recognized as the principal enemies of a successful old age (and ones which are often factors in determining whether that other enemy, dependency, gets the better of you), no argument should be needed to persuade individuals and families of the vital importance of maintaining health. The most exciting thing about this seems to be that nowadays, if one acquires the habit of health consultation, many of the evil effects of negligence and of ill-health may be staved off and often entirely prevented. For those who heed, the vigor of the middle years may be extended well beyond the point at which it now begins to wane, and the period of enfeebled old age may be reduced to a negligible minimum.

Parents who regularly consult the pediatrician about every apparent aberration in the health of their children are patently careless about their own health or that of their elders. And yet the medical men tell us that we should at no time of life take it for granted that a pain or an ache is to be expected just because in the past such aches and pains have been characteristic of old age. The first step in preparing for a healthy maturity is to keep healthy in youth, in young adulthood, and in middle age. The best way to do this is to have the *habit* of consulting one's own doctor or, failing the financial means to do that, the local medical or mental-hygiene clinic, either in the hospital of the community or through the public-health service. There is no substitute for regularity in this kind of consultation or checkup, even though the medical profession which urges it upon us as good practice is not yet trained or fully prepared to give it to us.

In rural communities there is real promise for a healthier future for many of us if residents can be persuaded to avail themselves of the multiphasic screening process being used by the public-health service in the community-organized clinics to detect the presence or absence of disease, acute or chronic. This is not a treatment process, but one which uses tests for detection purposes and gives the patient the opportunity of following up the original detection process for complete diagnosis and treatment. Similarly, in many of the cancer clinics, cancer is not the disease detected. Therefore the general health of the people is being raised, since the treatment of a heart ailment discovered in the course of a search for cancer may be just as important as the discovery of cancer in the long run in what it saves the individual and the community.

Central Information Services (Specialized)

In some communities in which there are information services there are also specialized services which maintain information as to resources for the treatment of illness and for the care of sick people. In the rural communities there are the public-health services and, in some instances, the public-welfare services. In large cities there are what are coming to be known as Central Services for the Chronically Ill, or for Convalescent Care, or Nursing Home Registries. These may be sponsored by the local Health and Welfare Council or by the local academy of medicine or institute of health. While there are a large number of specialized agencies, the central service will usually be the first point of contact, and referral is made by them to the others. This is a timesaving device and a protection for any of us; the habit of using such services is a good one to cultivate.

Mental Illness

These central services also have lines out to the services which must be used in the event of mental or emotional illness. Now that it is being recognized that such illness is curable in many of its manifestations, and that it is no more a disgrace than any physical illness, there is much encouragement to individuals and families who must seek help when such casualties occur. That they are treatable is something which many of us do not understand, especially when the patient is an elderly person. Shock therapy, nutritional therapy, or special nursing care in many instances can be restorative on either a temporary or a permanent basis. Confusion which results from accidents, from operative shock, from an overuse of barbiturates, can be reduced and usually entirely cleared up if there is understanding of the past habits of the individual patient and of what has happened to cause the confused state. For each of us this is important to know, and even more important to accept, for our feelings are usually so involved that judgment is warped and sometimes misguided when those nearest to us are the sufferers.

Nutrition

Perhaps the simplest and most essential health measure for any one of us to use is that of keeping ourselves nutritionally sound. Nutrition is more than a balancing of calories. It is the supplying to our bones and tissues of the elements which keep them healthy and firm and strong. Obesity, a real threat to man or woman in middle age or old age, because of the disease potential it harbors, can often be overcome by understanding which foods we need as we grow older. We have disproved the old theory that the aged need only toast and tea—and that they can get along by "gumming" their food, without teeth. Good nutrition is good sense; it is economy; and in the case of many an ailment it is treatment. It forms part of the rehabilitative therapy which is proving so useful with veterans of war and of life itself. Age is no reason for spending the rest of one's life "in bed," and frequently nutritional therapy is responsible for lifting a patient who might otherwise be condemned to such a punishment out of it. Local, state, and federal agencies are publishing pamphlets of great use to individuals on this personal aspect of aging. Libraries or information services will be able to direct one to source material.

Rehabilitation

Each of us can be grateful, too, for the application of the knowledge of rehabilitation, used so effectively with wounded war veterans, to people of all ages. A "stroke" which paralyzes no longer paralyzes for life, as it once did. Broken hips, which once meant being bed- or wheel-chair-ridden for the rest of one's days, now are set or pinned and the victim of the accident walks again. The greatest advantage flowing to the individual is his ability to do for himself—which is what each of us wants to do—and occasionally he is restored to serving others. Physical medicine, which includes in its treatment the whole person and personality and which considers the illness or the handicap in relation to the individual's capacity and his social world, is working wonders for patients of all ages, but it is revolutionary for the elderly, whose world formerly narrowed and narrowed until it finally ceased to be.

Mention is made of these services because they are not always automatically offered to an older person, nor is he told of them, for to many people there is no spontaneous thought that such a person should or could have the benefit of such hopeful services. This is part of the heritage from the past, in which the old and their families have been disease-conscious rather than health-conscious.

Counseling about Living Arrangements

"Somewhere to live" did not just happen to be the first on the list of the three needs of older people as stated earlier. It is significant that it occurs here, for it is around this need that most requests for help come to anyone who is attempting to help older people with their problems. What is the significance for any one of us in this? Surely it means that each of us should not fail to give careful thought to the matter of where we want to live, where we can live, and how and with whom we can live, in our later years. It also means that we must remember that what may seem to us in our youth or in our younger days an ideal plan may have to be qualified later by circumstances which will change our thinking and our desires. Standards of desirability which appeal to one in the full swing of a vigorous youth are apt to be out of tune with the standards of those later years when life has been tempered by experience and the human frame has been battered by the stormy voyage through the years. One's values do change and one's abilities to meet the demands of daily living change.

Home of One's Own

It is probably understood that the optimum plan would be a home of one's own, provided that can be kept suitable and livable. Whether it should be in the country or in the city will depend very much on one's lifetime experience. In either event no retirement away from familiar localities should take place without some previous trial to determine the validity of the proposed location, not only for the immediate present but for the uncertain future. Too many city dwellers attempt the little place in the country and the little plot for a garden without testing out either the place or themselves in it. Too many country dwellers dream of moving to town or the city, where warmth and comfort are assured and there are people who will help, only to find that loneliness and comfort have nothing to do with either the number of people around or the physical appurtenances of the house in which one lives.

The cost of upkeep of a house—in terms of dollars and cents as well as of human labor—needs to be carefully appraised and studied to determine whether either or both can be had from the resources available. Domestic help, even when it can be secured, comes high these days, and, as experience has demonstrated, labor from aging people may be dependable in the sense that there is responsibility for it but less dependable in the sense that one may not be able to deliver that labor when and if it be needed in an emergency.

Is one going to live alone or with one's family? What has been the experience in this? Does it lead to optimism for living together in friendly fashion when it is "for keeps"? What are the alternatives to this? Bleak as they may seem, they may be preferable in the long run to jeopardizing the affection which might not stand the strain of a combined household. Are interests and habits congenial? Do you like the neighbors, and do the neighbors like you? Are you an outsider or a member of the community? Can you hold your own with them? Can you handle the chores if there is no one else to do them? And does the community offer the possibility of care in the event of illness, and help when trouble arises, especially if you are on your own?

All these and many more are searching questions which need answer before a final plan is made.

Can you face emotionally the fact that perhaps the home you have always lived in—or at least for a good many years—may have to be given up? If this is a probability, then it is wise to prepare for the change over a period of time, so that it does not come as a shock. Maturity is a period of great changes, and most of them can be anticipated if there is the will to do so. Home is something we cling to at all costs, without reason, without good sense, but with a strength of feeling which cannot be explained by any logic. Reluctance to relinquish these tangible bits of the past is part of the common pattern of growing older.

And what about urban dwelling? With the reduced income which most older people will have, what kind of living arrangements which will even partially suit the old folks can be made in a city? Apartment living has much to commend it, for those who are accustomed to it and for some who are not —if they know enough of city life to understand it—for in the compactness of the living unit and in the common services which such an arrangement provides there is a peculiar suitability for older people, who can seldom negotiate tending the fire and shoveling the snow throughout all their later years. Apartment houses especially designed for older folks, with elevators, food service, and professional supervision of the house, have much to offer for future planning in most cities. They are capable of adaptation by both private real-estate owners and public-housing authorities, or by people planning cooperative residences in their own behalf. City planning commissions might listen to citizens' committees who make cogent arguments in behalf of a growing proportion of a city's population from whom investment return may not be large but which has every sign of being steady.

Cottage colonies, not too far distant from the center of things, have their advantages too, if the climate is balmy and there is assurance of another plan for living if and when the cottage becomes inappropriate, as may well be the case. Both cottages and apartments are fitting accommodations as long as they are what the residents want and as long as they can be maintained without harm or detriment either to the residents or to others.

Visiting Services and Home Medical Care

With a housing shortage which affects every community and many of the families who need the right kind of housing, and with hospital beds in equally short supply, especially for older people who do not require active medical supervision, the native ingenuity which has salvaged more than one serious crisis in the country has once more come to the rescue. Home medical care programs have been organized which, when it is in the best interests of the patient and of the hospital, make use of the patient's own bed as an extension of the hospital itself. By taking into the home the services of the physician on call, the nurse, and the social worker on a visiting basis, as well as a visiting housekeeper, the patient finds himself in his own home, where he usually prefers to be, and improvement, both psychological and physical, is the usual result.

Visiting services of this kind furnish the home with that "something new" which is needed, and many times even a lone elderly person can stay on at home with the help of these people who visit with a purpose. This kind of plan is "catching on" the country over, although it has had its major demonstration in New York City in Montefiore Hospital and in the municipal hospital system. It all sounds elaborate and expensive, but it seems to be costing the taxpayer and the hospitals less and satisfying the patient and family, where there is one, even better than continued hospitalization.

Not only does such a program offer care in more acceptable surroundings, but it also provides job openings for practical nurses and trained visiting housekeepers, who can be middle-aged or even older women without harm to themselves or the work they must do. In the country the counterpart of this plan is the town or country nurse and the country doctor. The visiting housekeeper is probably still the neighbor who comes in to help, when she can spare the time from her own home duties.

Boarding Homes

The alternatives to living in one's own home are at best compromises with what one would like to have, but in many instances they can be a great improvement in what they offer in the way of comfort and care. There are the family boarding homes, which are, after all, substitute family living arrangements. They are usually best when the plan is worked out between the older person and the family because of some bond of acquaintance or friendship, or when there has been careful exploration of the arrangement by persons skilled in such foster-home placement of adults. There are many families which have taken older people who have been discharged from mental hospitals, and there have been months and years of normal, contented living made possible for older people who might otherwise have spent their last days behind bars. It is being learned that such placement may well prevent the hospital experience, for none of us ever grows out of the early pattern of life so completely that this setting is uncongenial when the greatest need one may have is for sympathy and friendliness from others in a simple home environment.

Boardinghouses and hotels are filled with older people whose home ties have been broken by the years and by the growing mobility of a nation. They leave much to be desired, even for those who can afford to pay well for accommodations and service. They do little to relieve the lonesomeness which can be greater in these commercial hostelries than when one lives alone with one's own possessions. But the very fact that such situations exist points the way to similar ventures which are planned to give to residents a maximum of assurance, independence, and service when required, with the minimum amount of supervision or watchfulness that many older people should have, even though they may resent the mere suggestion of it. There is a wide-open market for those who will take the trouble to do a humane as well as a good catering job for countless elderly couples and single old men and ladies who would welcome the security of what might be called an "endowed" hotel. But the managers must like older people and must be willing to accept the crotchety with the gentle, the cantankerous with the mild, and the sick with the well.

Homes for the Aged

But what, may you ask, of homes for the aged?—which is what this last suggestion sounds like. There are a few homes which meet the qualifications outlined above for a profit-making venture, but most of them are non-profit and the charitable motive is still the predominant one. Time was when we might facetiously remark, in thinking or talking about the future, "Oh well, I'm going to buy my way into an old ladies' home when I get along in years. I'll save a few hundred dollars and set aside a good silk dress to be buried in, and I'll be no burden to anyone!" This could well have been the solution some fifty or even some thirty years ago. Today the story is different. Each of us must make plans well in advance if admission to a home for old folks seems to us the desirable way to end our days. Or it may be important to know the facts even when that is not our preferred plan. It is incredible how many people, and their children, in this day and age, in an emergency turn to look for a *"home"* for themselves or for their parents with no glimmer of an idea that waiting lists of such homes are years long and that admission requirements are strict.

The local or state information services can usually tell something about such homes, and frequently the local family agency can be of help. There is a national directory[1]—much out of date—which gives the important details of sponsorship, location, eligibility requirements as to church connection, residence, and state of health as well as fees. Local churches can supply the facts about homes that their denomination maintains. The important thing to know is that vacancies are limited, requirements are restrictive, and now in most states people receiving old-age assistance grants can continue to receive those grants in such homes if the home has worked out an agreement with the local public-welfare and state agency.

Homes for the older people themselves are going through a period of great change. The demand for residence, which a

[1]*Directory of Homes for the Aged,* U. S. Bureau of Labor Statistics.

short time ago was believed to be disappearing, has been mounting steadily, owing to both housing shortages and the lengthened time which people live. Homes are gradually recognizing that their residents are personalities—not merely charitable charges whose lives the administrators can "manage" in the literal sense of the word.

Life goes on in quite a different manner. The doors swing out as well as in. Entertainment is taken in and also is taken out by the residents. Diversional and occupational therapy —hobbies and recreational activities—is part of the progressive home's program today. Admission is not always the final step it once was. People may even leave without the stigma of "misbehavior" or disobedience. Boarding rates on a monthly basis have helped to make this possible, and it means better use of the valuable contribution which such homes make in the reservoir of resources of the community.

Health security is the usual reason which leads people to enter a home for the aged in these times. This is making it necessary for these homes to reorganize their infirmary equipment and their staffs. For anyone who is considering a home for this purpose, knowledge of the kind of medical and nursing care which the home can offer, and on what terms, is most desirable information to have.

Some homes are also finding themselves in a position to help people who are on their waiting list, during the period of waiting time, not with money, but with the guarantee of a watchful eye and of visiting service should this be required prior to admission. Some homes encourage people to remain on such a service, which is similar to the home medical care program, in order that the beds of the institution itself can be used for those who actually need the protection of the home. This is an extension of the fundamental idea that the organization wishes to provide the security of peace of mind to those

whom it accepts as eligible for its care. It is a healthy departur
from the old days, which are no longer abreast of the world i
which we live.

Nursing Homes

Nursing homes are another alternative for the elderly perso
who must be cared for outside his own home. These are, as
rule, commercial enterprises, operated for profit by the pr
prietor. They are generally expensive, and payment for car
in them when that care must be given over a long period o
time constitutes a great drain on personal savings or on th
means at the disposal of the family. Many of them are poo
places in spite of the price which must be paid. If they mus
be used, it is important to know whether the home is license
or certified and to learn of the quality of care which is giver
Some of the disasters which have taken place have arouse
public officials and private citizens, so that there is every reaso
to believe that conditions can be improved if action is de
manded. Proprietors have no right to traffic with the lives o
the helpless and the hopeless, and many of them have no wis
to do so. Standards can be set which are reasonable, and if th
community insists that such standards be met, enforcemen
will follow. Consultation with the local licensing agency o
information service is invaluable as a guide to the use o
nursing-home facilities.

The other alternatives about which we should all be in
formed are the public home and the state hospital—neither o
which is at present a place where any of us voluntarily seek
refuge. Only when the community begins to take seriously it
responsibility for these institutions will reforms be brough
about. The public home is becoming an infirmary or a hospita

for the chronically ill, just as is the private home for older people; the state hospital is housing a growing percentage of oldsters who have no other place to go. Both need better buildings, better equipment, and better staffs, but they will not have them until enough of the taxpayers are brought into personal contact with the condition, which is often one of inhumanity to man. The day is not far off when individuals will be paying in whole or in part for their care in either the public home or the state hospital. This may bring improvement, for when a patient pays for care there is an atmosphere quite different from one in which the care is "free."

Personal Plans

Knowing the best and the worst which may come, when plans go awry as plans so often do, it seems like good sense to look for the pleasant side of life. Leisure time—which, as one looks back upon youth, has such glamour and charm about it and which seems such an elusive factor in adult life—becomes in later life a drug on the market; one has either lost the knack of using it or has lost the zest for fun through having forgotten how to play. For this reason the habit of leisure—profitable leisure—seems the most worth-while habit one can develop for one's later years.

For people who are already old today there has been little opportunity to cultivate this habit, but for those who are having the benefit of five-day weeks and seven-hour days, with paid vacations regarded as health measures as well as investments for those for whom we work, there is no excuse for reaching old age without the habit of using leisure time in such a way that it will give to us occupation and a sense of contentment through usefulness to the community.

Such a habit does not come overnight. It takes a long time a-growing. And if there is no conscious effort rather continuously during one's earlier years, there will be a more painful period of adjustment in later life. William James, in his classical treatise on "habit,"[2] tells us that no matter how "good one' sentiments may be, if one has not taken advantage of every concrete opportunity to *act,* one's character may remain entirely unaffected for the better." And farther on in his summary of habit formation he emphasizes that it is wise to "keep the faculty of *effort* alive in you by a little gratuitous exercise every day."

A psychiatrist recently reminded a group of listeners of the same thing in practical suggestions by saying that acquiring the habit of listening to music fifteen minutes a day, reading a few paragraphs each day in the books one always intends to read, doing things with one's hands daily, as well as learning to rest with complete satisfaction for a time sufficient to be helpful each and every day, were all the bit-by-bit method of enabling one to do these things for longer periods of time later in life when those periods of time were ours. These are the "gratuitous exercise" of the faculty of effort.

The losses of age are compensable if one is prepared for their occurrence. And with preparation the actual degree of loss may never be felt. There is the loss of family and friends. By keeping one's associations with others, especially with others somewhat younger than oneself, there is a possibility of mending the circle of friends and keeping it satisfying. There are the losses of one's faculties, but if one is ready with several habits of leisure time which may involve performance of a range of skills, there will be no unnecessary period of anguish when eyesight, hearing, or locomotion may fail.

In almost every community there is a growing sensitivity to

[2] *Habit,* William James. Henry Holt & Co., 1890.

ie recreational needs of older people. Recreation, as used in
iis phrase, must be interpreted in its several meanings, since
ecreation is different for every human being. What is work
or one is play for another. What is tedious intellectual exercise
or one is the greatest relaxation for another. Fundamental to
iis sensitivity, however, is the awareness that association with
thers is a necessity for all people, especially older people with
ime on their hands. As one scientist has phrased it, "fission
iay be the word of the moment," but for human beings
fusion" comes much closer to reflecting man's natural be-
avior patterns. Social fission is what has taken place for so
iany oldsters. The movement to provide, through any num-
er of types of institutions and agencies, services which will
ive the older people the chance to foregather with others is
i the right direction of social fusion. To provide sociability is
ot the be-all and end-all of such plans, for sociability which
s not ultimately related to some sounder purpose than that of
ieeting for a cup of tea or a game of cards does not usually
rove to be a lasting basis for keeping associations alive. Since
ervice to others—being useful to someone else—is the salt
vithout which there is no savor to life, the mounting number
f golden-age clubs will find themselves a new resource for
ommunity service to their own members and to those in the
ommunity whose needs can be solved wholly or in part by
ersonal service.

Clubs for oldsters are being formed in many places under
ll sorts of auspices. The local council of social agencies will
ften have information about them. They may be sponsored
y the local settlement or by the young men's or young
vomen's organizations, by the church, by a business house, by
ie Junior League, either independently or in co-operation
vith one of the voluntary agencies, or by one of the men's or
vomen's service clubs. They may also be self-initiated or self-

sponsored. They offer a real opportunity for volunteers who wish to be helpful, and they are a most useful training ground for both members and leaders.

Program content varies. As groups become used to one another they know more and more what they want and how they may get it. They tend to become self-governing, to direct their thinking to altruistic activities rather than to selfish planning, and to take enjoyment in the fruits of their common labors. They are morale builders. They promote the kind of understanding which helps to unite groups with, rather than to divide them from, the community. Their members can "sell," on the basis of being satisfied customers, the need for community support of the social services which the ordinary citizen has not yet been convinced are needed because he himself has found no use for them.

The adult-education movement, by the flexibility of organization of staff and of educational material, lends itself to supplementing the programs of clubs and community centers. Its very informality is ideal for older people who have gone way beyond the formalism of the school system in their capacity to think of themselves as students in the ordinary sense. Forum discussion on all kinds of topics is a form of activity which is receiving much attention and which can be stimulating when good leadership is provided.

The opportunities for association with others which these clubs offer are an antidote for the withdrawal and isolation which is fairly common among older people. To overcome this universal tendency we must take advantage of every "concrete opportunity to *act.*" An adventurous attitude well counteracts the natural tendency to remove oneself more and more from free circulation with others. To prevent irksome readjustment we should keep ourselves in the mainstream of life, even though it takes a great deal of resolution and effort. It will

elp to ward off the kind of old age which most of us dread—
hat of the inward-looking, withdrawn, disoriented, and dis-
laced personality, with the even-more-to-be-dreaded eventu-
lity of care in a hospital for the mentally ill.

If one's interest is in crafts or hobbies of a tangible nature,
hen participation in the community hobby shows is another
abit to cultivate. Many of the large business houses and
rganizations are devoting some of their time and thought to
he hobbies of their employees. Here is a good place to begin
hobbies and creative activities for future retirement. The
public-library systems are finding an increasing demand for
organized shelves and bibliographies and readers' guides on
hese and related subjects. In some of them there are active
eaders' and discussion clubs; in others there are musical and
torytelling hours which are geared to older people's tastes.
Museums are responding to an older adult clientele and are a
esource of untold wealth for developing hobby, art, or cul-
ural interests. Home-bound travel is another hobby for later
ears, when the hardships of actually moving around the globe,
s well as the expense of it, are out of the question. In a world
which has rapidly increased in accessibility, in terms of communication and of transportation, this is a fascinating frontier
or the armchair explorer. The Church is grasping this oppor-
unity, also, to reach, both socially and spiritually, older folks,
or whom the church services and its pastoral visiting bring a
peculiarly gratifying solace.

One could go on at length with specific suggestions and still
not mention one which appeals to a particular reader. The
answer is that hobbies and leisure-time activities are as individual as are people themselves, but in the smallest community it is possible to find someone who can share your special interest. There is, then, no single formula or plan for using
one's time in later years. The common factor in the formula is

that time will have a new quantitative dimension, for all. It will have a deepened qualitative dimension only if there is preparation for the use of it when it becomes available. Living should be a continuous process, with as little interruption as possible. Inevitable changes can be anticipated. The sting of change can be removed by intelligent preparation.

The Individual and the Community

No individual in any community can remain healthfully isolated. That the past and the present have made this inappropriate disposition of so many oldsters is deplorable. It demands immediate and drastic reparation by the community. It is beyond individual control. Committees and services must be organized to relieve the crisis if the number of disadvantaged citizens are to be brought once more into the stream of life in such a way that their day-to-day lives may more nearly approximate in fullness and satisfation those of their relatives, friends, and neighbors.

To the basic needs of the individual, "Somewhere to live, something to do, someone to care," there should be added, "someone to care for." This gives everyone the possibility of response from the others in his community. The community is not a community in the true sense of the word unless there is that interchange of response which makes of it a whole and not a collection of individualists with no feeling for one another. The sense of belonging which is so essential to the well-being of each person is no less vital to the well-being of the community in which he lives. The need of each of the other is mutual.

The individual must make a deliberate effort to relate whatever planning he does to all of life, rather than to fractions or segments of it. Bertrand Russell,[3] in discussing whether an open or a closed mind is of greater help to the individual or the nation, concludes that a mind which is open, "despite its theoretical limitations," is to be advocated because of mankind's proneness to prejudice and bias. This seems to be sound reasoning for our approach to the years of harvest.

Old age may have historically been all that we are apt to think of it as being. This accounts for our prejudices and fears. However, we must remember that there are facts which warrant changing our minds about its misery, its discontent, and its uselessness. If we can keep our minds open to these hopeful facts and close them to the unpleasant whisper of the past, we can as individuals remain a vital part of the community. We can serve ourselves by serving others through all the ordinary institutions provided for that purpose. We need accept the specialized services only as circumstances indicate.

Keeping one's life well rounded at all stages of the journey through is the goal. The final stage may be brief in the sense of being a stage of enfeeblement. It must not defeat us. Nor can it if the early stages are such as to lead naturally along the path to that point where, philosophically, we can agree with the poet who tells us that "There is no difference between the quick and the dead—They are one channel of vitality."[4] Thus does each of us fulfill his own earthly destiny and shoulder his share in shaping that of his fellow men and his community.

[3] *Can We Afford to Keep Open Minds?* New York *Times* Magazine, June 11, 1950.

[4] *The Way of Life According to Laotzu,* an American version by Witter Bynner. John Day, 1944.

OCCUPATIONS FOR RETIREMENT

by

GEORGE H. WALTZ, JR.

Each year, as many thousands of men and women face retirement, they are confronted with one of the most difficult and important decisions of their lives. Should they accept that long-awaited final vacation and retire into retirement, or should they strive hard to keep relatively productive?

Obviously there is but one intelligent answer. To enjoy old age, and to extend it to the fullest, one must maintain three things—an interest in living, health, and an agile mind. Idle retirement is one of the surest roads to a short life. Complete inactivity after long years of work is the deadly blight that withers the final fruits of life. Sitting and waiting merely hastens the aging process. Leisure, as the late Dr. Alexis Carrel once pointed out, is even more dangerous for the old than for the young.

The one thing that many of us fail to realize, unfortunately, is that it is just as important to make plans for our retirement activities as it is to make plans for our retirement incomes. We start early in life buying annuities, paying money into pension funds, building up our investments, and paying Social Security to finance our later years. Yet too few of us have the foresight to start just as early to plan what we are going to do with our long-awaited leisure when it does come. It takes a great deal more than money for a successful and contented retirement. It takes ingenuity and work. A happy maturity requires activity in the form of an interesting hobby or some sort of agreeable part-time work as well as financial security.

Many business concerns are fast recognizing the need for creating definite retirement plans for their workers. As a result, more and more of the thousands of firms having employee pension systems are setting up retirement counseling services which not only provide aid in solving the financial problems of retirement but also give assistance in planning retirement activities. The Ohio Bell Telephone Company is one good example. It goes out of its way to encourage and help employees to organize hobby clubs and study classes, not just to provide day-to-day relaxation but to promote worth-while interests that will be valuable to the employees when they reach retirement age.

According to the geriatricians, we should start setting up and testing our "non-fiscal" retirement plan—our old-age career—at least ten years before we plan to leave active employment. Unfortunately there is no pat formula that can be applied to everyone. Each of us must find our own worth-while activity and then pursue it. It may be anything from building astronomical telescopes or collecting glass buttons to turning out attractive and salable needlework novelties. Above all, however, it must be something that we like, for what can be one person's favorite pastime can be another's favorite bore.

The art of finding your hobby or secondary career is largely a matter of careful sampling. An avocation can't be bought in a department store. The first step is to take an honest inventory of your interests, your likes and dislikes. It would be foolish, for example, for a man or woman who isn't tremendously interested in using his or her hands to attempt to take up model making or tapestry making. And by the same token, it would be an unpleasant waste of time for anyone to plunge into book collecting without some interest in books. The successful hob-byist, like the successful workman, is almost a fanatic about what he is doing.

The retirement consultant of one large midwestern store helps his employees to pick their future activities by asking them one question: "What one thing have you always wanted to do but have never felt you had the time to do?" The answers he receives range all the way from a desire to open a small gift shop to raising rabbits. The actual choice is not too important, but the fact that a choice has been made is. It is a start toward thinking about retirement in terms of activity.

Collecting Heads the List

The list of possible hobbies or retirement careers is just about endless. Perhaps the most popular hobby is the hobby of col-lecting, and that can mean collecting just about anything from odd bits of driftwood to valuable paintings.

Outnumbering all other collectors in America are the twelve million or more collectors of stamps. There are all kinds of stamp collectors. Philatelists who are interested in all issues of stamps. Specialists who collect only those stamps commenorat-ing historical events. Then there are others interested only in the freaks of the stamp world—stamps without perforation, with upside-down engravings, or with similar irregularities. Many times a stamp collection is closely related to the owners' own major interests—like the retired railroad engineer who saves only stamps depicting locomotives, the airplane pilot whose sole interest is in stamps that show airplanes, and the bedridden invalid who glories in her collection of stamps that show views of famous places in the world.

Stamp collecting, like most hobbies, can bring profit as well as fun. At last count it was estimated that there are more than thirty collections in this country worth $100,000 each. The late President Roosevelt's went for $212,847 at auction. Just how stamps, even ordinary stamps, increase in value is graphically shown by the fact that if someone at the turn of the century had had the foresight to buy a block of four stamps of every new United States stamp as it was issued up until 1920, he would today have a collection worth about $4,000. The actual original cost of those stamps would have totaled only $169.48! Quite an investment.

There is no great trick to starting a stamp collection. You can begin with stamps that business friends clip from envelopes and save for you, or you can buy assorted packets from stamp companies. Also almost every community boasts a stamp club whose members are eager to swap duplicates to fill out collections. By joining such a club you cannot only collect stamps, but, what is just as important, you can widen your circle of friends and enjoy the companionship of others who share your interest.

So you don't like stamps? Okay, then by all means skip it. There are a thousand and one things that can be collected, if collecting is what you want. It may be that a coin collection may hold more fascination for you. If so, you can start collecting gradually by concentrating on some of the many United States coins that already have increased in value (coin dealers will be glad to provide you with market and price lists). By watching the daily change in your pocket, and by asking any friends you have at your local bank to watch out for the coins you want, your collection will grow steadily.

The hobby of collecting knows no boundaries. There are thousands of hobbyists who collect matchbook covers. Other thousands gather in every new cigar band they can find. Still others collect political campaign buttons. Collecting is collecting, as long as you collect what interests you. One old gentleman in Indiana is as proud as Punch of his collection of automobile license plates. The walls of his garage are almost entirely covered with them, and they include tags from every state and for just about every year since "horseless carriages" were first licensed. Most of them have been sent to him by friends who know about his hobby.

Another man, a New Yorker, gets fun out of collecting samples of earth from all the famous places of the world. He has a bookcase stacked with small labeled vials containing varieties of ordinary dirt—sand from the Sahara, lava dust from the slopes of Vesuvius, soil from the Grand Canyon.

To many, the business of collecting license plates or samples of dirt may seem silly. Certainly neither of them is a thing of beauty and neither has any possible monetary value. Yet each of those collections has become a vital part of each man's life. Each provides an interest in living and each creates a day-by-day anticipation of what tomorrow may bring. Each new license plate and each new vial of dirt is an important goal achieved and an incentive to add more.

Workshops and Handicrafts

If you haven't the collector's yen, there still remains a wide choice of hobbyhorses from which to select a mount. There is model railroading, if you've always liked trains; jewelry making, leatherwork, and wood carving, if you like to use your hands; photography, if you've always felt at home with a camera; and gardening and nature study if you like the out-of-doors. Others include furniture repair, genealogy if you're interested in family trees, zoology, amateur radio, music, needlework, model building, ceramics, plastics, pottery making, dressmaking, sound recording, and even just plain everyday walking. There aren't many known activities that can't be turned into an engrossing hobby or secondary career.

More than ten million American men and women spend their spare time in their home workshops—some nothing more than a kitchen table stowed away in a closet, others elaborate basement arrays that boast the best in motorized equipment. The things these workshoppers turn out run the gamut from tiny wood and metal gadgets to elaborate suites of beautiful furniture. For those who like to work with tools, workshopping can be a particularly satisfying spare-time career. Best of all, it can be started in a small way with plenty of room for growth.

"The Sunday Painters"

More and more people, too, are joining the ranks of the "Sunday painters"—the army of middle-aged and older folks who sketch and paint, not with any idea of selling their paintings or having them hung in museums, but just for the sheer fun of doing it. Painting doesn't require a full art education to be enjoyed, and you don't have to know how to draw. Pleasing yourself is all that counts. As Winston Churchill—the dean of the Sunday painters—wrote in his book, *Amid These Storms:*

"Painting is a companion with whom one may hope to walk a great part of life's journey. One by one the more vigorous sports and exacting games fall away. Muscles may relax, and feet and hands slow down; the nerve of youth and manhood may become less trusty. But painting is a friend who makes no undue demands, excites to no exhausting pursuits, keeps faithful pace even with feeble steps, and holds her canvas as a screen between us and the envious eyes of Time or the surly advance of Decrepitude."

If none of the run-of-the-mill avocations appeal to you as a possible retirement career, dig down into your imagination. A hobby doesn't necessarily have to be something that can be handled or worked with in the strict sense of the word. Many big-time executives, for instance, finding time hanging heavy on their hands after retirement, have found brand-new and exciting interests by taking an active part in local politics and community affairs. By so doing they have not only provided themselves with new careers, but have performed a real public service for their fellow citizens.

Retired professional men and women, likewise, can do good for themselves as well as their neighbors by volunteering their services in their qualified fields. Dr. Helen Walbridge, a New York physician who five years ago, at the age of sixty-five, retired, provides a typical example. When her days began to drag she offered her services as a volunteer worker at New York Hospital, and since then has been putting in about twenty hours a week doing important clerical work. To her the work is her hobby and she loves it. At seventy she is active, doing a worth-while, productive job.

Profitable New Careers

Study and research should not be overlooked as possible retirement careers. Age is relatively unimportant. The psychiatrists have shown that a man or woman of sixty-five learns more easily than a youngster of twelve. More than one so-called oldster has succumbed to the desire to go back to school. When Dr. Frank Graves, the well-known educator and former Commissioner of Education in New York State, retired at the young age of seventy-one, he decided that he wanted to study law. So he went to law school, completed the course, and in 1943 was admitted to the Bar. At seventy-four he had found himself a brand-new career.

There is no reason why the hobby or retirement career you choose shouldn't more than pay its way by adding dollars to your retirement income. The products of most hobbies or avocations are salable. The woman interested in needlework can find buyers for her creations. The woman whose hobby is cooking often can build up a fair-sized business by catering to neighborhood bridge parties, small dinners, and church functions. The man who makes simple silver jewelry seldom has trouble finding takers for his hand-wrought rings and pins. And it doesn't take a great deal of ingenuity, for example, to transform a home workshop into a home factory capable of turning out birdhouses, jigsaw puzzles, or similar salable items. Several Californians have even made a profitable business out of gathering native weeds and grasses. They dye them in brilliant colors, mount them in deep frames in attractive arrangements under glass, and sell them for wall decorations!

The opportunities and possibilities in after-retirement careers are just about boundless if we approach them with an open mind and face them long before we face retirement. Many a businessman who once inwardly laughed at his friends who painted, who tinkered with a model railroad, who bought photographic gear, or who spent their time placidly whittling on a scrap of wood, has belatedly found out that such hobbies can provide invaluable anchors and calm ports in retirement.

The medical casebooks are cluttered with the histories of men and women whose lives have been so filled with their work that they had little time—or at least they thought they had little time—to develop an avocation. When their final quitting time did come, they had little else to do but to retire to an armchair and sit looking blankly out of a window to wait life out. In most cases they didn't have long to wait. Inactivity seems to be a deadly contributing virus to the degenerative diseases of age. Physicians call it "retirement shock," the inability to find oneself in retirement.

Senator Thomas C. Desmond, who has done considerable groundwork in trying to solve the problems of the aged and aging in New York State, recently summed it up nicely when he said:

"You have seen them; once they were dynamic executives or vigorous professional men; now they aimlessly putter around the garden or gloomily rock themselves on some hotel porch in a futile effort to find peace of mind in retirement. Many succumb. The doctor's certificates may read 'coronary thrombosis' or 'cardiac failure,' but the physician knows the real cause is 'retirement shock,' inability to adjust oneself to retirement.

"They are the victims of the myth that all one needs for successful retirement is ample annuities, a bulging investment portfolio, or an adequate pension. Financial preparation for retirement, an expression of high resolution and character, is the foundation on which a retirement structure must be built; but it is only one part of a livable edifice.

"Physicians today warn us to erase from our minds the phantasy of retirement as the period of The Great Loaf. Activity is a biologic duty. It is the violation of this fundamental precept that makes retirement, as currently envisaged by many people, as dangerous as toying with a high-voltage wire. Functions and living tissue that are not used decline and atrophy. Nature tends to eliminate those who have relinquished their functional usefulness."

The important thing is to approach your second career with

the same amount of thought and early preparation that you exercised in approaching your lifetime working career. Consider your retirement as just another new phase of life, a new chapter to be as well planned and as well executed as the one before. Retirement should not be an epilogue to a finished production, but a well-thought-out prologue to a brand-new adventure that can be pleasant and productive.

Finally, to borrow a well-known line from a well-known song, "It's later than you think."

TRAVEL IN THE HARVEST YEARS

by

RICHARD JOSEPH

SOMEDAY"—how many times have you heard your friends say it, how many times have you said it yourself?—"someday I'm going to retire, and travel. Someday, when I have enough money, and the leisure to enjoy it, I'm going to go places, and see the world, and treat myself to that trip I've always dreamed about!"

Travel is probably tops on the list of reasons why many thoughtful adults look forward with so much pleasurable anticipation to the harvest years of retirement—travel, together with the escape from the pressure of the day-to-day chores of making a living which is the happy reward of a well-planned maturity.

Also travel is one of the fields of civilized human activity in which maturity has very real and tangible advantages over youth. In practically every facet of travel, except for the obvious factors of physical energy needed to withstand an overrigorous itinerary and strength to wrestle heavy luggage instead of waiting for porters during an occasional minor crisis at railroad station or steamship pier, mature judgment is infinitely more valuable than youthful exuberance.

First and foremost, there's the sense of leisure that comes only with maturity. Leisure to travel slowly and to savor the mood, flavor, and atmosphere of the places you visit as you go.

Younger people are, inevitably, in a hurry. There's a living to be made, a job or a business to be gotten back to, family and friends with high priorities on their time. Frequently this is not true in the case of older people. With maturity comes the wisdom which tells a man or woman that the way to get the most out of life, the secret of working the maximum mileage out of the limited span of a lifetime, is to do first things first, to enjoy one thing at a time, to be able to afford leisure—the rarest of luxuries—rather than the futile attempt to squeeze the most out of the moment by trying to do as many things as possible at once, in a mad omelet of scrambled experience.

As a professional travel writer, I've had many letters asking such questions as, "How many European countries can I see on my two-week vacation?" or "Please tell me how I can cover the greatest amount of territory on my coming trip to South America." But never has any of this type of query come from an older person; always it has been from a young man or woman, or from a person in early middle age—old enough, really, to know better—who mistakes mileage for coverage and confuses mere scampering about the landscape with the intelligent and measured tasting of new scenes and new experiences which is the touchstone of the true traveler.

The Slower You Travel, the More You See

This unhurried sense of time of the mature mind has many practical, tangible advantages when you're traveling. The fastest means of travel is not always the best or the most enjoyable way of getting from one place to another. It is a truism of transportation that the faster you go, the less you see. Thus the walker knows best of all the country through which he travels; the motorist's impression is more blurred and fragmentary, less personal. When you go by train you're still further isolated and insulated from the landscape; and the newer and more modern the plane you're riding in, the higher and faster it will travel, and—generally—the less you'll see. At best your sight-seeing on the average plane trip is confined to some really thrilling vistas shortly after take-off and for a few minutes before landing, especially at night. At worst you'll see nothing, and you'll feel somewhat like a dollar bill being run through a pneumatic tube in a department store between customer and cashier. An airplane trip is the fastest means yet devised by man for taking you from where you are to where you want to be, but from a sight-seeing standpoint it frequently comes close to being a total loss.

The older traveler, unhurried by the pressure of the work-aday world and unharried by the demands of a timeclock itinerary, can use the plane as it is intended to be used, to carry him in speedy comfort over long distances which otherwise would mean long and arduous journeys, to fly him over and above seasonal storms which would make a sea voyage unpleasant at that particular time of the year. But for the interesting and scenic parts of his trip he can use the slowest means of transportation compatible with his comfort and his tastes. And often the slowest—and most enjoyable—transportation is the cheapest way of getting there.

The fastest ships do not necessarily guarantee the most enjoyable sailings for their passengers. Freighters and cargo-passenger ships, which are a cross between a freighter and a liner, have comfortable and often luxurious accommodations for the limited number of passengers they carry. And a loaded freight ship will give you a smooth ride, smoother than a liner sometimes, because its load keeps it low in the water, while liners ride high, where they can be buffeted by breeze and sea.

This is probably a good time to add a reassuring note about

seasickness. At long last this great bugaboo of the traveler—
which might have attacked you on land as car sickness or train
sickness or in a plane as air sickness—seems to be definitely
licked, once and for all. A comparatively new drug called
dramamine, developed right after World War II and tested
on thousands of soldiers on troopships as well as on a great
number of pleasure travelers during the past few years, is
reported to be practically infallible seasickness insurance. You
can get dramamine, a small yellow pill, with a prescription at
a cost of less than ten cents a pill.

Since the improvement of passenger facilities in the newer
cargo ships, they're no longer the shoestring bargains that
freighters used to be before the last war, but considering the
length of time you're partaking of their really handsome bed
and board, freighters are an excellent bet for the budget
traveler. And the more mature voyagers, taking a trip on an
unhurried schedule rather than trying to jam a trip abroad into
a limited vacation period, are in the best position to capitalize
on the advantages of travel by cargo ship. The older person,
too, is likely to find enjoyable the friendlier, more informal
atmosphere among the smaller group of passengers on a
freighter.

By the same token, you might enjoy a trip on one of the one-
class transatlantic liners. You have the run of the ship, which
is smaller and slower than the de luxe liners, and you'll enjoy
the luxurious accommodations for less than you'd have to pay
for first-class passage on the larger ships.

On land, the unhurried traveler can make use of the really
splendid facilities offered by new, modern, postwar motor
coaches. Some of these handsome land yachts, particularly the
tourist busses operated in Europe by Linjebuss, a Swedish
company, and the Italian CIAT company, offer such refine-
ments in bus travel as hostesses, open-view roofs, refreshment

and snack bars, toilet facilities, radio and public-address systems, and individual reading lamps. In France the French
National Railroads offer interesting combined rail-bus itin-
eraries, by which you're taken over the longer distances by
train to a regional center, where you continue on the more
scenic or historic parts of your trip by bus. Also bus travel is
particularly enjoyable in Great Britain and in the Irish Republic, where distances between points of interest are relatively
short.

Off-Season Travel Bargains

Another great travel advantage enjoyed by older men and
women who have been able to withdraw from the pressure of
the workaday world is the opportunity to enjoy off-season
travel. Most Americans take their annual vacations during the
traditional holiday months of July and August. For many it's
a matter of necessity rather than choice. Their vacations are
tied up inextricably with the school holidays; they have children in school or they are teachers themselves. Or midsummer
is the only time they can get away from business or job.

If your children are grown-up, though, and if you're not tied
down to a business schedule, then almost any other time of
year is preferable for your pleasure trip through the United
States or abroad. The July–August tourist traffic jam has
plagued transportation and resort people and vacationists alike
ever since the end of the second world war, and it was pretty
bad even in the late prewar years.

Space at all the best domestic resorts is booked far in advance
of the season, you generally can't get a tourist-class ticket on a
transatlantic liner unless you make a reservation as far as six
months ahead, plane space is scarce, and some of the more
popular cruises are booked months ahead.

If you're willing and able to break with the July–August ritual, though, you'll be able to make your initiative and your good fortune pay off in better accommodations, smoother travel arrangements, and a very considerable saving in fares, sight-seeing costs, hotel rooms, and even meals.

This is due to some very simple and basic economic facts of life in the travel and resort business. Many hotel owners have to keep their establishments operating throughout the year, during the months when they have comparatively few guests as well as in the relatively short season when their places are crowded with vacation visitors. And they are willing, and anxious, to attract more off-season visitors with the inducement of lower rates. In Florida, for example, you can enjoy a fine, ocean-front hotel room at almost any time of the year for a fraction of the cost during the January–March peak season.

Airlines and steamship companies have to stay in business during the off season too, even though some transatlantic liners are put into occasional cruise runs or laid up for overhaul during the winter and airlines schedule fewer flights than during peak seasons. Result is that off-season rates are considerably less than regular fares.

Also you can count on saving about twenty-five per cent on your hotel rooms and meals in most western European countries during the off season, in comparison to height-of-the-season rates.

The whole travel picture is different, too, before and after the July–August peak season. Hotel managers, clerks, bellhops, porters, concierges, waiters, cabdrivers, and chauffeurs of sight-seeing busses, all of whom are harassed into absent-mindedness and seeming discourtesy during the height of the midsummer rush, will give you that personal attention which means so much while you're traveling—if you're one of the relatively few but very welcome visitors who helps them earn a living during the slack season. If you're traveling abroad, you'll sense the difference at once in the warm, personal welcome you'll get from the travel-agency representatives who meet you at boats, trains, and planes.

The fact, too, that life is quieter in tourist centers during the off season should be an added attraction, rather than a disadvantage, for the older traveler.

Nor is the weather the prime factor you might think it is in creating the July–August vacation peaks, except for visitors interested primarily in beach life or active sports, and most mature travelers don't come under this category. Most of the United States is enjoying perfect sight-seeing weather from April through November. And Canada's season is only slightly shorter.

You can expect good weather for traveling and enjoying the European countryside from May through September all the way from Scandinavia south through Holland, Belgium, Luxembourg, all of the United Kingdom, Ireland, all of France, Switzerland, and Austria. Winter weather is sunny and reasonably warm in Italy from Rome south, in all of Sicily, Corsica, North Africa, Portugal, and, in Spain, Madrid, Granada, Seville, Valencia, and all of the southern part of the country. Practically any time is the right time for a visit to the cities of Europe.

Bermuda is an all-year vacationland. It is crowded during the summer, when the weather isn't at its best, but the real height of the Bermuda season is around Easter time. Hawaii is perfect, whatever the season, as the average temperature doesn't vary more than about eight degrees throughout the year.

You can take advantage of off-season rates in Latin America too, although our winter is the height of the tourist season in much of South America, since their seasons are the reverse of ours, and our winter is, therefore, their summer.

Seasons mean little, weather-wise, in Mexico and Central America and northern South America, where weather is usually a matter of altitude, rather than latitude, and there's little change in temperature throughout the year. October through May is the best time for a visit to the Caribbean area, although the Gulf Stream and the prevailing winds so moderate the weather that temperatures vary little between summer and winter in many of the islands of the West Indies.

How to Live Abroad for Less

With the postwar inflation that raised the cost of living so drastically at home, many older people living on fixed incomes began to consider the possibility of living abroad for extended periods in order to make their incomes cover their needs. There are a number of countries in which living costs— for someone whose capital and income are in dollars—are considerably less than in the United States. Devaluation of western European currencies in the autumn of 1949 made living costs even less in terms of dollars and cents, although prices have risen in the tourist centers favored by American visitors, especially during the height of the season. Thus you'll find that living expenses will generally decrease the farther away you go from the capitals, the larger cities, and the resort centers. And you'll be able to realize further savings by traveling during the off seasons and living abroad for extended periods.

Two hundred dollars a month is frequently quoted as an adequate retirement income by insurance companies in advertisements for their annuity programs. While it is becoming increasingly difficult to live on that amount in many parts of the United States, particularly in the large cities, there are a number of places abroad where a single person or a couple can live handsomely for that figure, and many of them—happily— have the sort of warm and sunny climate which is perfect for people enjoying the good life of retirement.

Mexico has become the best single bet in this respect, because it alone of the inexpensive countries can be reached by car or bus, so that you don't have to add any considerable transportation cost to your living expense in figuring your budget for an extended sojourn abroad. The Rio Grande is one of the world's most dramatic frontiers. Cross it and you're in a completely "different" atmosphere, in a different civilization, where people of different racial origins from yours dress differently, speak a different language, and lead different sorts of lives.

Here you'll find almost everything you could possibly ask for in a foreign vacation, or in a prolonged residence away from home. Mexico has color, scenery, glamour, art, music, a fascinating historical and archaelogical background, pleasant climate, fine hotels and comfortable and inexpensive *pensions,* good food, interesting native handicrafts producing wonderful things to buy, cosmopolitan and sophisticated cities, and charming remote villages you can "discover" for yourself.

Since the devaluation of the peso, your dollars will take you further in Mexico, in terms of transportation and living costs, than almost anyplace else in the world. Mexico City, of course, is more expensive than the rest of the country, as might be expected, but even there you'll find costs less than their counterparts in other world capitals. And living costs are apt to be comparatively high also in Acapulco, Mexico's most famous seaside resort, which draws a great number of wealthy Americans during the season. Anywhere else in Mexico, though, you'll be able to live well, even luxuriously, on $200 a month in a villa with a couple of servants or in a lovely and completely charming *pension*.

Most of the islands of the West Indies also represent bargains in living costs for dollar-bearing Americans. Living is inexpensive in the American Virgin Islands, which are rapidly coming to the fore as an outstanding tourist center. In the British West Indies, Jamaica is a favorite with American visitors, and Barbados is one of the least expensive islands of the Caribbean. In Grenada and Tobago, also, you can live very comfortably in a hotel for as little as five dollars a day, including meals, and living costs are considerably less, of course, if you hire a small villa or live at a *pension*. The Republic of Haiti has long attracted a number of American residents because of its climate, its low cost of living, its interesting historical background, and its recent exciting renaissance of painting and music.

For many years, interrupted only by wars, the South of France and the Italian Riviera have been the promised lands of Americans with leisure and the means, however limited, to enjoy it. Nice is a large city, and Cannes, Eden Roc, and Monte Carlo are expensive resorts. Aside from these four points, practically the entire French Riviera offers possibilities for splendid living at a cost considerably lower than anything comparable at home. There are the quiet, almost sleepy seaside towns of Menton, Cap d'Ail, Beaulieu, Cagnes, Golfe Juan, La Napoule, Cavalaire, and Le Lavandou; fishing villages like St. Tropez and Villefranche; well-known resorts such as Antibes, Juan-les-Pins, St. Raphaël, and Ste. Maxime. You can live in a *pension* along the coast for as little as $26 per week, including all meals, or you could rent a villa overlooking the sea for about $85 to $100 a month. A few miles inland, in the wonderful medieval hill towns of Vence and St. Paul, or in the perfume-factory town of Grasse, where the air is always scented with

the fragrance of crushed flowers, you can live nicely for a fraction of what it would cost you in the better resorts along the
coast.

Low costs and excellent living conditions are comparable in
such well-known resorts along the Italian Riviera as San Remo,
Alassio, Rapallo, La Spezia, and Portofino. And practically
every part of central and southern France and Italy offer excellent possibilities for comfortable and sometimes luxurious
living on a modest budget.

In Switzerland, too, despite the fact that the Swiss franc has
not been devalued, you can live very beautifully in the country
and in small villages for a great deal less than it would cost
you in many parts of the United States. Most attractive, from
the aspect of climate and scenery, is the section of the Swiss
Riviera along the northern shore of Lake Geneva from Geneva
to Montreux. Also Austria today is one of the least expensive
European countries for the American visitor.

In South America, Peru has attracted a large number of
American residents living on limited incomes since the slump
in the Peruvian sol a couple of years ago. Because of the exchange situation, it has been possible for Americans with dollar
incomes to live lavishly in Lima for a great deal less than at
home. The fly in the Peruvian ointment is, of course, the fact
that it costs so much to get there ($240 minimum one way on
tourist planes, $445 minimum by passenger-cargo ships), so
that the country is of interest—budgetwise—only to those
visitors who can remain long enough to liquidate the high
cost of getting there through the savings in living costs.

These, however, are very real and appreciable. You can get
a room in one of Lima's less fashionable though nonetheless
attractive hotels for $2.25 a day, including all meals. As a
further example of the cost of lavish living, the extra charge
for meals served in your room is seven cents per meal! Almost

everything about the life of the dollar-bearing American resident or visitor in the Peruvian capital is comparatively inexpensive. A five-course meal in one of the best restaurants in town, including native wine, coffee, and tip, will cost you between 75 cents and $1.50. You can see a reasonably recent American movie in the best film theater in town for 26 cents.

The *pensiones* offer wonderful bargain possibilities if you're staying any length of time, and don't make the mistake of associating them in your mind with anything like Mrs. Murphy's boardinghouse. They are lovely suburban villas in the best residential sections of Lima with a few rooms to rent to congenial guests. The guests live in clean and comfortable rooms and spend much of their time in the surrounding gardens, carefully waited on by squads of servants, for a total cost of about $10 a week, including four excellent meals a day. (The fourth meal is tea, which is almost as important a social function in Lima's international colony as it is in London.)

You can rent a flower-bordered six-room house in Miraflores, one of Lima's finest suburbs, for about $60 a month, furnished. Since the climate is so mild, your heating costs are nil. And you can enjoy having three in help—cook, *mayordomo* (houseman), and maid—at a total cost of little more than $20 a month!

In the food stores, Argentine beef sells for 32 cents a pound, fish at 2 cents a pound, domestic coffee at 40 cents a kilo (about 2½ pounds), sugar at 2 cents a kilo, butter at 39 cents a pound, rice at 2 cents a pound, and strawberries at 10 cents a pound. Cars in Peru are expensive to buy, but if you have yours shipped down from home you can run it at a cost of six to eight cents for a gallon of gasoline. Oil and tire costs are also comparatively cheap.

Now's the Time to See the World

Perhaps, though, you're more interested in seeing the world than in just living abroad and more or less staying put for a while. The dream of most travelers, active and armchair alike, is a trip around the world, and most people have to await the harvest years of retirement before setting about to make the dream come true. It will cost you upward of $1,200, the minimum fare on the Prince Line's British twelve-passenger cargo ships. All accommodations are in two-bedded outside cabins with hot and cold running water. (Rooms with bath are $120 additional.)

The voyage usually takes about four and a half months. Itinerary is dependent on cargo demands, but ports of call generally include San Francisco, Manila, Shanghai, Keelung, Hongkong, Saigon, Cebu, Davao, Macassar, Soerabaja, Batavia, Singapore, Port Swettenham, Penang, Belawan, Colombo, Port Said, Halifax, Boston, New York, Hampton Roads, Panama, and Los Angeles, with possible calls in Japan and Siam. Passengers might be required to find accommodations ashore at their own expense should the ship drydock during the voyage.

For those seeking more lavish accommodations, the American President Lines offers 110-day round-the-world cruises on the *President Polk* or the *President Monroe* for $3,200 to $8,400. The vessels are 10,000-ton sister ships with accommodations for ninety-six passengers each. Itinerary includes Boston, New York, Havana, Canal Zone, Los Angeles, San Francisco, Honolulu, Yokohama, Kobe, Shanghai, Hongkong, Manila, Singapore, Penang, Colombo, Cochin, Bombay, Karachi, Suez, Port Said, Alexandria, Naples, Marseilles, Leghorn, and Genoa. A shorter version of the round-the-word trip can be made in ninety-one days by leaving the ship at New York on the last leg of the voyage. Fares for the shorter cruise run from $2,525 to $6,620.

If you prefer to do your globe-girdling by air, Pan American World Airways has a round-the-world fare of $1,700 which allows you to stop over anywhere along the route for just about as long as you please. Some of the stopover possibilities include Newfoundland, Ireland, England, Belgium, Turkey, Lebanon, Syria, Iraq, Pakistan, India, Thailand, Hongkong, China, Manila, Okinawa, Japan, Guam, Wake, Midway, and Hawaii —although you have your choice of at least sixty-five different itineraries via the Pan American system, and the variations become practically countless when you consider the possibilities offered by joint itineraries with other international airlines and the combined air-sea round-the-world itineraries which may be arranged.

If you're interested in the travel and recreational possibilities in cruises, you'll find a complete menu to suit practically every taste and every pocketbook, from the baberuthian excursions described above down to six-day round-trip cruises between New York and Bermuda at minimum fares of $125.

Not that you have to go abroad to dodge the bad weather on your travels. Great numbers of retired people follow the sun around the seasons, spending the winter in Florida, California, or the Arizona or New Mexico desert country, then moving slowly north in the spring. When they combine their travels with life in a trailer, they usually find that they can live and travel well for little, if any, more than it would cost them to establish a home and live in any one place the year round.

Throughout this chapter I have tried to indicate some of the many advantages enjoyed by older people in their travels. They have the sense of leisure needed to travel slowly and to taste deeply of new experiences. They have the perception that

comes with maturity. Their cultivated tastes enable them to
know what they want on their travels and their vacations.
Their unhurried schedules enable them to take advantage of
slower means of transportation and off-season travel. Their
lack of home and business ties enables them to live and travel
abroad for periods long enough to enjoy the places where
living is cheaper than at home. Their mature tastes qualify
them to appreciate the attractions of places off the beaten
track; they're able to choose resorts distinguished by real
charm, not primarily for whatever night life, gambling, racing,
or sports facilities might be available.

Their shopping problems, needs, and expenses are not as
great as those of younger travelers, since they've passed the
acquisitive part of their life and aren't interested in encumber-
ing themselves with a great many souvenirs of their travels.
Moreover, their gift list is likely to be a great deal less demanding than those of younger people with great numbers of
friends and relations to buy presents for. Also, unburdened by
the necessity of maintaining appearances and keeping up with
the Joneses, they're not forced to be at the smartest resorts just
at the smartest (and most expensive) times, and they can take
advantage of the lower rates (and frequently greater comfort)
of lower-priced *pensions* instead of stopping at the largest and
most expensive hotels.

What You Should Know Before You Start

Against all these advantages, there are a few deterrents to
travel by older people. Those past middle age are, naturally
enough, more likely to be concerned about problems of health
than are younger people. Nevertheless there is little about
travel in most parts of North and South America, western

Europe, or Hawaii which should disturb anyone in reasonably good health, provided he uses the discretion in eating, drinking, and expending his energy which should be the accouterment of a wise maturity.

During the last war and shortly after, would-be travelers were disturbed by horrendous tales of the number and variety of immunization "shots" necessary for the foot-loose. They originated because of the regime of injections which soldiers had to undergo before shipment overseas, and partially because travel and health conditions in some parts of the world immediately after the last war did call for some special precaution. The situation has long since reverted to normal in most of the countries which would be of interest to the pleasure-traveling American. Today the only injection you'll need for your trip abroad will be a smallpox shot, if you haven't had one within the past three years, and this mainly because of the fact that you won't be allowed to re-enter the United States without an immunization certificate not more than three years old.

Beyond that, it's extremely advisable to see your own family doctor before you take any other immunization shots. As a matter of fact, a practical prerequisite for any long trip by an older person should be a visit to his personal physician for a careful checkup. Tell your doctor where you plan to go and what you plan to do, and he'll be able to give you the best counsel on the possible effect of altitude and changed environment on your own physical system, and he'll advise you on what you should and shouldn't attempt to do while you're traveling.

Sometimes typhoid shots are advisable if you're visiting certain rural sections of Mexico, Central America, and the Caribbean area, but your doctor will be the one to decide on that as well as to brief you on things to avoid, such as the drinking of unboiled milk and water and the eating of leafy vegetables, which might be necessary for the areas in which you expect to travel.

Much more important than possible questions of health as a deterrent to travel by older people is the lack of a proper traveling companion. Widows and widowers, bereft of their lifetime companions, are understandably reluctant sometimes to undertake a new and unaccustomed experience alone. They fear loneliness, and they're worried about getting caught up in the details of travel, the business of passports, visas, reservations, tickets, baggage transfers, language differences, foreign currency, et cetera.

Yet, far from being a deterrent, going alone is probably the best way to travel, except in the case of a married couple in no need of a vacation away from each other, or close friends who really know themselves well enough to be sure they won't get on each other's nerves during the course of a long trip or a prolonged stay abroad.

If change is one of the things you're seeking (and it usually ranks high in the reasons why people take a trip), then traveling alone is the best way to get the greatest amount of change out of your travels. Not only are you leaving your accustomed environment, but you're also discarding, at least temporarily, your friends and family, thus leaving yourself completely free to absorb new ideas and new impressions, meet new people and form new friendships. You will, in other words, be doing again the things which too often are done only in one's youth.

Planning a solo trip is really much easier than arranging an itinerary with companions, since you have only your own wishes to consider, but it takes a certain amount of careful thought to decide what your wishes and tastes really are. If you have a tendency to be shy and retiring and don't strike up acquaintanceships easily, then your best bet would be to

o on one of the many group tours organized by the larger
ravel agencies.

The problem of companionship is completely solved for the
ndividual traveler on the group or escorted tour. You'll be
ne of anywhere from a dozen to a hundred people. Some of
hem will be traveling with friends, but many will be making
he tour alone, like yourself, and will be just as anxious as you
re to meet people.

However, if you are reasonably resourceful, enjoy companion-
hip, yet like to take off on your own occasionally, then you'll
robably get more pleasure and satisfaction out of an inde-
endent itinerary, spending your time entirely according to
our own wishes.

Either way you go, you'll find plenty of experts whose help
s readily available to you in planning and arranging for your
rip. There is, first of all, a good local travel agent. He should
ive you personal guidance in tailoring your trip to your own
ersonality, tastes, and pocketbook, as well as the benefits of
is own travel experience in taking most of the burdensome
etails of travel off your mind. He will be able to book all
our ship, plane, train, sight-seeing, and hotel reservations. He
hould help you in arranging for your passport, visas, and
ealth certificates, setting up your baggage insurance and
ransfers. And he'll be able to issue you traveler's checks too.

Remember that, for the most part, it costs you little to make
se of the expert knowledge and experience of a good travel
gent. Commissions paid him by steamship, air, and bus lines
nd hotels are not added to the cost of your trip. In cases where
e charges a reasonable fee to cover his services in arranging a
etailed itinerary abroad, a good travel agent will actually save
ou money by planning your trip efficiently and preventing
ou from making mistakes which might add very considerably
o your travel expenses.

There are, in addition, a number of other excellent sources of information and help in planning your trip. Practically all the states, many resort regions, and a great number of foreign countries maintain tourist information offices, one of whose main functions is answering your questions and sending you leaflets, brochures, and literature about their areas.

The American Automobile Association is your best bet for information about motoring at home and abroad, and most of the large oil companies have good travel information offices. Airlines, steamship lines, and railroads are frequently of the greatest help, especially if you contact them when they're not at the height of their busy seasons.

Finally, good travel books will be invaluable aids in planning your trip, in heightening your anticipation during those busy, dizzy days just before you take off, and in increasing your enjoyment of your travels. Immodestly, but nonetheless sincerely, may I commend to your attention my own book— *Your Trip Abroad, the Handbook of Pleasure Travel.*

THE ANSWER OF CHRISTIAN FAITH

by

REV. DR. JOSEPH R. SIZOO

WE ALL have to learn to live just as we have to learn all other things. Life is a school which does not close until the last bell rings. We go from lesson to lesson, from teacher to teacher, from room to room. We are the pupils; the little world in which we live is our schoolhouse, and the periods of time, our teachers. Each teacher has his own peculiar traits. Some teachers are inspiring; some are difficult; some are hard to understand. Sometimes the classrooms are gray and dull; sometimes they are bright and cheery. Sometimes the classrooms are crowded; sometimes we are the only pupils. The day-by-day issues of life are our textbooks; sometimes the lessons are clear and sometimes they are so confused that it is difficult to find the answers. In each classroom we experience different frustrations and aspirations. Each period requires us to make new adjustments and fashion new patterns, new disciplines, and new values. So it goes on, from the beginning to the end, when the last bell rings and we are dismissed and go home.

Now one of the periods of life which many find baffling, but through which many must pass, is maturity. Why is that so? Who are the teachers and what are the lessons we are required to learn? What are the adjustments which we must make?

What does Christian faith do for us and what assurances does it give?

Each period of life has it own heartaches and misgivings. We look upon childhood in retrospect as a time of happiness, but children would not always agree to that. They regard it as a period of restraint and discipline. We think back upon adolescence with a kind of poignancy and homesickness, but to youth, given to self-expression, it often brings resentment toward those who would interfere with that pattern. Many regard the maturing years of life with satisfaction, but as men pass through that period it is often drab and commonplace. No one period of life is all sweetness. Each portion of time has its own dilemmas and pitfalls. So it is with the later years.

Now there are three attitudes you can take toward growing older: you can try to evade it; you can become embittered by it; or you can accept it.

I. You can try to evade it. In reading history, one of the strange phenomena which runs through the centuries is the way people try to run away from old age. The Egyptians were past masters in the fine art of that evasion. Cosmetics were extensively used by men as well as by women. They used rouge, penciled their eyebrows, plucked out gray hairs which refused to respond to henna treatment. They were dreadfully afraid of growing old and tried to hide it. Indeed, they buried their dead with all kinds of cosmetics, so that in the life beyond they would never show their years.

It is still so today. People often avoid the mention of old age and claim there is no such thing. They try to make themselves believe that old age is a state of mind, not a fact of existence. It is a pleasing illusion, and because it is pleasing, it is so fatal and deadly. You can no more run away from old age than you can run away from your shadow. Sooner or later it catches up with you. It is as certain a period in life as are birth, adolescence, and maturity. All the cosmetic counters in all the corner drugstores cannot hide it. You do not solve the problem of age by running away from it. It cannot be avoided. It comes to all alike, for it is no respecter of persons. It touches rich and poor. You will meet it in the humble cottage and in the palace of the king. It comes to savants and morons.

II. You can become embittered by it. There are people who when they become old become resentful. They chafe under the restraints and limitations which old age brings. They make themselves and everybody around them miserable. They become cynical when they can no longer do what they once did. This attitude poisons the roots of life and sours the soil of living. They turn in on themselves and wrap themselves in bitterness. They feel sorry for themselves. They pin crape on their arms and stand before the mirror admiring their own misery. They are about as comfortable to live with as a sand tick. They seem to repeat each day the Miserere of the jaded writer of Ecclesiastes, "Vanity of vanities; all is vanity."

But this attitude does not solve the problem of old age. Every period of life has its hazards and limitations. No period of life has a monopoly on problems. If old age cannot do everything, neither can youth. That is part of life. The Spanish proverb declares, "You cannot prevent sparrows from flying over your head, but you can prevent them from building their nests in your hair." You cannot prevent the years from crowding, but that is no reason why you should permit that experience to scourge you and rob life of its meaning.

III. You can accept it. We are not responsible for the conditions which crowd about us, but we are responsible for the way we react to them. God did not send us into this world to debate life, but to live it. Nobody promised that life would be a bed of roses. Only when the strings of a violin are pressed is the tone clear. The timber used in building sailing ships comes from the gnarled oaks which have stood up to a thousand storms and wind-swept winters. Most older people would take their first step out of misery into a normal pattern of living if they would recognize they are no longer young and deal with themselves accordingly. Growth implies change; change implies adjustment, and adjustment brings with it problems and strain. Life is a school. Don't be embittered when the lessons are hard. One day you will be glad you learned them. Life is a race. Don't whimper if the road is rough and the journey long. One day you will reach it. Life is a voyage. Don't complain if the storms batter the hull and winds tear the sails; you will arrive one day at your home port. Life is a growth. Don't find fault if the seeds lie smothered and submerged in the cold, dark earth. One day they will bloom and blossom and come to harvest. Take the luck o' the road and accept life where you find it.

> Whichever way the wind doth blow
> Some heart is glad that it is so;
> So blow it east, or blow it west,
> The wind that blows, that wind is best.

Heavenly Days

I wonder if people who are adding to their years fully realize how essential and important they are; how much they contribute to human happiness; what a benediction they are. The world would be a poor place, indeed, without them. We owe them much more than we will ever be able to express. It is true that every period of life has its rewards. The reward of youth is adventure. The reward of maturity is accomplishment. But there are rewards for the later years as well. The orchards are never so wonderful as when, having endured the cold, driven winds of winter, the storms of spring and the heat and drought of summer, the fall comes with its golden colorings. After the tedious plowing and planting, after April showers and summer suns have warmed the earth, after the seeds germinate and green stalks break through the ground, then, in autumn time, to see the fields of corn bending to the wind—there is no joy comparable to that. Charles Cotton put it in verse:

> To read and meditate and write,
> By none offended, and offending none.
> To walk, to ride, sit or sleep at one's ease,
> And, pleasing a man's self, none other to displease.

There come moments in every life when some new glory breaks upon the horizon. It may be a new book you stumbled upon, a new truth which stirs the mind, an unexpected promotion, or some undreamed-of opportunity of service. You never can tell at what bend of the road some new vision may break or some new power may be revealed. It is this which makes life so wonderful. And it can happen in maturity as surely as it happens in adolescence. Indeed, it is more apt to happen in later life because one isn't always running around furiously upon some errand.

Now what are some of these qualities of soul which are developed only in the autumn of life when the early frosts begin to fall? When people ask, "Can any good thing come out of Nazareth?" the voice always replies, "Come and see." Let me name some of them, so we may all look ahead with anticipation.

There is serenity. In later years one becomes conscious of living in two worlds. There is the world of which we are a part for a little while and which we leave, never to return. But there is also that other world which when we enter we shall

never leave. Youth is often a time of restlessness and aggressive-
ness, but with age there settles upon life a calm and the things
of this world are held more loosely.

I once had a friend who was for many years on the New
York Stock Exchange. He had a strange custom. He always
carried a penknife in one pocket and in the other pocket a
sliver of alabaster. When the tension and strain of business
became too great he would leave the floor of the Exchange, sit
for a little while in a chair in an alcove, and carve out of
alabaster the face of one whom he dearly loved and with whom
he had walked through the years. Then a strange calm would
settle upon him and he was ready for another task. It is this
serenity, this sure awareness of the world to come, which is the
reward of maturity.

There is perspective. In youth we are so apt to look at the
world through clothes, bank accounts, and material possessions that it is easy to lose balance and perspective. But in the
later years we are delivered from all that and we see things
more clearly. When Emerson was in his harvest years he wrote,
"Learn to know what the centuries say against the hours."
When we have accomplished that we will have attained perspective and greater simplicity. This simplicity does not mean
so much doing without things, but making the proper use of
the things we have at hand.

When Cecil Rhodes was under bitter attack in the British
Parliament and partisanship railed at him, he often would pull
out of his coat pocket an envelope upon which he had written
the outline and plan for an English-Speaking Union. It restored his perspective. Learn to sit back and say, "Why hurry,
little man?" The man who can take your place had breakfast
somewhere this morning. We must learn to see ourselves and
the world in clearer perspective. We must let the pieces of

life fall into their places and see the jigsaw puzzle as it begins to take form.

The fuller years have their accomplishments too. In the New Testament there is this magnificent sentence. "I will pour out my Spirit upon all flesh . . . and your old men shall dream dreams." Some of the greatest accomplishments have come from men who were old by some people's standards. They have written books, painted pictures, composed music, and written songs which will live through the ages.

What would England have been without its Gladstone? How much we owe today to elder statesmen like Bernard Baruch! Out of weakness strength is born; out of frailty a new faith may triumph; out of blindness may come a second vision. A blind old poet, sitting in abject misery in a household which scorned him, wrote *Paradise Lost* and *Paradise Regained*. Age may live with an eagerness, alertness, and expectancy.

Some time ago I was broadcasting over short wave to Europe with one of the great men of our time, Albert Einstein. Before we went on the air I said, "Mr. Einstein, it is a great honor to be sharing this broadcast with you." He smiled shyly, blushed, and gave me a bit of his philosophy, which accounts perhaps for his great vitality and many interests, "I always try," he said, "to keep the door open a little and to peek behind the curtain." On that basis the later years may well be one of the glorious periods of life.

With the growing years comes the opportunity for counseling. I know of no greater challenge to young people for noble living than to have in their midst someone whose serenity and perspective keeps them steadfast and strong. Their experience can be as a benediction to youth. That is why the picture of Whistler's Mother is hung in the homes of the rich and the poor alike. How many, in hours of despondence and frustration and confusion, run to some grandmother's home—that refuge for broken hearts. Sitting in a chair, taking part in the familiar small talk, gives to youth a sense of steadfastness and comfort.

I look back on such experiences in my own life as one of my best and richest memories. I was brought up in a Godly home. Each day, after each meal, some sentences were read out of the Book. On Sunday evening at twilight time my father would gather us together and read to us out of the Book and then he would lead us in the singing of the sabbatic songs of God and home and heaven. I would rather have that memory than all the bags of gold you can drag across Wall Street. It has become the most steadying factor in my life.

When I had become a minister I was sent to begin my work in Washington. My father, then in a midwestern community, became ill and sank into a coma. Then something strange happened. On Sunday morning, just before eleven o'clock, he opened his eyes and said to those who were with him, "This is Sunday morning. This is the morning Joe begins his ministry in Washington. We shall have to pray for him."

He sat upright in bed, offered his prayer, then closed his eyes, fell back on his pillow, and so passed away. That prayer of my father has haunted and hallowed all the days of my life. To those of you who are advanced in years, let me say: Let no one tell you that your lives do not count. Perhaps in these autumn days you have much more influence than you have ever had in the earlier years.

It Is Not All Gold

While no one can possibly deny the blessings of maturity, certain hazards also come with it. Every period of life has its own anxieties and difficulties. Old age is no exception. It is only when these are honestly faced that adjustments can be made to them and peace of mind be obtained. You never solve problems by being blind to them. What, then, are some of the anxieties that may accompany longevity?

I. There is the feeling of insignificance. People sometimes feel it does not matter to anyone what becomes of them. Many of them think they are in the way, which only makes their lives more complicated. There is nothing left for them to do. It is something, perhaps, akin to injured pride. On the other hand, it is never easy to be passed by. All their lives long they have been in the thick of things and then one day someone else takes their place and, with a pat on the back, an illuminated scroll, or an orchid, they are pushed off into pensioners. That is not easy to take.

There is a vividly illuminating story in the Gospels about this. Early in His ministry Jesus was calling men to become His disciples. One day on the shores of Galilee, He asked a pair of brothers to leave their boats and nets and follow Him. With great enthusiasm and pride they leaped at the opportunity and "they left their father Zebedee in the boat." Can't you see that old father waving a farewell to his sons who were now to become builders of a better world while he was left behind with nothing to do but to eke out an existence, alone! He was to have no part in a great movement which was beginning to surge through the world. I have always thought that Zebedee, left behind, is a picture of a great heroism.

In meeting with a group of ministers some time ago, I suggested that each in turn share with the group some sentence of Scripture which had come to have special significance for him. Among us was an elderly minister who had just been asked to resign his parish because of age. The young minister who was to take his place sat next to him. When the turn came for the elderly minister he arose and with a clear voice said, "He must increase and I must decrease." It was the testimony of a brave soul who met life's changes gracefully. But it is hard to take. To be in the midst of things, to toil and work with the best of them, and then, suddenly, to find that you are no longer to have a part in it, can be a bitter experience.

II. There is the sense of insecurity. Old people become dependent, and as the years increase that dependence upon others increases. They can no longer do everything for themselves. They must count on others to help them and provide for their care and shelter. Those with whom they have walked through the years are slipping away. Companions and friends of many years pass on; those with whom they could once take counsel are gone. They find themselves, therefore, increasingly alone and insecure.

III. There is the sense of regret. I mention this in great tenderness because the feeling of guilt haunts us all through life. But when people become mature they have more time on their hands to think about it. As they look back across the years they see where they missed the road and where they took the wrong turn. But for some blunder, so much more might have been accomplished. So many mistakes have been made which cut off so much of the abundant life. They seem to repeat again the spirit of Hamlet's prayer—O God, I could imagine myself king of the universe if I did not have such dark hours. Life holds so many disappointments. As the years crowd they become aware of their failings and imperfections. It may not do much good to think about all that, because the water which has gone over the dam will never turn the wheels of the mill. It may not help one to weep over opportunities which have been lost, failures which might have been avoided, and harsh words which should have remained unspoken. But there they are, and often in old age people brood over what might have been. In these hours self-criticism is not easy to evade.

IV. There is the fear of death. When the years crowd and people grow old they often repeat what John Burroughs wrote in his old age: "I wish someone would light up the way for me." There is a finality about death, and no mortal has come back from the other side to tell us what it is like. The sense of hesitancy always haunts as life stands on the threshhold of an unknown world. When we are young and life is before us, this is not a deep concern, but when we become old, with time on our hands, we often spend many anxious hours wondering what there is beyond.

The Answer of Christian Faith

What can religion do when the years crowd and time hangs heavy on our hands? What are the resources it makes available? How can it glorify the privileges of old age and also resolve its perils? What is the answer of the Christian faith?

It is well to remember that the Christian religion has no answer to the question Why? If you turn to it or to any philosophy for an answer to that question, you are apt to be disappointed. That is true of everything in life. Even Our Lord, in utter anguish of soul in the garden of His passion at Gethsemane, cried out, "Why?" and there was no answer. But while the Christian faith has no answer to the question Why? it does have an answer to the question How? It makes available unused and undreamed-of resources of power.

I. The Christian faith offers opportunities for service. God has given to each one of us talents. He has made an investment in every life. We are honor bound to make the most of them as long as we live. Because the years crowd is no reason why we should permit these talents to deteriorate by wrapping them up or burying them in a napkin. There is still too much to be done; our very existence implies an unfinished task. It may well be that retirement marks the beginning of a new and creative period in life. It is this attitude to life which lifts old people out of themselves.

Organized religion everywhere is looking for people who no longer do the work of the world but who have energy and talent to advance the interests of community life and the Kingdom of God. There are ministers in the church who throughout the years have rendered effective service. When, through age, they were compelled to give up some of these difficult and grueling tasks, they made themselves available to the Church, with the result that in some respects their influence is deeper and broader than it ever was before. They lead conferences; they counsel their brother ministers; they take part in preaching missions; they serve for younger ministers who are compelled to be away from their work for a little while. The result is that they are reaching more people than ever before and enriching the whole life of the Church.

That is especially true of lay people. There are many churches and community enterprises whose leadership is in the hands of those who have retired from secular work and who now are able to give themselves creatively to the building of these enterprises. Old age gives them the opportunity to do what they have never been able to do and to develop latent talents which enrich their personalities. Organized religion is in desperate need of people like that. I know many churches whose financial problems are in the hands of men of affairs who have retired from business. No church could possibly have afforded their services before, but now, with such funds as they have available, they can enlarge the income of those who have retired from active service and at the same time render a rich service. In my own church in New York for many years the treasurer was a man who had retired from active business; the affairs of the church were never in better hands. One wonders sometimes if we have not gone too far in this deadline of sixty-five. Many are still young at that age and able to serve, but industry and business have no place for them. The Church offers them an opportunity that will advance the interest of religion and make their lives increasingly effective. It may well be that for those who have retired such service will make them more productive and creative than at any other period of time.

II. Christian faith offers not only opportunities of service but opportunities of worship. I knew very intimately a distinguished and eminent jurist who at the time of his retirement suffered an added blow in the death of his beloved companion who had walked through the years with him. He began each day with a ritual. After breakfast he would go to his garden and cut a rose, put it in a little vase, and place it in front of the picture of his wife. Then he would sit in a chair beside it and read out loud a passage of Scripture, as they were accustomed to do through the years. Then he would offer a prayer, always as if his wife were still with him. I never knew him to be disheartened. He was always cheerful and serene. Through worship he had found himself. There are many churches which offer old people the opportunity of meeting for a luncheon, during which they enjoy one another's company and talk on some religious theme. Sometimes they form themselves into Bible-study groups. At other times they gather about a piano and have an old-fashioned hymn sing. Through worship there is made available to them resources of strength and peace.

What is even more helpful is the observance of a quiet time in the morning. Sit down with the Book; read a portion of it day after day until some one thought suggests itself in that reading. Then pause and meditate quietly upon it and pray about it. It is amazing what peace and comfort come to the soul. The Church has prepared month-by-month booklets with daily meditations and hymns and prayers. The church is rich in devotional literature, which it offers to all. Adopt the custom. When the day closes, think of all the evidences of God's care which you have experienced that day, and then, to quote Shakespeare, "To Thee I do commend my watchful soul, Ere I let fall the windows of mine eyes." Through meditation and worship you will recover a steadying faith and hopefulness.

III. But it goes deeper than that. The Christian faith makes available inner resources of power which will glorify the blessings of old age and resolve its hazards.

It has an answer for those who grieve over past failures and brood over their shortcomings. The fundamental affirmation of the Christian faith is that a God of love stands at the center of the universe. We are held by a love that will not let us go. What holds this world together is not chance, but eternal purpose. We are all God's children and never drift beyond His love and care. Nobody can take that heritage from us. We may deface the image of God, but we can never ultimately efface it. There is no grave deep enough to bury it; no darkness black enough to hide it. Underneath and round about us are His everlasting arms. The Christian faith makes available courage to face every difficulty and hazard unafraid. God does not tire of us as sometimes little children tire of their toys when they are worn and toss them on the scrap heap. He carries an eternal concern. He cares what happens to the reed that is bruised and the lily that fades. There are no forgotten with Him.

To all who have grown old carrying secret regrets and disappointments, the Christian faith brings the assurance of pardon, saying, "Go thy way, sin no more." When God forgives He forgets, and wipes out the memory of our shortcomings. "He knows our frame and remembers that we are dust."

Sometimes we become afraid of our friendships. We wonder if these friends would love us were they to know who and what we really are inside of ourselves. These friends place us on pedestals so high until they think we can do no wrong. But what if they really knew our secret foibles and shortcomings? Supposing we stood stark naked before them, without mask or pose. Would they still love us? The assurance of Christian faith is that we have a God who knows all about us and from whom we can hide nothing, and yet who, in spite of our blunders and shortcomings, holds us with a love that will not let us go. The heart of the Christian message is that He lifts the burdens from your back, emancipating you from fear and regret. He makes the miser magnanimous, the calloused compassionate, the sinner a saint.

> I cannot tell you how it came to pass,
> Enough that I am happy and for me,
> A brighter emerald trembles in the grass
> A whiter sapphire melts into the sea.

IV. Then, too, the Christian faith offers the assurance that God will never desert us. We do not make our way alone through the world. Faces may change, conditions may alter, but He is the same yesterday, today, and forever. We may change, but He does not. He is not an indifferent spectator standing on the side lines, judging us. He is too good to let us alone and too great to let us drift. God is love. The symbol of that love is a circle which has neither beginning nor ending, but goes on forever and ever. He does not cease to be God because we grow old. He is as much in the dusk as in the dawn. Darkness and light are both alike to Him. He does not bow

Himself out of life when the night closes in upon the weary pilgrim.

Sometimes with age you feel yourself let down and look back over the years and run your finger over the threads of memory. Has He ever failed you? Never! You can see the pieces slowly, but surely, falling into place. There are a few more which puzzle you. Give God time. He will show you where they belong until the picture is perfect. The end of life is not a mournful elegy, but a hymn of victory. Behind the mutable stands the immutable. We change, but He remains abiding and forever, bridging the chasm of the years and spanning the gulf of the centuries. So wide and deep is the concern of God, so sure is His inexhaustible power, that though the mountains fall and the hills be removed, yet shall His kindness not desert us. He is still the refuge of the weary, a shadow of a mighty rock within a desert land. The love of God is greater than the sorrows of men, and the redeeming power of Omnipotence mightier than the sins of men.

V. There is one final assurance which Christian faith brings to strengthen the inner resources in old age. It is the assurance of immortality. We know that we were not born for death. Through the long ages men in every generation have asked, "If a man die, shall he live again?" The Christian faith replies with the assurance, "Because I live, ye too shall live also." This lies at the bottom of everything that makes life worth living. One need not be afraid of growing old. In his *Pilgrim's Progress,* Bunyan describes Christian standing on the hill called "clear," looking for the gate of the eternal city: "They thought they saw something like the gate and also some of the glory of the place—which when I had seen I wished myself among."

I once had a friend whose name was Albert Payson Terhune, the inimitable writer of inimitable dog stories. One day he contracted with a publisher to write a book on immortality.

Shortly after his death his family found this incomplete manuscript, like an unfinished symphony. The last sentence of the last paragraph of the last chapter of that manuscript was: "God always finishes His sentences." That is the deathless assurance of Christian faith. In reality there is no death; at best it is only a transition. One day the boatman with silver oars will take us across the river that has no bridge to the shores of Emmanuel's Land, where we never grow old and never know pain, and where "Nearer, My God, to Thee" is no longer a hymn of hope but an everlasting experience. If once again this assurance could lay hold on life when the years roll on, there would come a new sense of expectancy as we wait for daybreak when the shadows flee away.

THE CATHOLIC VIEWPOINT

by

REV. JOHN L. BONN, S.J.

EVERYBODY knows that we Catholics have tremendous respect for antiquity and for authority. We have been complimented on our two thousand years of culture and on our veneration of tradition. There have even been some charming things written about our policy of being governed by a group of wise old men in Rome.

Now while there is a good deal of truth in these flatteries, like most flatteries, we set precious little store by them. The difficulty is that they disregard distinctions which we believe fundamental—the distinction between reverence and obedience; between experience and the right to command. We do not obey because our superior is wise or old but because he has received his authorization from Almighty God, and this, we think, is a very important philosophy for our age and for our aged.

In the service, as I well know, the "gripes" of the enlisted men were all based on the idea that they knew more than their officers, and while this may well have been true, it was quite beside the point. The officers, for their part, often assumed that their commands were not merely statements of objective law but were personal prerogatives and that any disobedience was a direct attack on themselves. The difficulty with both officers and enlisted men was that most of them had been trained in the "Mother-knows-best" school of authority, the only trouble with that being that Mother may not know best.

In present first-generation education, the son, at an early age, surpasses the intellectual and social level of the father. If obedience is based on respect for superior wisdom, the entire domestic structure crumbles, bringing untold heartache to the old and heartbreaking catastrophe to the young.

We Catholics believe, therefore, that the distinction between reverence and obedience is important. We believe that obedience is not to be identified with the expediency of respecting the judgment of one's elders. It is a duty correspondent to that authority vested by Almight God in one who has the right to command. The superior is the vessel of God's law; the subject obeys God, not the whim of man. The superior's orders are valid only when they are just; the subject's obedience is virtuous only if it is to a just command.

What is more pertinent here, of course, is the application of this theory to the home. We believe that God bestows authority on parents through the Sacrament of Matrimony, so that they possess not only natural but also supernatural rights. God gives them special helps called graces in their governance of their children, and as our history shows, Catholic parents are tremendously aware of these rights and tremendously and properly jealous of them.

Again, in our philosophy, while the father is the head of the house in a very strict and Pauline sense, yet authority over children is shared by the mother. It is a mutual right, and trivial disagreements and incidental attractions cannot lightly sever this common bond of duty toward children. It is this, I think, that goes far toward explaining the superior marital concord of our people.

Then what of the later days? Inevitably, at some time of

life, rights must be surrendered. Parental prerogatives over the child are ceded; even the power of position must be given up with retirement. It is here that the long years of thinking with the Church assume importance.

The Authority of the Parent

First of all, the child has always had obligations toward the parent—to love him as the author of his existence, to reverence him because he is his superior, and to obey him as the delegate of God. The first two obligations never cease. The parent may justly expect to be supported in moderate comfort through his old age, and there is no social stigma attached to this. It is quite usual and is expected in modern society. Indeed, we look on anything else as shameful.

As for the relinquishing of authority, remember that the parent has held it only as a delegation from God. Now God removes the delegation. That is all. It is hard for a man to surrender authority when he has exercised it in tyranny, but renunciation is not difficult when it is the abandonment of a burden.

Besides, the authority of the Catholic parent has always been limited. It has been limited by several inalienable rights which the child possesses. The choice of vocation is the child's choice; the choice of a partner in marriage is the child's, and it is here particularly that the parent can only assert his advisory right, his right to be respected and reverenced, the rights of his greater age and experience and wisdom, but not the right of command. Indeed, where such authority is assumed without justification and coupled with threats and violence, the Church will declare null the marriage of the child. It did so in one very famous American case.

So the parent has always known the limitations of his authority. He has known, too, that this authority was circumscribed by ecclesiastical and civil law. Therefore it is no new thing that is facing him—this knowledge of the transitory and limited nature of his power. Add to this his fundamental concept of delegation by God and he is saved the heartache that is just retribution to the dictator.

Now there remains to the elders the right of receiving reverence and love. It is perhaps our practice of these virtues, so obvious to those outside the Church, which has caused the confusion about our whole philosophy, for only as a quality distinct from a just concept of obedience can that other virtue, which we call filial piety, truly emerge. As a separate virtue it has a special beauty. It is resplendent in all the antiquity of our tradition, though even the word *tradition* has for us a special and dogmatic meaning above the mere transmission of beliefs. Yet our love and veneration of age has been so apparent and so magnificent that it has, as I have said, somewhat obscured the major issue of our doctrine on authority. There is clear cause beyond moral duty why these virtues should flourish among us.

In its very beginning Christianity brought about many changes. It was a pagan custom to abandon the useless old on a hillside where they might die by exposure to the elements, a fad which I am distressed to discover is again advocated by modern pagans in moderated and less painful medical forms. If the aged and the useless have anyone to thank for their preservation in life, it is most certainly the Church.

With Christianity the whole attitude toward old age changed. One has only to read the strictures of Horace, the rather more mild caricature of Nestor in Homer, the challenge to contemporary opinion present even in Cicero's "De Senectute," and compare them with the accounts written two hundred years later about the Fathers of the Desert. It is significant that the Christian concept of veneration and love was to replace the savage ridicule of the old until the renaissance of paganism —to which even Shakespeare partially succumbed.

There is no purpose here in tracing the development of Catholic veneration of the aged, but it is noteworthy that Christ did not present us with an example of old age, leaving that one thing to his followers.

The genealogy of Christ begins with the story of the aged Sara bearing to her aged husband, Abraham, the child Isaac, who also prefigured on the mountain the sacrifice of Christ offered to His Heavenly Father. The Gospel of Luke tells of the aged Elizabeth bearing to her incredulous husband Zachary the fruit of their old age, John, the precursor of Christ. Then the story has grown, and has been generally credited for centuries, that Anne and Joachim, in their great old age, gave birth to Mary, the Mother of Jesus. Perhaps even with less authenticity the figure of Joseph has grown older and older through the years and in the popular mind until now he is depicted as a very old man indeed. In this connection I cannot refrain from mentioning a more modern figure, and one still more familiar, who was after all a genial old saint of ours and whom we venerate as Saint Nicholas, but whom, out of pleasant familiarity, the world at large has nicknamed Santa Claus.

It is no wonder, with this tradition of devotion for the aged saints, and because of the surrounding of age with a halo of affection, that the old have shared in the warmth. I have always thought it rather a touching little story that a child once shouted in delight when he saw Mr. Monty Woolley, who was certainly revered for attributes other than benignity, "Oh, Mama, look at Santa Claus!" I really believe that there is something a little beyond humor in the association of white whiskers with wonder and trust.

Now this is a far cry from the attitude of youth toward the pagan old men, but then the Fathers of the Desert were the very antithesis of the pagan old men. Far from praising times past, they repudiated them roundly; far from shuffling around in the slippered pantaloon, they wore no shoes at all; and far from being garrulous, there was one of them who reproved himself for having broken silence once in seven years. When they did speak, their speech was extraordinarily pithy. Their sentences crackle like whips over the centuries. And the odd part of it was that the younger monks accepted their rebukes and built their cells nearer and nearer to their fathers until the desert was a desert no longer. So it was that Christian civilization itself was born and the new world was begotten of the aged. We of the Church give tribute to these old men for our Harvest Years.

At the same time there was another group of men also called by that peculiarly Catholic and distinctively Pauline name, "Fathers." They were the Fathers of the Church. Some of them were also Fathers of the Desert, but in addition they were the great teachers, the transmitters of primitive tradition. The Apostles themselves had instructed the earliest of their number, and through an unbroken succession the apostolic truth comes to us. What the Fathers teach universally we hold as matters of faith. Before every new pronouncement of dogma their ancient doctrine is investigated. In every textbook of theology their argument has preponderant value. We do not let them die. These are our fathers.

There is, of course, an even more familiar use of the word Father. It is the fatherhood of the priest, something so intimately Catholic that it is almost impossible to expect anyone else to understand the relationship of the Catholic layman to his priest, his father. For this man, like any father of the flesh, has the true prerogatives of fatherhood. As the instrument of spiritual existence and sustenance, he is entitled to love; as the delegate of God, he commands obedience; as a superior, he is reverend, and by that title he is also called. In the venerability of his position, he is given the respect due to the aged. He is, whatever his actual years, by office an ancient, and so we call him the priest, the presbyter, which word means old, the old one.

The young priest performing his sacred ministry is not young—he is immeasurably old. As he vests for the celebration of the Mass, clothing himself in the symbolic garments of ancient Rome, he casts aside his youth and becomes not a man but a symbol. He is the kind of symbol that passes from metaphor into spiritual actuality. Soon he will stand in the place of the ageless Godhead and be of no age and of no time but of the eternal priesthood of Melchisedech. All about him, as in the actions he performs, will be reminders of his antiquity.

Before this, when he was an acolyte, three times at the foot of the altar he said the words of Psalm 42, "To God who giveth joy to my youth." But now, as celebrant, he will say them no longer. As a deacon, he genuflected without support, but now he will lean on the altar and assist himself to rise. As an officer of the Mass, he had had many changes of position, often going up and down the steps in the rubrics of the ceremony, but now he rarely descends, and then only to sit.

Now the priest is no longer young, but a symbol, and the symbol is that of the old man. Everything he does proclaims his venerability. He will expect from his people that respect which is not due to himself but to his priesthood, and the old kneeling before him will not think it strange to call him father.

In the confessional, where for hearing some classes of persons he is bound by canon law to have reached at least middle age, he will be not only a judge and a doctor but also a father. In witnessing the marriages of his people he is directed to give them that fatherly advice that is proper from the old to the young. In Holy Communion he feeds his children with the Body of God. In his preaching he directs not as one voicing opinions but as one speaking with authority. In all his actions, in all his functions, he is the priest, the old man.

He himself is subject to another—to his Bishop, whose pectoral staff is not only a symbol of the shepherd but is in fact something for him to lean upon; and the Bishop is subject to the common father of Christendom, who, though a thrice-crowned emperor, is known only as the Pope, *Il Papa,* The Father.

The Veneration of Age

Here, then, is the whole hierarchy of veneration for age. This Church, ruled so exclusively by at least the symbolically aged and generally by the actually aged, considers old age as the harvest years of life. Has it not given itself over for its governance, its protection, its very existence, to the aged? It hears with sublime amusement the talk of the necessity of young blood in the politics of nations and smiles at the repudiation of old men upon the supreme bench of justice, while its elders carry on the affairs of their two worlds, the lasting and the everlasting. And it is always young. But that is because the Holy Ghost which abides in it is beyond time.

The Church can never forget the services of the old. We have had Pope Leo, on his ninetieth birthday, replying to a cardinal who had whispered, "May Your Holiness live to be a hundred," the very apt rejoinder, "Why should Your Eminence put limitations to divine providence?" Pope Leo reigned for more than twenty-five years. He was an old man who, if the myth of the aged had been true, should have been reactionary but who actually drafted the encyclicals on labor which contained social contributions that the world took only about half a century to catch up with. Achille Ratti, Pius XI, thundered away against Nazism and warned till his dying breath against encroaching Communism. There were no symptoms of senility in him. Newman, who was made a cardinal at seventy-eight, wore the purple for twelve years, writing in the English of angels. The president of Manhattanville College ran upstairs to greet me and said, "Oh, I keep forgetting I'm seventy! The trouble is that the body ages but the soul never grows old." And we believe this on faith.

But these are, of course, people of the Church. There is the laity as well.

It was in her youth of seventy that Miss Agnes Repplier was chosen to represent the United States at the Spanish Exposition, and though she seemed to be doing a great many things, her only complaint was that she did not have enough to keep her busy. At eighty, of course, she produced a book of essays ranging from a delicate handling of the episode of Byron's daughter Alegra to a defense of the character of cats, but, most important, she gave an account of Catholic boardingschool life so thoroughly saturated with humor and youth and spirituality as to be utterly timeless. Speaking of her eighties, she thought it foolish to talk about facing them bravely, remarking that hundreds of people were facing them necessarily and she saw no particular reason for being heroic about it. Her contribution toward the philosophy of growing older was simple sanity.

Then in the literary world we have only recently lost Mr.

Meynell and Mr. Bruce, who, pressing on toward their centuries, gave shining examples to their intimates and to their world—for this also is a duty of the aged too often overlooked, to be an example to following generations, and in this both Mr. Bruce and Mr. Meynell were heroic.

Of course no mention of the outstanding and exemplary aged would be complete without a word about Mr. Connie Mack, and I should hesitate indeed to offend the small and large boys of America by omitting him. As I believe that he is at the moment turning his hand to autobiography, we may well let him tell his own story, though I am a little regretful that he is finding time for this indulgence. I would rather recall what Mrs. Charles Perkins said to me recently—and I hope she will forgive me for suggesting that she is somewhat beyond middle age. She showed me a painting which she had just done and which had been hung and of course had won a prize; she pointed to her piano, where a pile of musical manuscripts lay; she gestured toward plans for carrying on the liturgical movement in which she is now engaged and she said, "Someday I hope to write my memoirs. But you see there isn't time yet! There is so much that is going to happen that I want to wait until at least most of it is done."

The keynote of this activity is perhaps more than the mere looking forward, the anticipation of the immense amount of work that still remains. It is the absolute, settled assurance that true life does not begin at forty but with eternity, and that the nature of that eternal life depends a good deal on the employment of every moment squeezed out of this life.

Speaking of forty reminds one inevitably of Rose Hawthorne Lathrop, who at forty had already lived two full and seemingly adequate lives. At that age she decided to begin her cancer foundations, and thirty-five years later, when the cornerstone of her great hospital was blessed, she said, "Tomorrow, the real beginning!" For her it was the real beginning, for it was on that day that she entered into eternal life.

Yet when we Catholics think of the contributions of our active older people and the planning beyond their own lifetimes, there is, of course, one figure which stands out above all the others, and that is Michelangelo, to whom his followers, aged seventy, were mere whittling schoolboys.

He was nearly ninety when he put away his chisel, and the work was still not finished. He would never see it finished, he knew, and the problem of time had always haunted him even when he was much younger. They had wanted him to hurry. They had torn down the scaffolding to see how far his work had progressed. But that was years ago. They had told him that he was too old then. If he had let himself believe them he would not have had the scaffold put up again and have finished the ceiling. Now, at eighty-nine, there could be no scaffolding, no more strong strokes of the chisel against marble or cuts of pigment with the knife, like slashes against stone. Yet, he smiled, he was still not through. He had fooled them again with this host of unfinished things, with his clay models, with the plans still lying there from which any drudge could construct. No. Not any drudge—but this younger talent which he had trained, going on and on forever through men yet unborn who would continue what he had started until St. Peter's, the center of the world, would stand forever fresh and new and young.

Then Michelangelo Buonarroti, in his ninetieth year, laughed and cried out, "My youth has been renewed like the eagle!"

Certainly these are but a few of the contributions the aged have made to the Church—the pontiffs, the builders, the writers, the sportsmen, all of them exemplars of the young. Theirs has been the same spirit which animated all our active nuns in their cloisters and our unknown priests laboring in the jungles. It is the work, not for self, but for Christ. What labor for self is worth while to the very old? They will never see it finished. Theirs must be the divine cloistered motive which they have seen all around them throughout their lives—zeal for the Kingdom of Christ.

So they go on. But what of those who cannot—those whose age has brought infirmities and incapacity? We offer them no panacea, no assurance that medicine or machines will extirpate debility. We think that we bring them something better—we offer them a definite place in life; we give them value and dignity; we welcome them into the human race.

We offer them four freedoms from the fear of loss—of position, of loved ones, of physical well-being, and of life.

Our whole teaching on the performance of the duties of one's state now becomes important. From earliest infancy our people have been taught that the only thing worth doing is what God asks of them. As a cultural group we are not noted for ambition, and indeed our acceptance of poverty is frequently charged against us. Our defense is that this minor vice is a corruption of a major virtue. To us the things of the world are quite secondary to the things of eternity, and we have pondered so much on the simile of the lilies of the field and the parable of Dives that perhaps some of us have forgotten the simile of the barren fig tree and the parable of the talents. In any case, we really believe that it does not make very much difference whether we *do* anything or not, provided that we bear and suffer all in Christ.

Having this attitude of mind, it is not too difficult to give up worldly position. Since the job we held was only one way of saving our souls, we are now quite willing to try some other way. We remember Thomas More and how, when he ceased to be chancellor and lost his home, he replied to his wife's worries, "But, my love, we have never been beggared and perchance we shall be more joyous in beggary." As everyone will admit, he was the model Catholic layman.

However, in this adaptation to enforced idleness, our times give us an advantage, and we hope that we have learned how to fill our extended leisure with prayer. Remember, we think prayer is better than work, having also read the gospel of Mary and Martha.

Yet with the loss of position comes inevitable dependence. But almost the first lesson we learned in our ascetics was the tremendous social lesson of the reliance of all creatures on each other and all on God. What is this myth of independence, anyway? Are we not dependent for everything we have, for the clothes we wear—did we sew the cloth or card the wool or shear the sheep? Did we, by a wild surmise, create the lamb? This trivial degree of further dependence upon those who love us is no matter at all. We have our own way of rewarding them, better than we have done before, in the beads that slip through our fingers hour after hour. Can we feel needless and useless when always we have put the proper value on spiritual over temporal actions?

Freedom from Fear

Now we can rest. Now, in the harvest time, we can pray. As in that lovely story that James Truslow Adams tells of the South American Indians who would not press on until their souls caught up with them, now we too can sit down from the overanxieties and the hastes of our past when there was no time at all and distraction in everything.

Next we have freedom from the fear of suffering the physical handicaps of the old. We Catholics do not fear suffering. Above the bed is the figure of the Crucified, and at the end of the rosary, the Cross. Over and over again we have asked Our Lord to let us share in His agony that we might have part in the redemption of the world. The little pains and aches we have now are small enough, God knows, and scarcely do for our own sins, let alone for the sins of others.

You see, we believe in the value of suffering; we are not one with the pagans who think it worthless. We know that Christ was God. He suffered, so suffering must be good.

But what of the bystanders? We Catholics believe that the care of the aged presents opportunity for patience and service and charity such as nothing else does, or why should our women dedicate their lives to the abandoned old? The sisters in orphanages and schools see growth and a life ahead; but the sisters in homes for the aged see only advance into a future unending, and their consolation is in the freed souls in heaven.

There remains, then, the fear of the loss of loved ones, not only by death but by the transference of affection from parent to wife or husband or children. In a true Catholic home this cannot happen. There is not a transference of affection, which means a loss of affection, but a new and different affection that is healthily distinct from the love of a child for its parent. God, Who demands that husband and wife love one another, also demands that children retain their love for their parents. He cannot make either duty impossible. The love must be different, and if it is not, even worldlings know now what we have always known—that then it is a psychic disease, or what we, in our quainter terminology, have called an inordinate affection.

True love is not a disease. Beyond being the most beautiful of emotions, it is also the most beautiful of virtues and it is a virtue infinitely diffusive. A true and ordered love extends the relationship of the aged to their children-in-law and to their grandchildren. It is a widening, an expansion, not a contraction or a deprivation. The position of the grandparent in a Catholic home is indeed a golden one.

The most joyful recollections of my childhood are connected with an old gentleman named Mr. Burke, who lived in our neighborhood and who adopted me as a kind of extra grandchild. He used to come around every sunny afternoon, always with a youngster on his shoulder, and tell us endless stories about Watergrass Hill and the Bells of Shandon in a language that Yeats would have envied. And the details of his inventions! There were no wee folk, no pixies, but the angels that came and went, the holy ones who performed their incredible miracles, peopled all our land then with an illumination until the Island of Saints lived again in Waterbury, Connecticut. The audience, though always increasing, was basically the same—for, save for myself, they were all his own grandchildren. As soon as he could set the one down, there would be another ready for the shoulder.

I do not suppose he ever knew what he did. He was too old then to work and him telling stories all day to the young ones around him! But when one small boy grew up and read his Blake and came to the part about the angels in the trees, he put down the book and said to his own surprise, "Oh, shure, they have better than that in Watherass Hill."

The angels, you see, live all about us, and the saints in the heavens are waiting for us and praying for us too. Our Lady is there, the mother of us all. There are some whom we have sent on before, but we have prayed for them and have known we could help them as the Maccabees taught us, and after we go they will be waiting in the bright glory of God for our coming.

We believe in all that. We believe in the resurrection of the dead and the life everlasting and the communion of saints— in which we believe that we truly have communication because we believe very simply in immortality and are confident that our loved ones are alive. For us there is no fear that death will be only a dreamless sleep and annihilation—only the certainty of God's grace and the hope of His mercy and the truth of eternal reward.

I have seen our people die, so many. There is one death though, above all the others, that I think was most typical.

She was a very old lady, and I tried to break it to her gently, and I said, "Aunt Lizzie, as long as I'm here, wouldn't it be a good idea to bring you the Last Sacraments?"

She rose up on her pillow and looked at me squarely. "Now, see here," she said, "I've been a Catholic for eighty-six years, and I've paid my way all the time, and I want everything that's coming to me." So I anointed her, and then we recited the Rosary and the prayers for a happy death until there was no more to be said, and the family rose from its knees and went out. I leaned over her then. "Is there anything else I can do for you?" I asked her.

She rose up again and said, "Yes, there is. I've always celebrated every sacrament I've ever had and I'm going to celebrate this one. Go on downstairs to the cellar and look under my gardening gloves, where no one can get at it, and fetch me the bottle of champagne that's there. We'll drink it to this."

She was right. It was something to celebrate. She was ready to receive what we call the *Magnum Donum,* the great grace of final perseverance. Of the deaths I have witnessed, I think this was the most edifyingly Catholic and the most truly valiant.

So this is the way we are. I fancy sometimes that we are most fortunate because through long lives our aged have believed that prayer was more blessed than deeds and sacrifice more holy than possession. They have sent their girls off to the cloistered convent believing in the vast value of their prayers. They have said farewell to their sons at the gates of La Trappe because they have credited the injunction to penance. Now they themselves can cultivate the cloistered virtues. Never before could they practice them, because of the endless activities, the constant distractions. Never the great silence for prayer. But now it is here.

It seems to them, then, that all the little details of their living, their envies and ambitions, their bothers, were trivial. Before this their world was circumscribed, limited to their own cares, but now it is enlarging and the great interests of God come into them. Their beads slip through their fingers for the Intention of the Pope, for the Spread of God's King-dom, for the Conversion of Russia. Things once read hurriedly in headlines are now concerns of their spirit. Now there is time. Now there is cloister.

Our aged have risen through renunciation and sacrifice, through all the monastic virtues of penitence and prayer, into the wide zeal for the saving of the world, until at last they are ready to be admitted into the celebrating love that is the desire of union.

Then, indeed, come their Harvest Years.

MATURITY IN JEWISH TRADITION

by

REV. DR. DAVID DE SOLA POOL

NATIONS pride themselves on their age. The immemorial tradition of a people such as the Jewish or the Chinese gives to that people mellowness of character, deeply rooted strength, a sense of assured status, and something of the mature wisdom that is born of experience.

As it is with a people as a whole, so should it be with individuals. Age should be something in which a man can take pride because it brings to him fulfillment of the promise of his budding years, a status of honor, and the calm perspective which the experience of years can give.

This is axiomatic in the thought of the Jew. The millennial Jewish tradition rooted in the Bible bids one turn to the elders to learn the true values of life. "Remember the days of old, contemplate the years of the many generations. Ask thy father and he will declare thee, thine old men and they will tell thee." (Deuteronomy 32:7.) For three thousand years Jewish tradition has accorded to elders special recognition, honor, and function.

It has also consistently counseled men and women to make a full and wise use of their advancing years. For the tradition that is based on the Bible is realistic in its recognition of the physical limits to the number of our years. Man is but "flesh and his days shall be 120 years." (Genesis 6:3.) This is regarded as the utmost limit of life which we can ever hope to attain. Ordinarily one hundred years is considered the most to which man may look forward. In the happy, restored Jerusalem, "there will not be heard any more the sound of weeping or the sound of outcry; there will never more be thence an infant of days or an old man that will not fulfil his days, for the youngest shall die at a hundred years . . ." (Isaiah 65:19, 20.) The Psalmist, considering the fleeting character of life, allots us still fewer days on earth: "The days of our years are threescore and ten years, or with vigor fourscore years." (Psalms 90:10.)

Moreover, the Biblical tradition vividly recognizes that length of days necessarily brings with it increasing limitations. After the Psalmist has allotted to man the hope of attaining a maximal fourscore years, he adds, "yet is their boast only toil and sorrow, for quickly life passes and we fly away." (Psalms 90:10.) Neither the Psalmist nor the Preacher of old knew today's miracles of medicine and health conservation which make it possible for us to live through our advancing years with only slowly diminishing physical vigor. The Preacher, Ecclesiastes, drew a vivid picture of the physical disabilities and decrepitude to which the aging could look forward: "Remember thy Creator in the days of thy youth, ere the days of evil shall come, and the years draw nigh when thou shalt say 'I have no pleasure in them,' ere the sun and the light, and the moon and the stars are darkened and the clouds return after the rain [failing eyesight], in the day when the keepers of the house [the hands] shall tremble, and the strong men [the legs] shall be bent, and the grinders [the teeth] cease because they are few, and those that look out of the windows [the eyes] shall be darkened, and the gates on the street [the lips] shall be closed as the sound of the grinding is low, and one shall start up at the voice of a bird [inability to sleep], and all the daughters of song shall be low [increasing deafness]. Also one shall fear a hill [shortness of breath], and terrors shall be on a journey [difficulty of walking]. And the almond tree [grey hair] shall blossom, and the grasshopper shall be a burden [inability to carry even a small weight], and the caper-berry [appetite and passion] shall be weak, for man will be going towards his eternal home and the mourners go around in the street; ere comes the time when the silver cord is severed, and the golden bowl shattered, and the pitcher broken at the fountain and the wheel fallen shattered into the cistern, and the dust shall return to the earth as it was, and the spirit shall return to the God who gave it." (Ecclesiastes 12:1-7.)

This was the picture of physical breakdown that was familiar to our ancestors in Bible times. Centuries later it was the same as seen by the rabbi who in characterizing the fourteen ages of man said of the later years of human life, "60 is age, 70 old age with the hoary head, 80 survival for exceeding strength, 90 bent decrepitude, and 100 as though one were already dead and passed away completely from the world." (Mishnah, Aboth 5:24.) Similarly, another rabbi, looking on the physical disabilities which beset old age, could exclaim, "Youth is a crown of roses; old age is a crown of rods." (Talmud, Sabbath 152a.)

Today old age has largely lost these physical terrors. Many of the encumbrances of advanced years which the Preacher saw as inseparable from age have been largely overcome by the techniques of modern science. Eyeglasses correct defects of vision that come with the years. Artificial teeth and dentures preserve the "grinders" in the mouth and hold firm their lips, "the gates on the street." Today many are the venerable elders who know the blessing signaled out as so exceptional in Moses that in extreme old age "his eye was not dimmed, nor his vigor abated." (Deuteronomy 34:7.)

In our days maturity need seldom fear such physical handicaps. In an era of total world wars it should rather fear the unhappiness of which it may be the witness and the living memory. When the patriarch Jacob first came before Pharaoh, he was asked by the king, "How many are the days of the years of thy life? And Jacob said to Pharaoh, 'The days of the years of my earth's sojourning are one hundred and thirty years. Few and evil have been the days of the years of my life . . .'" (Genesis 47:8–9.) Jacob had known enforced flight from home, years of toil for a deceitful and exacting master, bereavement in the early death of his beloved Rachel, and mourning for his darling son Joseph.

Life's True Perspective

Growing old is not simply a chronological condition of arteries, tissues, and organs physiologically aging with the passage of time. Privations, hardships, excessive toil, insufficient sleep, homelessness, bereavement, mourning—all such experiences as these, which Jacob had known, made him look back on his length of years as on something quite other than an unmixed blessing.

But here again our greater capacity today to control the physical forces and conditions which surround us can lengthen our expectation of life and rob old age of many of the accumulated sorrows and burdens that have traditionally been considered as inseparable from longevity. Scientists have shown that length of life can be materially affected by controlling outward conditions. Thus, on the purely physical plane, the life span of an insect has been varied from twenty days to six months, according to the temperature in which it is kept. So may our life span vary according to the fever or the restful coolness with which we live, the excitement or the calm of the spiritual atmosphere in which we habitually move, the sorrow or the joy, the worry or the serenity which we allow to possess our lives.

We can largely control and make beautiful the character of our individual living so long as the world remains sane. Only if it gives itself up again to the suicidal madness of total war will those of us who may escape with our lives re-echo the despairing words of the Preacher when he looked out on life and saw the torturous cruelty of oppression which marked social and economic life in his days: "Then I praised the dead who have already died above the living who still are alive." (Ecclesiastes 4:2.)

We misjudge life's perspectives when we set old age at the center of its panorama. Only for a nonagenarian or a centenarian may length of years become a primary consideration. For others it is often quite an unimportant concomitant of a full and interesting life. Let us not forget the proudly hopeful mother who went to visit her daughter's violin teacher and asked him how the child was progressing. The answer that she received was, "If enough time is given her, she will become very famous." "Ah! She will be a great musical artiste!" "No! If she is given enough time and she lives long enough, she will be very famous—for her exceptional age." Old age must not be allowed to become the paramount value in life. It must be an incidental in a life that has rich values in its own quality of living.

On the other hand, age may not be disregarded or negated. Not even a woman should yield to the weakness of concealing or disguising her age. It is told that, exasperated by a nagging wife, a husband lost his temper and, turning on her, said, "You are a troublesome, nagging, bad-tempered, disagreeable old woman." "Old," she replied, "whom are you calling old?" We have to recognize the centrality of character in the values of life, and we must put old age in its commensurate place among them. "For honorable old age is not that which standeth in length of time, nor is its measure given by number of years; but understanding is gray hairs unto men, and an unspotted life is ripe old age." (Wisdom of Solomon 4:8, 9.)

The relation of character to age is fundamental also from the negative side. It has long been recognized that physical age descends prematurely on man when he allows himself to be the victim of vice or carking cares. Many centuries ago the Talmud declared that old age descends rapidly on those who give themselves up to sexual excess. (Talmud, Sabbath 152b.)

Rabbi Joshua ben Nachmani declared that old age comes too rapidly to four classes of men—those who are possessed by fears, those who give way to anger with their children, the one who has a bad wife, and to everyone in time of war. (Midrash Tanhuma—Hayye Sarah 2.)

Many of such life-shortening troubles are humanly controllable, and therefore much of the psychic and the physical disabilities of age can be averted and avoided as we learn to live more serenely and with peace in our hearts. It is truly within our own power, through the quality which we give to life, to make our mature and advancing years the blessing which they should be and may so well be.

We have no right to look for a happy old age if in our living we habitually violate physical and spiritual law. The full blessing of length of days comes to those who have known how to live, and the beauty of the years of maturity can be assured only by maintaining high standards of living. Thus the Psalmist has a simple formula for happily living out the harvest years of advancing age: "Who is the man who delights in life, who loves length of days in which to see good? Keep thy tongue from evil and thy lips from speaking guile. Depart from evil and do good; seek peace and pursue it." (Psalms 34:13–15.)

His prescription is as valid today as when it was first written down.

The master of Proverbs suggests several other ingredients with which to fill the cup of happiness for length of life. "The one who hates ill-gotten gain will prolong his days." (Proverbs 28:16.) He calls also for moral wisdom: "Length of days is in its right hand . . . Hear, my son, and receive my words, that the years of thy life may be many." (Proverbs 3:16; 4:10.) "Reverence for the Lord will increase days, but the years of the wicked shall be shortened." (Proverbs 10:27.) "For length of days and years of life and peace shall [God's command-ments] add to thee." (Proverbs 3:2.) "A crown of glory is the hoary head; it shall be found in the way of righteousness." (Proverbs 16:31.)

The rabbis of the Talmud take up the refrain. In their gen-eration they also sought to find a formula of living that assured a happy old age. Thus Rabbi Zaccai, when questioned why he had reached a ripe old age, attributed it to his respect for the synagogue and to his never having spoken harshly of others. Rabbi Eleazar ben Shammua also attributed his blessing of years to the respect he had shown the synagogue, and also to the fact that he had treated others with deference. Rabbi Nehunya believed that he had lived long becouse he had never humiliated anyone, nor had he ever harbored resentment over-night, and because he had been generous in helping others. Rabbi Zeira attributed his length of days to the fact that he had always treated the members of his household with gentle-ness, he had shown respect to others, he had never rejoiced in another's misfortune, nor had he used opprobrious nicknames. (Talmud, Megillah 28a.)

What is remarkable in these statements is that in every case the venerable rabbis give credit less to their personal piety than to the considerateness they had shown in their social relations. "Would you live long?" they say, "then treat others in a kindly and generous way." Truly, old age comes to us most readily as a blessing when we have lived unselfishly and have built up for ourselves a kindly, warm, comfortable, and cushioning world of friendship through our considerate relations with others.

There is valid and potent wisdom for our days in all such diagnoses. One of the delights of walking in our city parks on a weekday is to see how many of those who are there are little children alongside men and women whom the world calls old. Youth and the more vigorous adults are busy in their workshops or offices. But the little child is there while the venerable elder sits on the bench and smilingly watches him at play. It is the picture of a city at peace that we have already seen painted by Isaiah. The same picture of happy age as the very symbol of outward and inward peace is depicted by another prophet: "Once again old men and old women shall sit in the open places of Jerusalem, every man with his staff in his hand because of his great age, and the open places of the city shall be filled with boys and girls playing in its open places." (Zechariah 8:4, 5.)

But advancing years do not compel one to spend one's time doing nothing more than sitting idly in the park. There are qualities in maturing years which traditionally bring to elders their own distinctive obligations as well as leisurely honors. The high-pressure youth of our days do not ordinarily give respectful attention to their elders. They hardly wait in silence for the words spoken by older lips, as did Elihu who "waited for Job with his words, because they were older than he." (Job 32:4.) Nor does modern youth usually know of the injunction to "rise up before the hoary head and honor the face of the old." (Leviticus 19:32.) In past centuries, however, this respect for the aged was demanded of the Jew. Indeed, it is told of one of the greatest of the rabbis, one before whom everyone would deferentially rise, that he never failed to stand when in the presence of an old man, even though the old man was unlettered and ignorant, and of Rabbi Jochanan it is recorded that he would always rise up before the aged, even though the old man might be a heathen. (Talmud, Kiddushin 33a.)

Our generation is not alone in its failure to accord such deferential gestures to age. The master of lamentation weeps that in his generation of catastrophe "the face of the elders is not shown honor." (Lamentations 5:12.) Isaiah similarly deplores that in his day "each oppressively pushes against his fellow and against his neighbor, the young act insolently towards the old, and the base towards the honored." (Isaiah 3:5.) He felt that his was a generation like that of the heathen among whom "none showed countenance to the aged nor pity to the young." (Deuteronomy 28:50.)

In our days we feel less strongly about this failure to rise up before the old, because the aged are now less likely to be physical and mental wrecks and pitiful wash-ups on the marginal shores of active life. Today old age should hardly demand this formal deference from the young, for advancing years do not automatically bring on a debility and a senility that arouse our pity. The education which we receive when young, and its continuation in later years and even in old age, through newspapers, books and magazines, moving pictures, radio, television, and other twentieth-century instruments of mental stimulation, makes rare indeed that type of the illiterate old villager who then asked how he filled his time replied, "Sometimes I sits and thinks, and sometimes I just sits."

Formerly, physical infirmity and blindness would often compel the aged to live as virtual prisoners shut in by the walls of their room. Today the telephone, with the radio and television, and the elevator and the automobile, very often rescue them from being prisoned within narrow, inbred confines of living and open up for them the outer world with all its personal touches and wide vistas of interest.

The mechanizing of so much of the physical drudgery of life by such willing slaves as the electric laundry machine and vacuum cleaner in the home and the automobile at the door takes away from today's maturing woman and man many of the handicaps and physical limitations of advancing years. In our era everyone can take an eager, zestful part in life to a degree that men and women of similar years in earlier generations could not have dreamed possible.

Age, however, can now rejoice in something more than that many of its physical and mental disabilities have been overcome. It has retained many of the special advantages which come with advancing years. Foremost among these is the maturing wisdom which may come with the ever-deepening experience that the years bring. It will be recalled that King Rehoboam, when coming to the throne, took counsel with the elders as to the policy that he should follow. He consulted also with his young contemporaries, and by following their advice and rejecting the sage counsel of the elders, he came to disaster. (I Kings 12:1–15.) For, as was said by the rabbis many centuries later, "building by the young may be tearing down, while tearing down by the old may be upbuilding." (Talmud, Megillah 31b.)

Of old it was almost axiomatic that "with the aged is wisdom, and with length of days understanding." (Job 12:12.) Jesus ben Sirach declared, "How beautiful is the wisdom of old men . . . Much experience is the crown of old men." (Ecclesiasticus 25:5, 8.) In angry expostulation Eliphaz said to Job, "What dost thou know that we do not know? What dost thou understand that is not also with us? For the hoary

head and the aged are with us, older in days than thy father."
(Job 15:9, 10.)

Then it was almost assumed to be true, as the Arab proverb
expresses it, that he who is older than you by a day is wiser
than you by a year. When Moses was building up an incipient
organization for the Jewish people that he had created, he was
bidden, "Gather sixty men of the elders of Israel." (Numbers
11:16.) Because of their age and experience, elders were regarded as the men best fitted to guide the destinies of their
people, in the same way as the ancient Romans set duties on
their "senators," a term meaning "elders."

The rabbis sometimes express this point of view with a
stinging disparagement of youth. One of them said, "He who
learns from the young, to what may he be compared? To one
who eats unripe grapes and drinks wine fresh from the wine
press. But he who learns from elders, to what may he be compared? To one who eats ripe grapes and drinks old wine."
(Mishnah, Aboth 4:26.) However, they realized that not all
the advantage is on the side of years, for another rabbi said,
"One who learns as a child, to what may he be compared? To
ink written on fresh paper. But one who learns when old, to
what may he be compared? To ink written on rough blotting
paper." (Mishnah, Aboth 4:25.)

The Wisdom of Maturity

We must be on our guard against thinking that length of
years necessarily and automatically brings wisdom. If we are
not watchful, old age may bring us only a garrulous dotage.
"Better is a poor lad who is wise than an old king who is a
fool and who no longer knows how to accept admonition."
(Ecclesiastes 4:13.) The greatest of the rabbis declared, "Look

not on the flask but on what it contains. For there may be a new flask containing old wine, and an old flask which contains not even new wine." (Mishnah, Aboth 4:27.)

The recognition that wisdom does not necessarily go hand in hand with the length of days is needed to keep those who are aging constantly alert. We have to put forth continued effort not to fall behind and become outdated as the years creep on us. Unless we consciously and consistently keep ourselves mentally wide-awake, we may find that there is bitter truth in the saying of the rabbis that while the wise grow wiser with the years, the older the ignorant get, the more foolish they become. (Talmud, Sabbath 152a.)

Perhaps the happiest way for the maturing to keep astir and not settle down into fusty old fogyism is for them to maintain contacts with the young and associate themselves with the interests of the younger generation. When we are aging we must watch out against a facile living in the past. The young who live in the present and the future will have little patience with those who habitually look backward and have praise only for the days that are gone. As we become veterans in the art of life we must preserve a forward-looking spirit if we would give our best as the heritage of those who come after us, and would see our highest purposes carried on by the next generation. There can be no stop signal set up by age or even by death itself unless there is a stopping of the next generation.

There was a moment in the life of the patriarch Abraham when he believed that Isaac, his beloved son and spiritual heir, must be sacrificed. He had to be taught by a vivid and dramatic demonstration that age must not try alone to complete life's work. There must not be the sacrifice of youth by old age; old and young must go on "both of them together."

Age must not allow a break to develop between the generations. None of us, however old, may say, "I have done my

work, I do not care now what happens. *Après moi le déluge."*
Life has continuity. Interesting, gracious, and useful advancing
years will be those where the elders think, counsel, and plan
together with the more vigorous, inventive younger generation.
Life needs both the radicalism of youth and the conservatism
of age. It needs the fire and enthusiasm of youth to get things
done and the experience of age to see that they are not overdone. Fullness of living, with the divine spirit richly poured
out on all, will be when "your old men shall dream dreams
and your young men shall see visions." (Joel 3:1.)

If, then, men and women are to grow old without losing the
zest of living and are to feel that life still has for them a niche
where they can be useful, they must stand behind the young
to give them guidance and encouragement and cheer them on
their more active course. In this way those who have lived
through their more vigorous years can fulfill for themselves
the prayer of the Psalmist, "Cast me not off in the time of old
age; when my strength fails forsake me not . . . Yea, to old
age and hoary head forsake me not, so that I may tell Thy
power to the next generation, Thy might to all who are to
come." (Psalms 71:9, 18.)

The years of early struggle and groping purposes can with
age yield to an assured inner quiet and comfort. The difficulties
and asperities of our overeager youth can be smoothed down
with the years to a mellow richness of personality that has
matured. The ardent discontent of questioning youth can yield
with the passage of time to a calm philosophy of ripened
experience. Our usefulness is not measured primarily by chronological considerations. We have to learn to look on our
advancing years not as our *declining* years but as our *progressing* years, which we can make meaningful with fitting purpose
and stimulating interests.

Not everyone can be a Goethe who completed his *Faust* at

eighty, or a Verdi who was writing brilliant music, or a To-
scanini interpreting it when past eighty. As the decades pile
up we have to make concessions to time. Baseball and tennis
will yield to the more leisurely golf, and that in its turn to
gentle walking on the level without the burden of the clubs.
For with the increase of our years our physical processes do
slow down. A wound or a broken limb heals more rapidly
when we are young because the physical coursing of life within
us is more active. Time seems to pass slowly for youth because
when young we are eagerly impatient to get things done. But
with the old, as their physical processes slow down and their
pace of living slackens, time seems to rush by and outrun them.

Therefore, growing old must be made a triumph of inward
forces over outward handicaps. If we lose courage at the first
twinge in our stiffening joints, we shall yield prematurely to
the growing limitations imposed by increasing years. But if we
face the future with courage and indomitable spirit, and cling
to life with its brilliant wealth of interests, then we shall keep
it sensitively filled with meaning and purpose. As the years
rush on us, we shall regard each new day as borrowed time
and fill it with significance for ourselves and for others. As the
flow of time catches up with us, we can cry out with the Psalmist, "Blessed be the Lord who each day bears our burdens," or,
as the phrase may be translated, "who each day places a
responsibility on us." (Psalm 68:20.)

While age may progressively necessitate our giving up our
work, we must not let it mean giving up our interests and our
joie de vivre. As the years accumulate, we should with grateful
recognition check our expenditure of the energies that were
born of a more youthful venturing spirit. But we can keep alert
our eagerness to have new experiences. We must beware of
settling down and accepting things as they are or as they were.
While with the years we become more restrained and calmer,

we must be on guard against becoming *passé* and allowing our enthusiasms to be dampened. We must wisely put fewer demands on our heart and on our physical strength, but without weakly submitting to the psychological limitations of increasing age. If we fight against growing rigidity of mind, we can maintain much, if not all, of our resiliency of spirit even though the years crowd in upon us.

The rabbis of old remind us that when we reach the end of the final chapter of life on earth, no one of us has fulfilled even half of his plans, desires, and hopes. There is no room for smug satisfaction in a ripening age. With true instinct of the poet, Robert Browning put into the mouth of a *Rabbi Ben Ezra* the stirring call:

> Grow old along with me!
> The best is yet to be,
> The last of life, for which the first was made:
> Our times are in his hand
> Who saith, "A whole I planned,
> Youth shows but half; trust God; see all, nor be afraid!" . . .
>
> Therefore I summon age
> To grant youth's heritage . . .
>
> Youth ended, I shall try
> My gain or loss thereby;
> Leave the fire ashes, what survives is gold . . .
>
> My times be in Thy hand!
> Perfect the cup as planned!
> Let age approve of youth, and death complete the same!

In this spirit we can look out on the advancing years without apprehension. So long as we retain our interests and preserve even residual physical and mental strength to meet the challenge of each cumulative day, and so long as we delight to be with the venturing young and feel that we still have something to give to tomorrow, so long will life have no terrors for us and old age will be a blessing. Only when the years weigh so heavily on us that we can no longer bear their burden and we crave quiet, rest, and peace, then, and only then, will our days truly be numbered. Then there will be fulfilled on us the words of blessing spoken of old by Eliphaz to Job, "Thou wilt come to the grave in ripe old age as a shock of corn comes up in its due season." (Job 5:26.)

The rabbis tell much of a legendary character about the historic city of Luz. It was a city, they say, into which the angel of death could not enter. Therefore those within its walls could not die. They would grow older and older, and so long as they had work to do and a function to fulfill, all was well. Life without the possibility of death was a glorious and brilliant adventure. But inevitably the time would arrive when to everyone in Luz the weight of his eighty, ninety, one hundred years or more would become heavier and heavier. Life would become for them more and more a burden, a physical existence dragged out without the ability to work or play, and without the mental strength to take an interest in anything. Then the worn-out inhabitant of Luz, from sheer weariness of a hopeless, aimless existence, would drag himself or ask to be carried outside the walls of the city, there to be welcomed by the angel of death in the soothing sleep of peace. (Talmud, Sotah 46b.)

Life to be truly life must at every age be lived fully, richly, meaningfully. As wise and as true today as when uttered more than two thousand years ago are the words of Ecclesiastes (11:6, 8): "In the morning sow thy seed, and until evening rest not thy hand, for thou knowest not which shall succeed, this or that, or whether both shall alike be good . . . So if a man live many years, let him rejoice in them all."

INDEX